Shield of David

The Story of Israel's Armed Forces

overleaf: Israel armoured units
in position as dawn breaks, Suez
Campaign, 1956

Shield of David

The Story of Israel's Armed Forces

Yigal Allon

Weidenfeld and Nicolson
in association with Vallentine, Mitchell

Weidenfeld and Nicolson
5 Winsley Street London W1

Weidenfeld and Nicolson Jerusalem
19 Herzog Street Jerusalem

Designed by Alex Berlyne for Weidenfeld and Nicolson Jerusalem

SBN 297 00133 7

Printed in Israel by Central Press, Jerusalem, and Japhet Press,
Tel Aviv, 1970

To Ruth

Contents

Acknowledgments

The authors and publishers are indebted to the following institutions and individuals for help in providing the illustrations:

Government Press Office 41, 126, 160, 196, 200, 206, 212, 224, 232, 233, 234, 237, 240, 241, 243, 245, 246, 247, 251, 253, 254, 255, 256, 258, 260, 263, 266, 267, 268; Israel Defence Forces Archives 112, 125, 189, 192, 195, 197, 198, 200, 208, 209, 218, 220, 221, 222, 223, 225, 226, 227, 230, 232; Micha Bar Am 228, 238, 257, 259, 261, 262, 264; Jabotinsky Institute 172, 178, 187; Jewish National Fund 87, 115, 126 (top), 138, 181, 231; Illustrated London News 57, 94, 107; Associated Press 154–5, 168 (left); Werner Braun 19, 21, 56; Leonard Freed frontispiece, 248; Shimon Fuchs 114, 140 (top); Jewish Agency 16, 68; British Information Services 147, 189; Photo Gross 61; Laser Duenner 99 (right); Dr. K. Meyerowitz 127; Yad Vashem 131; BBC 146; Acme Photo 182; 'Bamahane' 235; UPI 250; Keystone 252; Mrs. O. Michaelson 116; Photo Ilani 188; Mr. Reuven Mass 195; Ministry of Defence Photo Laboratory 209; United Nations 221; The Technion 123; Yigal Allon 66; Yeruham Cohen 122

All other illustrations have been kindly provided by the History of the Haganah Archives, Tel Aviv

The maps have been prepared by Carta, Jerusalem

The soldiers on page 108 were drawn by Alex Berlyne

Author's Note

In recent years, most particularly since the Six-Day War of June 1967, people throughout the world have asked themselves how it happened that the Israel Defence Forces won so resounding a victory over the Arab armies. What suddenly endowed the Jewish people – traditionally non-martial – with such impressive military skills? What is the secret of the prowess of Israeli soldiers, airmen and sailors?

The answer, of course, is that nothing happens 'suddenly'; that the modern story of Jewish self-defence in the Land of Israel dates back some eighty years, and is the result of the commitment and dedication to national survival of many men and women – most of whom, seeking no publicity, received none. This book is my attempt to tell part of that little-known story – as simply, briefly and clearly as possible. It is not a study in depth of the growth of Israel's armed forces, nor is it a historical analysis of the military doctrines which those forces developed. It is rather a sketch, a profile of the people and of the events which moulded first the resistance movement and then the army of the Jewish State.

In much of what is described in the following pages, I have been an active participant myself; first as a young and raw recruit; later as a seasoned commander; still later, in a ministerial capacity, as a decision maker. Some of the pioneers I have written about here were my mentors; others formed the stuff of the legends upon which I was brought up. Some were part and parcel of my childhood memories, while others, my contemporaries, were comrades-in-arms. But, in no sense is this book an autobiography. I have tried to keep myself out of the story altogether; to tell it as it really was, so that the questions asked after 1967 can be answered more clearly, so that history be given its due, and those, whose courage and endurance were integral to a great tradition, can become more familiar figures beyond the borders of that State for whose existence they fought and all too frequently died.

I wish to express my deep appreciation to four people: first and foremost, to Rinna Samuel for her invaluable help in writing this book; to Asher Weill for his editorial advice; to Nathanel Lorch, former head of the Department of History of the Israel Defence Forces for having carefully checked the whole manuscript; and to Alex Berlyne whose help in graphic design and illustration contributes so much to the book. It goes without saying that, all of this assistance notwithstanding, any errors or misjudgments and the responsibility for them are entirely mine.

Ginosar, August, 1970   *Yigal Allon*

1 From Pogroms to Palestine

*The rebirth of Jewish self-defence — Pale of Settlement to Palestine–
Bar Giora ·and Hashomer — NILI*

The men, and women, who created the first military formation in modern Jewish history – the founders of *Bar Giora* and *Hashomer*, who took up arms in Palestine at the beginning of the twentieth century, and who were to become the direct forbears of the Israel Defence Forces – were, more than anything else, people who deeply understood that inherent in self-defence was self-reliance. They were many other things as well: they were East European Jews determined to rebuild a Jewish National Home in the Holy Land; they were socialists, flexible enough to accept, and to insist upon, the idea of the self-determination of nations; they were revolutionaries, able to dedicate themselves to the twin goals of social and economic equality and the brotherhood of man, on the one hand, and to the realization of an ancient and romantic dream, which had nothing at all to do with class warfare, on the other.

But mostly, and finally, they were people convinced that the real meaning of Zionism lay in their own direct personal participation in every aspect and area of the Jewish return to Zion; and in this grand sweeping statement of aims, they gave priority to self-defence. Their attitudes and their commitments did not derive, as might perhaps be expected, from a sense of historic connection with the warriors of the Bible, nor were they nourished by any combatant mythology. They were, instead, very much the products of their time and of their geographic location. Children of ghetto dwellers in the small Jewish townships of Russia, Rumania, Poland and Lithuania, they were, however, responsive to and moulded by the winds of liberalism that blew through Europe and marked the end of the nineteenth century. By the same token, they were Jews impelled to reject martyrdom, Jews who could no longer remain passive in the face of anti-Semitic violence.

Unlike their grandparents or even their parents, these young Jews had broken out of the restrictive environment of traditional

Jewish self-defence

opposite: An early photograph of members of Hashomer – the forerunners of ZAHAL – The Israel Defence Forces

11

Jewish life. They were not orthodox Jews; they spoke Russian, they had had some modern schooling, and they felt themselves to be part of a universal ferment for the betterment of human society. This being the case, their reaction to the Czarist pogroms which punctuated the years of 1903 and 1904 was also unorthodox.

Where other Jews before them had huddled together, praying that the storm would pass and finding solace in their own spiritual values and beliefs, these young Jews were unable to resign themselves to the inevitability of being victims. And in the spring of 1903, when the Czar's officials unleashed a major and brutal attack on the Jewish community of Kishinev in Bessarabia, the members of the tiny Zionist Socialist Party of a town called Gomel, between White Russia and the Ukraine, decided to ready themselves for defence. It was obvious that the new wave of pogroms would spread throughout Russia; but this time, in this one town, the rioters would somehow be held at bay. It seemed unlikely that any self-defence could be effective; but the young Zionists of Gomel made careful plans. Defence in depth was impossible, but nonetheless they bought weapons; they did their best, sometimes ludicrously disguised as Russian peasants, to set up an intelligence-gathering organization so that they would not be taken by surprise; they amassed and assessed information about the rioters' mood and preparations, and they divided the Jewish streets of Gomel into small defendable blocks. When the pogrom, at last, burst on the town, the Jews were ready to face their tormentors. For the first time, anywhere, in hundreds of years, armed Jews fought in the streets to protect themselves. In the beginning they fought against drunken barbaric hooligans; then, when the Czar's troops intervened to protect the rioters, the Jews of Gomel returned their fire.

The pogrom, which lasted for three days, attracted no attention in the world outside; it attracted very little attention within Russia itself. But it was, in fact, to prove an historic event. The first revolutionary pioneers to leave Russia for Palestine in 1904 were a group of those same young Jews who had, unprecedentedly, given battle to the Czar's army a few months before.

The Palestine to which they arrived was, in some respects, a shock. Envisioned as the fertile, lovely land of milk and honey, paradisial and eternal, it was, in reality, a neglected province of an already crumbling Ottoman Empire. Ruled inefficiently by corrupt Turkish officials, for whom service in the Holy Land was neither glamorous nor prestigious, the Zion which received the eager idealists of Gomel was depressing. Palestine's total Jewish population then numbered some 50,000. There had, of course, al-

Pogroms and self-protection

opposite: Map of the Jewish Pale of Settlement in Russia showing some of its principal towns and villages

13

Mounted Bedouin watchmen were hired by the Jewish settlers before the foundation of Bar Giora

Beginnings of Jewish pioneering

ways been Jews in Palestine; for long periods they clustered mainly in the Land's four holy cities – Jerusalem, Tiberias, Hebron and Safed – where they devoted themselves to the study of the Law and were supported by a sort of charitable dole raised on their behalf by pious Jews in far-off communities throughout the world. In the Middle Ages, various attempts at a mass return of the Jews to Palestine had taken place, but all had failed. Towards the end of the nineteenth century, however, a new spirit of practicality set in, given impetus by the worsening conditions of Russian Jewry.

In 1870, an agricultural school, Mikveh Israel, was founded not far from what was then the Arab town of Jaffa; and in 1878, a Jewish village called Petach Tikvah ('The Gateway of Hope') was established. It consisted of some eight hundred acres of malaria-ridden land, and eventually it too failed. For years, it was abandoned, but it represented a departure. In Petach Tikvah, inept Jews, unaccustomed to the climate, unused to agriculture in any form, and strange to the Land itself, nonetheless, began once more – after a hiatus of more than a millennium – to work the soil of Palestine. In 1882, a group of newcomers from Rumania founded Rosh Pinah, a village in the Upper Galilee, and the first modern wave of Zionist immigration was started by the *Bilu* pioneers, who had formed the name of their society from the initials of four Hebrew words which meant 'House of Jacob, come, let us ascend'. They had made their momentous decision to settle in the land of Palestine as the result of their membership in the Zionist clubs which had sprung up throughout Eastern Europe, groups which

14

called themselves 'Lovers of Zion', and were the first to send agricultural pioneers there.

A member of Hashomer stands guard in the village of Rehovot, founded in 1890

By 1900, a chain of villages existed and the beginning of a definite pattern of resettlement could be discerned. The birthdates, and
often the names, of those early settlements are as noteworthy as
are their locations: Rishon Lezion ('First in Zion'), 1882; Nes
Ziona ('Zion's Standard'), 1884; Gedera ('The Sheep Pen') and Rehovot ('Broad Acres'), 1890; all in the coastal plain. To the north
was Zichron Yaakov ('Jacob's Memorial'), 1882, and Yesud Hama'alah ('Start of the Ascent'), 1883.

In 1904, none of these colonies was flourishing; all were dependent by now, in one degree or another, on the energetic philan-
thropy of Baron Edmond de Rothschild and other members of that
wealthy and powerful family. In many respects, these villagers had
created a planter society in which part of the hard work was done
by Arab labourers, and in some cases their safety deposited in the
often treacherous hands of hired Arab watchmen. But by purchasing land and actually settling on it, they had nonetheless established bridgeheads, and had done so, consciously, in order to
redeem and reclaim the Land which they firmly believed was the
Land of their Fathers, the land promised to them and to their seed
in the ancient covenant formed thousands of years before between
God and Abraham. They despaired of reinforcements ever appear-
ing; they lived in perpetual danger, their security was threatened
by brigands; they were isolated, not only from the mainstream of
Jewish life in Europe, but also from any meaningful contact with

15

Dr Theodor Herzl, 1860–1904,
Founder of the Zionist Movement

the hostile Turkish regime. But they had been the first to equate farming not solely with the production of food but with the reclamation of the land; perhaps even, at some distant future point, with its political liberation. They had spoken and thought and written in national terms, and they had regarded their unimpressive little villages as outposts; outposts which had no headquarters, no centre, and no hinterland, but which would, one day, help to fix the boundaries of a Jewish State. Viewed close up, they were innovators, but also, and no less, observed across the full sweep of Jewish history, they were successors; the continuers and the implementers of an age-old yearning.

From a certain point of view, these early pioneers were strategists, the first strategists of the Return, although they were looked at askance by the more dynamic settlers who were to arrive from Gomel in 1904 with an entirely different, far more radical set of ideas. Had they thought in terms of military operations, and very few of them did, and had they asked themselves how best to achieve the goal of settlement behind what were essentially enemy lines, they would have done exactly what, in fact, they did. They would have set up their walled, fortress-like villages all over the country; in the north, in the coastal plain, and in the south; they would have tried, as indeed they did try, to create corridors of settlement, to carve a common territory, to start the process of bringing land into Jewish hands, and constructing a modern Jewish economy.

In their diaries and letters, we find over and over again the same exalted note sounded, the same sense of having embarked on a history-altering path, formally charted by the Zionist Congress of 1897 which had been convened by Theodor Herzl in Basle.

But the Gomel group, more sophisticated, infinitely more discerning, and capable of much deeper self-criticism than the first settlers, viewed these pioneering efforts with scepticism. They looked about them and beheld a dry and shadeless land, cracked soil and thorny trees; here and there a few eucalyptuses, olive trees, an orange grove or an almond plantation, planted through the good offices of the Baron, which testified to the start of Jewish agriculture. But the labourers, almost everywhere, were Arabs.

They dealt with the Turkish *gendarmerie*, and saw for themselves the extent of bribery. They travelled from the port of Jaffa to Petach Tikvah and realized that they were in a country overrun by, and terrified of, robbers. They looked for work in the fields of Petach Tikvah and found none – for Jews. Jews, it was made clear, were overseers, not labourers. Ploughing, hoeing, the tough necessary aspects of real farming, all these, as was right and proper, were carried out by Arabs. Arab labour was inexpensive, said the

opposite: Palestine under Turkish rule. *inset*: The extent of the Ottoman Empire

16

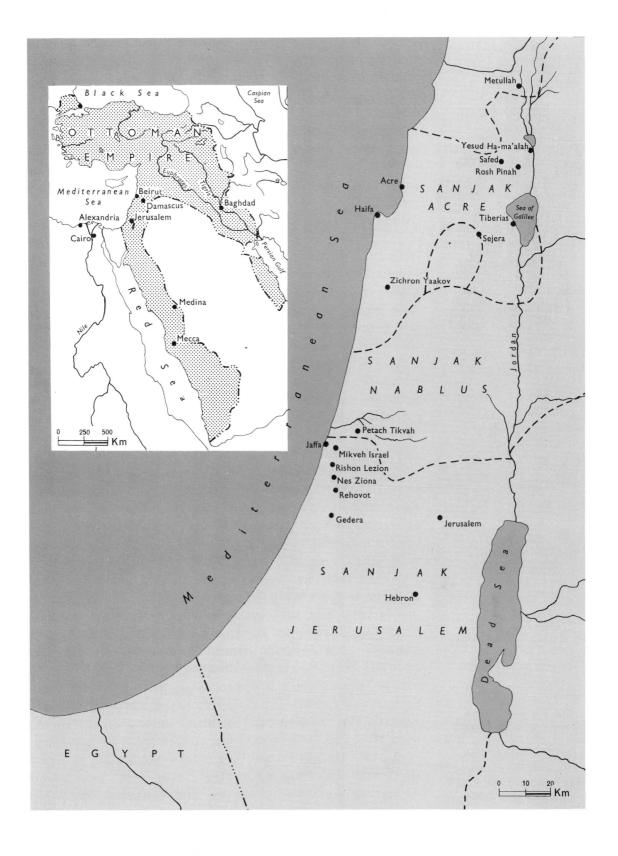

Black Sea

Caspian Sea

OTTOMAN EMPIRE

Mediterranean Sea

Euphrates

Tigris

Beirut
Damascus
Baghdad

Alexandria
Jerusalem

Cairo

Persian Gulf

Nile

Red Sea

Medina

Mecca

0   250   500

Km

Metullah

Yesud Ha-ma'alah

Safed
Rosh Pinah

Acre

SANJAK ACRE

Haifa

Tiberias

Sea of Galilee

Sejera

Zichron Yaakov

Jordan

SANJAK

NABLUS

Petach Tikvah

Jaffa

Mikveh Israel

Rishon Lezion

Nes Ziona

Rehovot

Gedera

Jerusalem

SANJAK

Hebron

JERUSALEM

Dead Sea

EGYPT

0   10   20

Km

Mediterranean Sea

Israel Shochat, one of the founders of Bar Giora and Hashomer, typified the young visionary immigrants of the Second Aliyah

farmers, and, more relevantly, the Arabs were experienced.

A vivid description of the impact of Petach Tikvah, and of its basically feudal order of life, comes down to us in the writings of Israel Shochat, a young Russian Jew who was to become one of the founders, first of Bar Giora, then of Hashomer, and who typifies the pioneers of 1904–14, a period that has come to be known as the Second *Aliyah*, or wave of Zionist immigration.

'Petach Tikvah,' wrote Shochat, 'looked like any village anywhere; small stone houses, or wooden huts; unpaved streets; villagers in their work clothes. Around it, orange groves, vineyards, cultivated fields, and eucalyptus trees. Even the young people gave no hint of being involved in any sort of national enterprise. They seemed like the children of farmers anywhere else; except that their main job was seeing to it that the Arabs worked properly. After a week or two, my wonderment at being in a Jewish village in Palestine began to fade and blur. The magic evaporated. In the market in the centre of town, all the produce came from Arab villages in the area, was sold by Arabs. Before dawn, hundreds of Arab labourers daily streamed into Petach Tikvah to look for work, and mostly they found it. Then there was the matter of language: the villagers all spoke Yiddish. To speak Hebrew was regarded as absurd, as a Zionist affectation. And the most serious thing was that Jews were considered virtually unemployable.'

When Shochat and his friends protested the state of affairs, the Petach Tikvans rushed to proffer advice: go to America, they said, and earn enough money so you can come back here and buy your own orange grove; others talked of Canada, and even of Australia. But the young people of the Second Aliyah decided to stick it out. Somehow or other, they would find work; somehow or other they succeeded.

Within several months, the numbers of Jewish workers in Petach Tikvah grew; new arrivals were met in Jaffa and told that, although employment for Jews was not to be taken for granted, it did exist. At night, jammed into a small room, they drank tea, talked for hours about Socialism, and argued about whether how and when they themselves could alter and purify the way of life in the Jewish colonies. Redemption of a people? Liberation of an ancient homeland? Equality of man? Productivity and independence? What had happened to the dreams they had dreamt on the crowded miserable ships which had brought them to Palestine? Were they to remain lofty, unattainable concepts, devoid of any meaning or potential in Zion? What had happened to the idealists, the *Bilu'im* who had come to the country before them? What had staled *their* vigour and distorted *their* aims? Why were the farmers of Petach Tikvah,

opposite: At the old Crusader port town of Atlit, the Aaronson family conducted espionage activities on behalf of the British and against the Turks in the First World War in the NILI group (see pages 36–40)

who had once drained swamps, endured brigandage, been symbols of courage and perseverance, now so devitalized, so reluctant, perhaps even unable, to affect change? Was it because the Baron, in his magnanimity, had removed the burden of survival from them? Or was it because, weary of struggle, they had too quickly settled for the visionless life?

Perhaps, after all, Petach Tikvah was not typical: hopefully, they journeyed to other colonies. In Rishon Lezion, founded in 1882 by members of the First Aliyah and centred around wine cellars built by the Baron, they walked into what seemed to their astonished eyes to be a parody, a musical comedy version of bucolic life: large cool villas; well-dressed, even elegant 'villagers', a population that chattered in French, Arabic and Yiddish, but spoke almost no Hebrew; girls dressed in frills and furbelows. Here, too, the entire labour force appeared to be made up of Arabs. Asked where the Jewish workers were, the villagers answered that Jews only worked in Rishon seasonally, at harvest time, and then not many. Israel Shochat nonetheless managed to find himself a job, and even a place to live. On Saturdays, he walked for hours in the countryside around Rishon, practising his Hebrew with whichever of the young men of the village agreed to accompany him.

On one of these hikes, he happened upon an aspect of life in Palestine which made a great impression on him, and which was soon to lead to renewed stress, in the incessant conversations of the Gomel group, on the importance of Jewish self-defence. Passing an Arab village, Shochat saw Arabs who looked quite different, and were dressed quite differently, from any Arabs he had ever seen before. It turned out that these were Circassians, not Arabs at all; remnants of a proud and truculent community of Caucasian Moslems who had been brought to Palestine by Abdul Hamid in the second part of the nineteenth century.

Shochat was curious about them, and he listened attentively when an oldtimer explained the special position of the Circassians in the country. Although they were only a very small group, several hundred in all, the Arabs held them in considerable respect. Not that they liked them, but they left them alone; and the Bedouin were actually frightened of them. They could do everything the Arabs did – and do it better. They were crack marksmen, spectacular horsemen, and, most of all, they were known to be tough and plucky. So much so, in fact, that some of the Arab villages near Rishon had even petitioned the Circassians to defend them from robbers, and in many of the Jewish colonies the Circassians were the most trusted and reliable watchmen.

Afterwards Shochat thought long, and pensively, about the dif-

20

ference in the relative status of the Circassians and the Jews. The trouble was not so much that the Arabs had singled the Jews out as victims, but that they scorned them, and thought of them as being inherently weak and defenceless, The commonplace synonym for 'Jew' among the Arabs of Palestine then was 'The Children of Death' and at all possible opportunities the Arabs demonstrated their contempt for the immigrants. Years later, recalling that Saturday morning, Shochat wrote: 'There was much to be learned from the Circassians. Here they were, a tiny minority in the sea of Arabs, and nonetheless, they had managed to earn an honourable position for themselves. They had rooted themselves in the land, they had set up their own villages; perhaps all was not lost for us yet. It was possible, after all, I thought, to strengthen ourselves, to settle and to hold on to the land, to force our Arab neighbours to respect us. But for this we ourselves needed to be brave, and to persevere.'

As Socialists, heirs to a new world, foes of exploitation or discrimination, the idea of a Jewish élite in Palestine was, of course, anathema to the pioneers of the Second Aliyah. But there was little point to the perpetuation of a society, here too, which would be dependent upon the mercies of a hostile majority. What the Circassians had accomplished, the Jews must accomplish, too. The struggle for the 'conquest of labour' was primary; without Jewish workers, there would be no Jewish homeland. But the right and duty of the Jews to defend their own farms and homes themselves was surely part of that struggle.

In the next few months, Shochat travelled around the country; he argued with his friends and he argued with the colonists. At least, let us try to stand guard, he begged; give us a chance. Even if we make mistakes, in the end it will be worth it. But the doubters were many; the farmers found it impossible to believe that a handful of young men, barely familiar with the landscape, alien to the ways of the sheikhs who controlled the Arab villages, unable even to talk to the Arab watchmen, could be entrusted with Jewish life and property. Besides, said the estate managers, the relationship between the Jews and Arabs in Palestine would be utterly destroyed. The Arabs would be resentful, and would become more destructive. Better by far, in this part of the world, to pay *baksheesh* than to upset established tradition. It was all very well to be imaginative and enthusiastic, but it was preposterous to 'go native'. The Jews had one role to play in Palestine, the Arabs, another.

The Gomel group, however, was determined. It met dozens of times, drafting and redrafting a programme, laying foundations for a secret society of Jewish watchmen. Its seven-point programme was practical and succinct, free of rhetoric, even of eloquence. The group,

above: Much of the Jewish community of Palestine was supported by the charity of Baron Edmond de Rothschild
below: The Circassians were considered to be the finest fighting men in Palestine. A group of modern-day Circassians in Israel

21

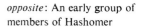

The first members of Bar Giora. Second from right: Zvi Becker, and third from right, Israel Shochat

Alexander Zeid led the mounted members of Bar Giora in Galilee

still undecided as to name, declared itself opposed to the maintenance of the '*Hallukah*', the charitable relief fund on which most of the Jews in Jerusalem and the other sacred towns still lived. It upheld voluntary work, the attempt to find new work methods and to embark upon a new life style, put itself on record in favour of Jewish self-defence and the establishment of a Jewish militia, and vowed to participate actively in Zionist-Socialist education and in the unification of the workers.

In September, 1907, in a top-storey room of an old house in Jaffa, which was lit by one candle, sitting in a circle on upturned orange crates, fully aware of the significance of their action, the members of the Gomel group officially founded their society. They called it *Bar Giora*, in memory of a famous Jewish fighter against the Romans in that final rebellion which preceded the destruction of the Second Temple in 70 AD. Despite the drama of the moment, the proceedings were matter-of-fact. Ten men stood up, took an oath of loyalty to the Jewish national cause, swore fealty to each other and unconditional obedience to the rules of the society, and raised a blue and white flag on which Bar Giora's motto, 'By blood and fire, Judea fell; by blood and fire, Judea shall rise again', had been embroidered. They chose Israel Shochat to be their leader.

Although they had much, almost everything, in common, there was also much that was dissimilar among the ten men. In their photographs, so posed and formal, the differences stand out clearly. Israel Shochat, the intellectual, the unquestioned leader. First, romantic in a wide-brimmed hat and flowing cravat, he looks like any member of the Russian intelligentsia of the time; like any educated romanticist in the years before World War I. Then, in other pictures, the face has thinned, hardened, the eyes are less

23

Mendele Portugali

dreamy, the beard is gone. Now, a rifle is held easily at his side, a bandolier slung loosely across his chest, the ubiquitous Arab robe, the *abaya*, hangs from his shoulders as though he has always worn it. He has become the prototype of the Watchmen, head of a conspiratorial organization, a changer of history.

Alexander Zeid is Bar Giora's blond, blue-eyed 'Buffalo Bill'; hunter, scout and amateur botanist *par excellence*. He came to Palestine from a Siberian village; probably had Zionism not lured him so absolutely, he would have remained a Russian revolutionary, become a Socialist hero. He too seems wholly at home in the Arab dress Bar Giora had adopted, at home in the adventurous, dangerous role he chose. Zvi Becker is another of the founding members; for a moment, we see him, misleadingly, as the young squire, weary after the hunt: one hand lightly strokes his dog, while another feels for his holster. He lies, relaxed, near a stream, or pond, a member of the gentry somewhere. Tall, broad-shouldered, he is known as Zvi the Giant. There is a childish and endearing quality about him, and in different photographs, he experiments with different hats. Then, there is Mendele Portugali, hot-tempered, warm-hearted, self-confident, Bar Giora's *enfant terrible*. Restless and candid, he is impatient with fools and has a tendency to be overbearing. But his physical strength and courage are to make him the central figure of local sagas. And Israel Gileadi, dapper, calm; like Shochat, from the start a leader; his clothes, simple peasant blouse and trousers, bespeak plainness and tidiness. Like Shochat, he, too, has an aura of ordinariness, of knowing what he is about, of efficiency.

Their wives, in some respects, were like the wives of frontiersmen in the Wild West; they moved from one place to another whenever circumstances demanded; they made homes, reared children, farmed and stood on guard, with the minimum of fuss and the minimum of reward, other than a fulfilled sense of duty. They were dry-eyed and stoic in the face of grief, comforting in situations of uncertainty, and calm when danger struck, as it frequently did. But unlike the women who crossed the great plains of the young United States, their role was in no way passive. Many of them were members of Bar Giora and later Hashomer in their own right, and not a few became famous both within the organization and in the country as a whole.

Contemporary photographs, unflattering, have smoothed much of the character from their faces; somehow in albums of the period, the women of Hashomer look like teachers, middle-aged housewives, practical nurses. But Rachel Yanait Ben-Zvi, Manya Shochat, Keilah Gileadi, and Esther Becker were women who were

24

part of a remarkably valiant sorority, and their contribution to the saga of Hashomer was both meaningful and substantial.

Mounted members of Bar Giora leave for a patrol

They were new people in an old land; explorers committed to a great discovery. Of that night in Jaffa, one of them, Yitshaq Ben-Zvi who was to become President of a Jewish State nearly half a century later, wrote: 'We felt we were standing before Mount Sinai at the Giving of the Law, and all of us were ready to sacrifice ourselves. We knew that words could not rebuild the nation, only our deeds.'

The plan of action called for the assumption of a triple burden: to take over completely the defence of a village or a colony, as soon as possible; to abandon the familiar nuances of the Russian language and the comfortable tang of Yiddish, and become entirely Hebrew-speaking; to live together, whenever feasible, in their own way, according to their own light, creating models of a co-operative and fraternal community. By now, the watchmen had trained themselves to use arms, they had learned to ride competently, they had wandered in and out of Arab villages and picked up a working Arabic vocabulary. They had even stood guard in one or two colonies, patrolling outside the village walls at night, side by side with Arab watchmen. They had forced themselves on the consciousness of the Jewish population of Palestine and though they were still regarded as wild men fired by a naïve vision, they had begun to prove their worth. Now, the time had come to take full responsibility.

In the Galilee, in the north of Palestine, where the scattered Jewish colonies seemed less smug, less hidebound, and where Jewish

Bar Giora moves to Galilee

25

A group of Hashomer members showing Russian, Turkish and Arab clothing and a medley of weapons

farmers did more of their own farming, the members of Bar Giora thought they would find a more congenial and more accepting atmosphere. To Galilee, then! In the foothills of Mount Tabor, in Sejera, a small farm which had once been planned for use as an agricultural school, Bar Giora found and took its first full-fledged chance to work the land, and to guard it. Today, every schoolchild in Israel knows of Sejera, and of its place in Israel's history. But in that early autumn of 1907, when Bar Giora settled there, the experiment seemed, to most of the Jews of Palestine, to be foolhardy and almost certain of failure. But the watchmen themselves were confident. The Galilee – its wild beautiful scenery, its climate, its multiple associations with biblical days and their own isolation in it – all these fortified them and added to their sense of purpose.

Sejera   Everything they did filled them with pride; they cleaned and polished their personal weapons, they learnt to accommodate eyes and ears to the night, they rose before dawn to plough and to sow, and they went on talking. Some of the watchmen thought perhaps they had taken the wrong direction; perhaps they should concentrate on raising cattle, live in tents, adopt for themselves the easier, more authentic Bedouin way of life, about which they were coming to know more and more. Others maintained that Sejera must be modelled on the Cossack villages, where farmers left, when necessary, to fight, and then returned to work the land as free men.

One thing was clear; theirs would be a collective, in which they themselves would do everything. In Sejera, there was, at last, only Jewish labour; within a few months, for the first time anywhere,

26

the job of defending the Jewish farm was turned over entirely to the watchmen. The Circassians and the Arabs were displaced. Disgruntled, angry, they threatened retaliation, organized raids on Sejera, vowed to avenge themselves on the Jewish guards. But the watchmen stayed their course, and the Arabs, at first with disbelief, then with growing wonderment, saw that the Jews were serious, after all, and that the safety of Jewish property and Jewish lives was now the concern of Jewish guards. In the spring of 1908, Sejera feasted its success. At Passover that year, it was picked as the site of the convention of the Labour Party and Jews from all over Palestine came to the farm to celebrate.

David Ben-Gurion has described the celebration vividly: 'We gathered in the upper *khan*, the old Arab staging inn in the farm compound. The large hall, which was once a cowshed and afterwards became the workers' dormitory, was decorated in "Galilee style": the two long walls were draped with eucalyptus and pepper branches, and looked like an avenue of trees. On the inner wall hung farm tools and weapons: ploughs, spades, harrows and hoes were wreathed with bright spring flowers, and rifles, pistols, swords and daggers were hung above the windows. The faces of the young men who sat and sang around the table testified that this arsenal was more than a decoration'.

The spring festival ended in tragedy. Arab robbers set upon a traveller on his way to Sejera, and in the fight, an Arab was badly hurt. Later, he died of his wounds; and the watchmen of Sejera gravely faced the possibility of a blood feud. The law of the Middle East called for the family of a murdered Arab to avenge his death; Sejera waited for the first blow to fall. Two of the farmers were killed in the ensuing, inevitable Arab attack. Sejera buried its dead in a single grave, mourned them without orations, and went back to work. Good relations with the Arabs, the comrades assured each other, would be worked out in the course of day-to-day dealings. The watchmen would have to learn to defend themselves, wherever possible without killing; the chain of blood feuds would be broken if the Jewish guards excelled in caution.

But Arabs were not the only problem: there was a perpetual financial crisis. To buy arms one had to have money. Israel Shochat started a pleading correspondence with Zionist leaders abroad; he suggested the creation of a special loan fund from which weapons and horses could be bought. In the end, a small sum of money was given to Bar Giora by the World Zionist Organization, and the watchmen set up a fund for arms and put money aside to care for the families of comrades who were killed.

1908 was marked by a further success. Impressed by the skill

A Yemenite member of Hashomer in the village of Ben Shemen, 1910

Death in Sejera

Mes'cha

27

and devotion of the watchmen, another Jewish village took them on as guards. This was Mes'cha, today Kfar Tabor, which was in trouble with the Arab village nearest it, from which Mes'cha's watchmen traditionally had been selected. The farmers of Mes'cha turned to the Sejera commune for help. The defence of Mes'cha was painstakingly planned: Jewish workers came from all over Galilee, and Bar Giora took command. In Mes'cha's tiny schoolhouse, a headquarters was set up, weapons were collected and checked, and guard duty organized in shifts. During the day, the 'troops' were mercilessly drilled, marched back and forth in the blazing sun, taken on gruelling route marches. Again, the Arabs stared, incredulous, at the farmers-turned-warriors, noted the new professionalism, and calmed down.

The self-defence unit was disbanded, the volunteers returned to their respective colonies, and Mes'cha formally entered into a contractual relationship with Bar Giora. From now on, Mes'cha's defence was officially the responsibility of the watchmen. The contract is interesting: it stresses that Bar Giora will undertake the colony's defence only, if and for as long as, Jewish labour solely is employed in Mes'cha. Other conditions have to do with payment, fines if farmers are negligent about locking up their property, and wages to the watchmen. The colony, for its part, agreed to supply the watchmen with one Martini rifle, 162 bullets and four bandoliers. Bar Giora chose four of its most experienced men to go to Mes'cha: among them, Zvi Becker and Mendele Portugali. Also, Bar Giora mobilized Jewish workers for the colony, knowing that it could rely on them as reinforcements in the time of need.

A year later, in the spring of 1909, a secret meeting took place in Mes'cha. In the kitchen-cum-dining room of the watchmen, members of Bar Giora reviewed the past, and planned the future. A small clandestine society was no longer sufficient; reorganization was needed so that the watchmen could branch out to other points in the country, recreating themselves as the nucleus of what one day might become a national self-defence force, a true shield for the homeland. The new society would be given a new name: *Hashomer* (The Watchman); and its programme reflected its broadened scope. It would work more openly than Bar Giora had; it would, in effect, be the cover organization for Bar Giora, at least where the Turkish Government was concerned. It would deal less with the professional aspects of self-defence, more with the national ones. It would represent an *avant garde* whose specific mission would be to make the entire Jewish population conscious of the needs, and implications, of self-defence. It would emphasize the dynamics of self-defence, constantly clarifying the relationship between this and be-

opposite: The village of Mes'cha became the first Jewish settlement to enter into a contractual arrangement with Bar Giora. One of the watchmen can be seen on the right of this 1910 photograph
below: Tel Aviv, founded in 1909, also had its own watchmen. Four of these are seen in this photograph from 1911

29

Nisanov, one of the founders of Hashomer, in Arab dress

tween the creation of new social and national values.

From their experiences in Gomel, in Zhitomir, from the service of some of the members of Bar Giora in foreign armies, from the hard-won lessons of the immediate past in Palestine, they drew up the main planks of the Hashomer credo: the inculcation of personal responsibility, vigilance and readiness for sacrifice; the equation of hard work with military training, of military ability with the maintenance of high personal moral standards; Hashomer would continue Bar Giora's tradition of defence, settlement, the conquest of the wilderness and the upbuilding of the country. Lastly, it would dedicate itself to the development of friendly and honourable relations with the Arabs.

In this programme, in this combination of an ideology of self defence and Socialism, in this emphasis on the value of each individual component part of an army-to-be, Hashomer clearly relates itself to that army which was indeed to come into being within another four decades.

Defence 'contracts' began to come; occasionally, a Jewish colony, though agreeing to Hashomer's terms, and anxious for Hashomer to take over its defence, would stipulate that although the Jewish watchmen might guard the village, they should try not to use their arms. Now and then, quarrels broke out between the members of Hashomer and the colonists, who were scared by their 'extremism' and worried by their radical point of view. But the Sejera model had taken root. By 1910, members of Hashomer participated in the creation of Palestine's first fullblown settlement or *kibbutz*, Deganiah, founded on the shores of the Sea of Galilee. The cooperative way of life, the idea of voluntary work, the egalitarianism of Israel's kibbutzim all stem directly from the experiment first carried out in Sejera by a dozen or so Jewish watchmen.

In the course of time, Hashomer formalized its organization. It maintained Bar Giora's principle of selectivity. Not all of Palestine's Jewish watchmen could become Hashomer members, only those whom the society agreed to include in its ranks. A year's probation was demanded of all would-be members, and often extended to two years. Ordeals were contrived to test the stamina and talent for improvisation of candidates, and special places were chosen for Hashomer's swearing-in ceremonies, which took place during its annual conclave. Sometimes, new members would be inducted in fields, sometimes in woods, sometimes in caves. But always these rituals took place at night; two horsemen silently escorted the candidate to the selected site, where by the light of torches, armed watchmen circled the newcomer, with him repeating Hashomer's terse oath: 'I swear to abide by this oath of loyalty

30

to the principles of Hashomer and to this society'. Then, in the dark, four shots rang out: the ceremony was over.

The Hashomer also thought up ways of lessening Arab suspicion. Impressed by the warmth of Arab hospitality, and noting that each Arab village had its own *Madfiyah* or guest tent, Hashomer set up Madfiyahs of its own, where passing Arabs might, and did, stop for coffee, and where they engaged in the long flowery dialogues which delighted host and guest alike, and in which the Arabs were so expert, as well as in down-to-earth discussions about horses, cattle and weapons.

But Hashomer did not exist in a vacuum; it was part of a community which daily struggled against the corruption and deviousness of the crumbling Ottoman Empire. It was not sufficient for Hashomer to support itself, or to increase its numbers or to acquire new weapons. It needed legal assistance against the time when it ran foul of the slack, bribery-ridden Turkish courts. There were only two or three Jewish lawyers in Palestine then, and these were neither very interested in Zionism, nor particularly gifted. Hashomer raised enough money to send its own law students to Constantinople. It would be good, decided the society's steering committee, if the number of Jewish intellectuals in Palestine were to increase, and important to prove to the community that there was no essential contradiction between education and working the land.

Hashomer in the struggle against Ottoman corruption

Besides, Hashomer believed that the Jews should start to play a more active role in Turkish society, should be better integrated into the governing circles, should be ready, when and if a Turkish revolution came, to participate in it as Turkish citizens, as Socialists, and as conscientious Jews. Hashomer therefore encouraged medical students, budding engineers, and young economists to study at Turkish universities, and then, their studies finished, to return as pioneers to Palestine. Israel Shochat himself was sent to Constantinople where he, Ben-Zvi and Ben-Gurion helped to set up a Union of Jewish Students, and continued planning expansion of Hashomer's activities, including a further and more precise projection of how Hashomer could turn itself into an overall defence organization.

By the spring of 1914, this question was no longer academic. The shadow of World War I fell across the Ottoman Empire, and within the Zionist world, important new alignments were taking place. A great deal had changed since 1904. There were now some 80,000 Jews in Palestine, living in small towns and on some fifty-odd agricultural settlements. Tel Aviv had been founded on the sand dunes outside Jaffa and was already nearly five years old. Theodor Herzl, who had founded the World Zionist Organization

World War One

31

and was the recognized father of modern Zionism, but who had failed to win international or even Turkish support for the idea of a Jewish National Home in Palestine, had died, worn out by his unsuccessful efforts. Chaim Weizmann, a Russian-born chemist who made his residence in England, was to become the acknowledged leader of Zionism.

Zionist attitudes to World War One
Zionist leaders, throughout the world, were divided in their allegiance: some hoped that Germany would prevail, and that Turkey would eventually change her attitude towards the Jews. Others, including Weizmann, believed that victory would go to Britain and France, and that although Britain was allied to hated Russia, it was not impossible that the British, long interested in Zionism, might actively and overtly support Jewish claims there.

In Palestine itself, there was considerable tension. The Turkish Government, tense and apprehensive, stepped up its restrictive actions where the Jews were concerned, and the Arabs, sensing this, accelerated the tempo of their raids on the Jewish colonies. The members of Hashomer met in almost endless secret meetings to discuss the worsening situation. To them, it seemed quite clear that the Jewish community of Palestine (the *Yishuv*, in Hebrew) would have to prepare itself for total defence, reassure the Turkish Government of its loyalty, and, at the same time, deal with the increasing menace of Arab brigandage. And all of this would have to be done without jeopardizing Hashomer's attempt to lay hands, as rapidly as possible, on arms.

It was becoming difficult to purchase arms abroad, and even more difficult to buy them in Palestine. Eventually, Hashomer contrived a machine which could load cartridges with gunpowder; the beginning, actually, of a local weapons' production. The precious machine, and whatever rifles and revolvers Hashomer managed to buy in Beirut and Damascus, were stored in regional caches, the location of which were only known to a few members.

Hashomer is outlawed
But despite all their attempts to placate the government and co-operate with it, the Turkish administration continued to suspect the Jews. All local organizations were disbanded and Hashomer, which for several years had enjoyed semi-legal status, was now outlawed. The watchmen were forbidden to sign any contracts with the colonies, and those agreements which *were* drawn up during the war, bore only the names of individuals. There appeared to be no way in which the Yishuv could persuade the Turks that its hopes for Palestine were predicated on Turkey's winning the war – although, this, in fact, was the truth.

Along with the security situation, the economic situation in Palestine became critical. The Turks had quartered a vast garrison

32

in the country with which they hoped to take the Suez Canal. To supply these forces, they confiscated mules, horses, camels, and cattle; demanded and received huge war levies of food and money from the population, particularly from the Jewish community. Provisions became scarce, and the Turkish officials more and more demanding. Whatever else happened, the Turks were obviously committed, once and for all, to doing away with Jewish nationalism.

Hashomer emerged from its conclaves with a plan, with a list of priorities, and determined to dig in. Whatever else happened, said Hashomer, for *its* part, the Jews of Palestine must stay put, must survive the war, and must remain intact. One way to do so was to stop the Turks from expelling the entire population. Mass expulsions had taken place often in Jewish history, and their memory had remained fresh. This time, the Jews would not be extirpated from Palestine. Hashomer took the lead in urging upon the entire Yishuv that it take Ottoman citizenship. Additionally, it made known a specific programme for action in the sharpening emergency. All members of Hashomer were ordered to stay at their posts under all and any circumstances. Their duty, declared the central committee, was not only to remain where they were, but to organize the young people of the colonies so that, together, they

The 1914 graduating class of Tel Aviv's Herzliya Gymnasium as Turkish officers

33

could defend the Jewish settlements from attack either by the Arabs or by the bands of desperate Turkish deserters who now roamed the country, terrorizing the population. Also, in addition to the campaign to persuade the Yishuv to Ottomanize itself, Hashomer decided to try to persuade the Turks to permit the formation of a Jewish militia, of a fighting unit which could also include the Arabs, if the Turkish authorities were so to decide. The job of this militia, explained Hashomer, would be to protect the Holy Land itself.

Relations between Hashomer and the Turkish authorities

It seemed most unlikely that the Turks would even consider this proposal, but it was worth trying. Hashomer believed that various Arab leaders might be equally interested, and also, that in the chaos that currently reigned throughout Palestine, it was even possible that one Turkish official might agree to this without the others necessarily knowing about it at all.

One of the most extraordinary decisions taken by Hashomer was also the most secret: plans were made for the conquest of Jerusalem by the Jews. By this time, going on the assumption that the British would win World War I, Hashomer assumed also that Jerusalem would fall to the British. The Turks would almost certainly retreat, and in the ensuing panic, a well-knit, well-trained cadre of Hashomer members would take and hold Jerusalem until the British arrived to claim it. Somewhat unrealistically, Hashomer was convinced that if this happened, the British would then gratefully note the special contribution of the Jews of Palestine, taking it into account when the future of Palestine was discussed. Accordingly, a carefully chosen group of watchmen was sent to Jerusalem to reconnoitre; to study its topography, learn its fortifications and report on the size and location of Turkish barracks there.

Open defiance of the Turks by Hashomer

At first, to everyone's astonishment, the Turks were inclined to favour the creation of a militia. They stipulated that two separate units be formed: one of Jews, the other of Arabs. Only Turkish citizens would be accepted and, of course, the Officer Commanding would be a Turk. At the last minute, however, the government changed its mind. It would be an act of criminal insanity to arm the Jews. The idea of the militia was rejected, and in its stead came a tidal wave of new restrictions. Foremost, and most serious of which was the order that all arms be turned over to the administration at once. Terrified of the consequences of disobedience, some of the colonists complied with the order, and despite Hashomer's pleas, handed over all of the arms in their possession. When nothing availed, Hashomer raided the arms stores of a number of Jewish villages to keep the weapons from falling into Turkish hands. Some farmers, unable to face telling the Turks that there

34

Many young Palestinians served as officers in the Turkish army. Moshe Shertok (Sharett) shown with his sister, was to become first Foreign Minister of Israel after the establishment of the State and its second prime-minister

were no arms left to turn over, organized special purchasing missions, paid exorbitant sums to the Arabs for a few Mausers and Brownings, and dutifully delivered them to the government.

The strong, lighthearted young men and women of Hashomer, those who had run races, played their flutes, and at night sung: 'Three friends have I; my gun, my horse and my people'; the self-ordained defenders of a nation, the would-be establishers of a new social order, now squared their shoulders to prevent the disintegration of all that they had helped to build. They stood guard at night, worked all day, felt as though the burden of the survival of the Yishuv was theirs, exclusively; and wondered how much longer they could continue to replenish their meagre supply of arms, avoid conscription, keep from being expelled from Palestine. The days of the wedding canopies held up by rifles, of the swash-buckling honour guard they formed for Baron Rothschild when he visited his colonies, the adventure and sweet novelty of their life in the past, all gave way now to grim anxiety lest the Jews of Palestine suffer the fate of the Armenians at the hands of the Turks, lest the Yishuv be exterminated.

It seemed possible: the expulsions continued, so did near famine, so did ravaging disease. Tel Aviv emptied slowly; family after family was driven away by Turkish decree, or thrown into Turkish jails. Soon, the Jewish community might be brought to a standstill, cut off from all outside aid, starved to death.

The months of war dragged on, taking their toll of Palestine. Hashomer, or what was left of its leadership (by 1916, Shochat, Ben-Zvi, Ben-Gurion and many others had been exiled) intensified its efforts to create small partisan units which would fight to the end, regardless of what happened to the rest of the Jews. Rachel Yanait's diary evokes the intensity of the times.

'If the worst comes to the worst, at least some of us will be left, some of the Jews of Palestine, and at the end, they will defend the honour of the nation, and by doing so, they will raise the hearts and the hopes of future pioneers who will come from the lands of the Diaspora and rebuild all that has been destroyed.'

The Aaronsons and
NILI

But Hashomer was not alone in its concern for the future; nor did all the Jews in Palestine share its way of thinking. In Zichron Yaakov, not far from Haifa, a prosperous village, in whose vineyards the watchmen had first stood guard in 1906 together with Arabs, a well-to-do, attractive, educated family called Aaronson had taken the initiative in spying for the British. The leader of the spy ring was the family's oldest son, Aaron, a distinguished botanist whose name and experimental station at Atlit, on the coast, were known far beyond the limits of Palestine.

36

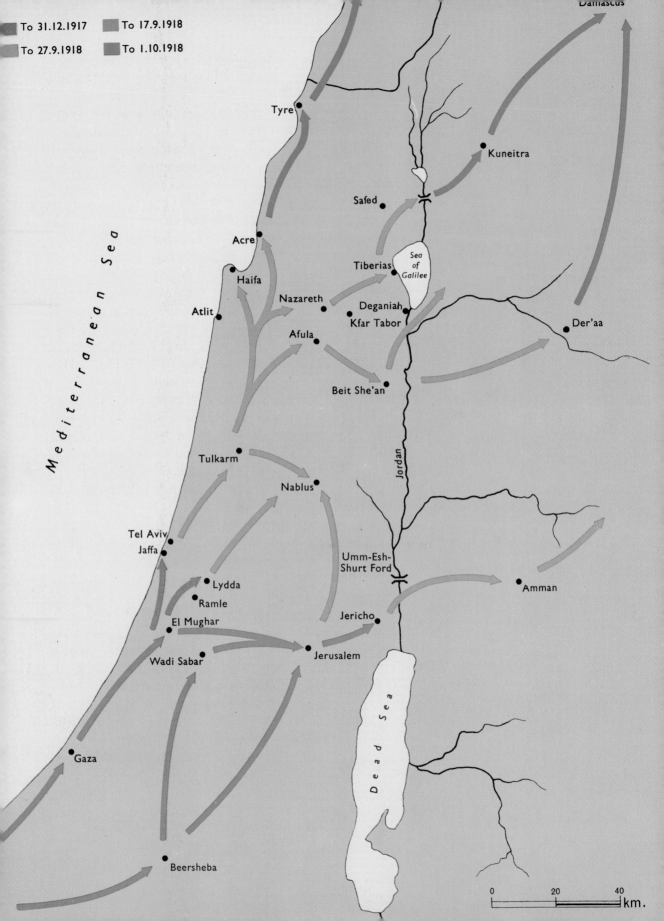

To 31.12.1917
To 27.9.1918
To 17.9.1918
To 1.10.1918

Damascus

Tyre

Kuneitra

Safed

Acre

Haifa

Tiberias
Sea of Galilee

Atlit

Nazareth

Deganiah
Kfar Tabor

Der'aa

Afula

Beit She'an

Jordan

Tulkarm

Nablus

Tel Aviv
Jaffa

Umm-Esh-
Shurt Ford

Amman

Lydda

Ramle

Jericho

El Mughar

Wadi Sabar

Jerusalem

Gaza

Dead Sea

Beersheba

Mediterranean Sea

0   20   40
km.

The Aaronson family: *above*: Sara, *below*: Aaron, *right*: Alex, were all members of the NILI group working on behalf of British intelligence

Aaron, his brother Alexander, his sister Sara, and a few loyal friends, among them Avshalom Feinberg of Hadera and Na'aman Belkind from Rishon Lezion, had volunteered to provide British headquarters in Egypt with information about Turkish troop movements and battle strength. At first, the British had been sceptical about the group; spies who refused to take money for themselves and whose motivation seemed purely altruistic were not necessarily a desirable commodity. But Aaron Aaronson was convinced that the Allies would win the war, and was anxious to speed the moment of victory. Besides, he too felt that in the peace talks that would follow Turkey's defeat, the voice of the Jews of Palestine would be more likely to be heard if the Jews could point to active participation in the war.

Avshalom Feinberg of NILI was killed by Bedouin in 1916. His grave was discovered in the Gaza Strip after the Six-Day War of June, 1967

The group which called itself *Nili* (the acronym of the Hebrew words 'The Eternal One of Israel Does Not Lie'), contrived an ingenious code composed of Hebrew, English, French and Aramaic, and succeeded in setting up and maintaining communications with the British. Apart from its actual value to the Allies, Nili, through Aaronson's experimental station in Atlit, had access to money raised abroad and for a while constituted the Yishuv's only access to the world outside, and to funds of any kind.

In the beginning, very few people in Palestine knew anything at all about the spy ring. Inevitably, however, rumours spread; the comings and goings of the Aaronsons began to attract attention; money which reached the experimental station and was turned over to the Yishuv's emergency committee to help the hundreds of hungry and homeless families had to be explained somehow. Despite Nili's attempts to achieve complete secrecy, the Jews began to whisper about the existence of spies in their midst. Not only was the idea of spying abhorrent, but they were sure that if the Turks got wind of Nili's activities, the entire community would be brutally punished. Those who did know regarded the Aaronsons as dangerous, considered them lacking all political judgment. Hashomer, in particular, opposed Nili. Aaron Aaronson was notoriously disinterested in employing Jewish labour; when Hashomer representatives berated him, he answered: 'When you produce Jewish workers as efficient as my Arabs, I shall be delighted to take them on. But, until then, I shall do things my own way.' His attitude appalled the pioneers; they felt him to be alien and uncommitted; he represented the very bourgeoisie against whom they had fought for so long. In every respect, Hashomer disapproved of the Aaronsons, of Nili, of all it stood for, and most of all, of the perilous work the spy ring had undertaken.

One day, the espionage would be discovered; in their resultant rage, the Turks would know no bounds. If anything was needed to convince the government that the Jews were indeed untrustworthy, it was the perilous activity conducted at Atlit. And, one day, the espionage *was* discovered. A carrier pigeon, specially trained to take messages to and from Atlit, lost its way, and ended up in the hands of the Turks. It took time for the Turks to grasp fully what had happened, but within a few days, the order went out: get the Jewish spies, dead or alive!

NILI *is uncovered and its members tortured and executed*

The dragnets covered all of Palestine. There was not a farm, a village, a collective settlement or town that was not searched, its men hauled off in chains to be tortured and endlessly interrogated, its women and children threatened and molested. The Turkish rampage – its many victims, the news of the execution of Nili leaders and of Belkind's hanging in Damascus, the death of Sara Aaronson who killed herself rather than reveal Nili's secrets to the Turks – brought the life of the Yishuv to a virtual standstill for weeks.

Then, Yosef Lishansky, a Nili leader, caught and subjected to the bastinado, (an excruciating Turkish form of flogging) avenged himself on Hashomer before he died. Hashomer had tried, towards the end, to put a stop to the spying. In various clandestine and urgent gatherings, suggestions for active intervention were brought before Hashomer's leaders. Perhaps it would be possible for Hashomer itself to hold the members of Nili in protective custody until the end of the war? Perhaps, all sentiment aside, it was the duty of Hashomer to do away with Nili's leaders before the entire Yishuv paid the penalty for their irresponsibility? It was the lives of a few weighed against the lives of many, against the continuity of the Jewish effort in Palestine, against the very future of Zionism. The debate raged back and forth; it was protracted and painful. But before any final decision could be taken, Nili was found out, and the Turks had started their manhunt. Yosef Lishansky was finally trapped by the Turks, and tortured beyond endurance. The names of dozens of Hashomer members fell into the hands of the Turks.

Turkish reprisals

Hashomer burrowed deeper underground, but the Turks unearthed many of the watchmen, sent scores of them to jail, and expelled many others from Palestine. Leaderless, diminished, and in ever-worsening physical condition, it seemed impossible that the Yishuv could recover from the Turkish terror. From the south, however, the sound of guns heralded the approach of the British; and news reached Palestine of the Balfour Declaration.

The Balfour Declaration, so termed because it was signed by Britain's Foreign Secretary, Arthur James Balfour, was issued in London in November 1917. It followed prolonged negotiations

Lord Balfour together with Dr Chaim Weizmann, destined to become first President of the State of Israel. Balfour was instrumental in the issuing of the 'Balfour Declaration' of 1917 which promised British support of a National Home in Palestine for the Jewish people

with Zionist leaders in England and was to become one of the most important documents ever issued concerning the Holy Land. It declared that the British Government favoured 'the establishment in Palestine of a National Home for the Jewish People', and would use 'its best endeavours to facilitate the achievement of this object.' The Declaration was couched in the form of a letter addressed to Lord Rothschild; one of its prime architects, Chaim Weizmann, described it as a 'great act of restitution', and despite its ambiguous phraseology, its intent, at the time, seemed clear to all concerned. The foundations had been laid for a Jewish Commonwealth in Palestine.

The excitement and elation among Zionists in the Diaspora was great, and in Palestine itself, the Jews, half-disbelieving, rejoiced. But, by the winter of 1917, hunger, exile, and execution had critically reduced the Jewish population. There were now only some 56,000 Jews left in the country. But these rallied, tended their wounds, and began, once again, and in great earnest, to plan the formation of a Jewish Legion which would help Great Britain to conquer the Holy Land and free it of the Turks.

41

2 Jews in Uniform

The Jewish Legion — The Zion Mule Corps — Trumpeldor and Jabotinsky — Tel Hai — The Haganah

The impulse of the Jews of Palestine to bring into being a Jewish Army that would take part in the Allied campaign against the Turks dovetailed, as is often true of such historical imperatives, with a similar impulse generated many miles away, under far more favourable circumstances. Although the Yishuv, cut off, under Turkish control and on the verge of famine, was not to learn about the formation of the Jewish Legion for several months, by 1917, in fact, two Jewish battalions within the British Army, under their own and the British colours, were already preparing, in a training camp in England, to take part in the conquest and occupation of Palestine. Within a year, a third all-Palestinian Battalion was to be added.

The idea of the Jewish Legion is born

All three – the 38th, the 39th and the 40th Royal Fusiliers, after the war to be known as the Judean Battalion – were destined to become the first practical expression of the British commitment to the Zionist cause; their disbandment was to mark the first bitter confrontation between the Jews of Palestine and the new Palestine Government; and they were to have a radical and lasting effect on the course, style and dimensions of Jewish self-defence.

The Jewish Legion was born in the crowded Egyptian barracks of Gabbari and Mafruza where, idle and discontented, over a thousand Jewish refugees from Turkish Palestine, given shelter by the British, had set up an autonomous community, supported mainly by the bounty of Egyptian Jewry. Two men, both remarkably gifted and both endowed with singular determination, met in these barracks and there jointly conceived the idea of an identifiably Jewish fighting force to signal the official emergence of the Jewish people from their traditional state of neutrality in a European war; which would, in effect, make Jewish proclamation of belligerency on the side of the Western Allies necessary.

It is likely that both these men – Vladimir Jabotinsky and Joseph

opposite: The emblem of the Jewish Legion. This unit of the British Army eventually consisted of more than 5,000 Jewish volunteers, eager to fight against the Turkish enemy. The motto below the emblem reads *Kadima* — 'Forward'

Trumpeldor – would have functioned separately towards the same end, even had they not met in Egypt. Together they formed what turned out to be a virtually irresistible, highly dynamic combination of imagination, will-power and personal courage. To these qualities were added, in equal measure, a shared sense of history, of the manifest destiny of the Jews returned to their homeland. Like the founders of Bar Giora and Hashomer, both Jabotinsky and Trumpeldor understood that the time had come for the Jews to abandon a national posture of passivity, and that activism, even when and if it involved militarism, was an essential factor in the struggle for independence. In brief, they believed that only if the Jews fought for Palestine, entered the lists on their own behalf and in their own name, would they be able to stake a claim to it, come peace.

Zeev (Vladimir) Jabotinsky

Despite these similarities of approach and basic temperament, the two men were very different. In 1914 Jabotinsky was a correspondent for a Russian newspaper: his assignment was reporting on what he called 'the moods and sentiments produced by the war'. In this capacity, he had wandered around Europe, filing brilliantly-written stories about what people were saying and thinking in the various capitals of the continent. One wet, blowy morning found him staring at a billboard in Bordeaux. There, flapping in the wind, a damp poster informed him that Turkey had just entered the war as one of the Central Powers. Jabotinsky, then thirty-six, had long been a Zionist; also, he had lived in Constantinople for several years. He had no doubt at all that Turkey would be defeated; he was familiar with the internal condition of the 'Sick Man of Europe', and while the fate of Germany was far from sure, he was convinced that Turkey would not only be beaten, but dismembered. In the dismemberment lay, he thought, the first real chance for the Jews of Palestine to attain independence. In the same moment of insight, Jabotinsky decided that now the Jews must make an immediate effort to participate in the inevitable fighting for Palestine – and do so under the aegis of the British.

Joseph Trumpeldor

Accordingly, he set off for the refugee camps in Egypt. At Gabbari he met Trumpeldor for the first time. Joseph Trumpeldor was a rare example of a thoroughly professional Jewish soldier. He had fought, and lost an arm, at Port Arthur during the Russo-Japanese war, and after its fall had been a prisoner of the Japanese for many months. Decorated for valour, he had also been permitted, despite his injury, to become a reserve officer in the Russian Army. It is possible that he was, in fact, the *only* Jewish officer in the Czarist forces. Like Jabotinsky, he had long been a Zionist; even in prison camp, he had organized Zionist groups and raised money for the Yishuv. It was natural that, after a while, he settled in Palestine

44

Joseph Trumpeldor (1880–1920) studied to be a dentist, but volunteered for the Russian army, losing an arm in Port Arthur in 1904. One of the key figures in Jewish self-defence, he was instrumental (together with Jabotinsky) in founding the Jewish Legion, the Zion Mule Corps, and the pioneering movement, Hechalutz. He was killed leading the heroic defence of Tel Hai (see pages 63–66). He is shown here as an officer in the Russian army.

himself, in a collective settlement on the shores of the Sea of Galilee. By 1914, one of the displaced Palestinians of Gabbari, Trumpeldor was a pacifist, a Socialist, a vegetarian – and an exile. Unlike Jabotinsky, he was handsome, Nordic-looking, tall, slim and not given to garrulity. His most celebrated idiosyncracy was his favourite expression, in the Hebrew which he spoke with difficulty: *Ein Davar* – Never mind, which Trumpledor said about almost anything that went wrong, and *ein davar* were the last words he spoke before he died, some five years later, defending a small settlement in the Galilee against Arab attack.

The notion of a Jewish unit is suggested to the British

In the Egyptian barracks, Trumpeldor and Jabotinsky found that their views on action to be undertaken were identical: they would, they agreed, approach the British at once and put forth the case for a Jewish military unit. First, however, they called a meeting of the barracks' population and put the issue to a vote. On a piece of paper, torn from a child's exercise book, and signed by a hundred of those present, they wrote a terse resolution in Hebrew: 'It is resolved to form a Jewish Legion and to propose to England to make use of it in Palestine.' The formalities finished, they organized a delegation to present itself in Cairo before the British authorities. Trumpeldor wore his uniform and all four of the St. George Crosses awarded him for heroism by the Russian Imperial Army.

The British, though impressed, denied that there were any plans for an offensive in Palestine; but, nonetheless, made a suggestion. To the crestfallen delegation, it was proposed that a detachment for mule transport be formed to be used somewhere on the Turkish front. It was a far cry from anything the delegation had envisaged. Characteristically, Jabotinsky was affronted by the notion. A 'donkey battalion' was hardly appropriate for the entrance of the Jewish people into the armies of the world. Were the Jews then to enter Zion, leading mules? But Trumpeldor, less given to histrionics, less sensitive to the outward appearance of things, favoured accepting the offer. After all, he argued, all fronts lead to Zion. Besides, wasn't the French Camel Corps universally romanticized, considered by many to be the ultimate in glamour? Should this opportunity be passed by, because of the apparent indignity?

The Zion Mule Corps

Trumpeldor triumphed: by April 1915, all Palestinian volunteers who had enlisted in the barracks, the Zion Mule Corps, 650 Jewish muleteers (and their 750 mules) were in Gallipoli. They created a small working Hebrew vocabulary of military terms, made themselves a blue and white Zionist flag, and although their primary role involved transport, were all trained and equipped for battle.

After less than a month of training, therefore, the muleteers

found themselves in the trenches of Gallipoli, on the firing line where, at last, they met the Turks in battle. Nightly, under heavy Turkish bombardment, they led their loaded mules to the front and back. Some of the muleteers were killed, others wounded; and a few decorated. Those who lost their lives in Gallipoli were the first Palestinian Jews to be buried later in the tranquil British War Cemetery on Mount Scopus in Jerusalem; the Star of David on their tombstones bespeaking their role as the precursors of Israel's army.

The Gallipoli debacle took nine months and cost the British Army nearly a quarter of a million men. The operation was abandoned and the troops evacuated. The Jewish muleteers paid formal tribute to the graves of their comrades, prayed over them, slashed the throats of their mules, and left. Those who returned to England were ordered on to Ireland, told that they were to help quell the anti-British riots that had broken out there. To a man, the muleteers refused and in May 1916, the Corps was disbanded.

But it had not existed in vain: to begin with, it had attracted attention; it had reminded the preoccupied Allies that the Zionists might be useful, that they formed a real entity, that they had a potential. Gallipoli was not a glorious campaign for anyone; in the dust of the retreat, the small band of Palestinian Jews from the barracks of Gabbari and Mafruza whose insignia contained a Star of David made good copy for journalists and the General Officer Commanding in Gallipoli, Sir Ian Hamilton, praised the Corps for 'showing a more difficult type of bravery than the men in the front line who had the excitement of combat to keep them going.'

One hundred and twenty Palestinian members of the Zion Mule

The Zion Mule Corps, founded by Joseph Trumpeldor, played a distinguished role in the bloody battles of the Gallipoli peninsula against the Turks

Vladimir (Zeev) Jabotinsky (1880–1940), Zionist orator, writer and leader, together with Trumpeldor founded the Jewish Legion. Later, he founded the Revisionist Movement and the Betar (Brit Trumpeldor) youth movement. In a split from official Zionism he also founded the New Zionist Organization. He is shown here with a group of soldiers of the Jewish Legion

Corps re-enlisted in the British Army; although they had no way of knowing it at the time, they were slated to become the nucleus of the 'real' Jewish Legion to be formed shortly. But perhaps the greatest single asset of the Corps was its Commanding Officer, Lieutenant Colonel John Henry Patterson, who was to become the Commanding Officer of the 38th Royal Fusiliers and who was to help bring the Legion into being. Patterson, a slender, elegant Irishman with elegiac eyes and a deep interest in the Jews under his command, had been best-known until then as the author of a popular book about man-eating lions in Africa. He was a career soldier, with a creditable past behind him and assured promotion ahead of him. The Zion Mule Corps represented a minor posting for him, but he accepted it with goodwill and gradually became fascinated by the intense national feeling which supported and motivated its men. Patterson fell ill before the Gallipoli campaign ended, and Trumpeldor, his second in command, took over from him. It was logical, therefore, that when Trumpeldor and Jabotinsky renewed their efforts to obtain British consent for the formation of another and larger Jewish force, they turned to Patterson, among others, for assistance. Trumpeldor, disappointed by the British refusal to delay disbandment of the Mule Corps and his request for re-enlistment turned down by the British Army, decided that the best hope for a major Jewish formation lay in Russia itself, and eventually attempted to mobilize an army of 100,000 men which, he believed, could be sent to the Caucasian front, there to break its way through Armenia and Mesopotamia

Lieut. Col. John Patterson became first commander of the Zion Mule Corps, and was active in the formation of the Jewish Legion. Col. Patterson who died in 1947, is here shown in his command post on the Nablus front

on into Eastern Palestine. But in the meantime he stayed in London, trying with Jabotinsky, to find an entrée to the British Government. When all doors seemed closed, and the British, led by Kitchener, who was firmly opposed to any offensive on the Eastern front, were disinclined to talk to these strange Russian Jews about a 'fancy regiment', Jabotinsky began to travel, as Herzl had done before him, throughout Western Europe, to try to interest the heads of other governments in the creation of a Jewish Legion.

Everywhere, he met with opposition, even among many British Jews. A Jewish Legion was an inherently separatist idea, they said; it boded no good for the integrated future of Jews anywhere; it would be conspicuous, and risky. What if it did *not* distinguish itself? Who would pay the piper? But a small core of British Jews, Zionists themselves, encouraged by Dr Weizmann's wholehearted support, backed the project; Colonel Patterson helped Jabotinsky to meet members of Lloyd George's Secretariat, and Jabotinsky himself lent force to the argument he was propagating by joining the army. He enlisted as a private in the 20th Battalion of the London Regiment, where he gathered around himself Platoon 16, the one hundred and twenty men who had formerly served in the Zion Mule Corps.

At last Jabotinsky, in private's uniform, was summoned, with Trumpeldor, to the British War Office. Lord Derby, then Britain's War Secretary, looked with astonishment at the two self-declared emissaries of the Jewish people but listened to what they said. Then he asked some questions. Chiefly, he wanted to know whether

49

Yitshaq Ben-Zvi (1884–1963), later to become second president of Israel (succeeding Dr Chaim Weizmann), joined the Jewish Legion as a private in 1917. His wife, Rachel Yanait Ben-Zvi had herself been a pioneer of Jewish self-defence, as well as a member of Ha-shomer

the British could count on a large number of volunteers. Trumpeldor, in thickly accented English, answered. 'Your Lordship', he said, 'If it is to be just a regiment of Jews – perhaps. If it is to be a formation for the Palestine front – certainly. If, together with its formation, there will appear a government pronouncement in favour of Zionism, the response will be overwhelming.'

At first, the War Office agreed that the new units should be distinctly labelled as Jewish, both as to name and insignia. By the summer of 1917, however, when the 38th and 39th Royal Fusiliers were officially gazetted, the British had changed their mind. But a Hebrew sign hung outside the recruiting centre in London, and on their sleeves the Jewish soldiers wore the six-pointed Star of David. The 38th was to be commanded by Patterson himself, the 39th by Colonel Eliezer Margolin, a Jew who had once lived in Palestine and had later emigrated to Australia.

One of the commanders of the Jewish Legion was Lieut. Col. Eliezer Margolin

The bulk of the recruits from England were Jewish immigrants from Russia, most of them living in Whitechapel, as aliens exempt from British conscription. It had taken weeks of persuasion to interest them in the Legion. They were men to whom Britain itself was still foreign, who spoke Yiddish, who worked mainly at sedentary occupations, primarily tailoring. Pale, round-shouldered, influenced by bitter memories of enforced soldiering in Russia, and, like most exiles, on the defensive, they were unlikely material for the Legion of which Trumpeldor and Jabotinsky dreamed. But the Legion's 'tailors', as they came to be called, turned out to be first-class soldiers. Hours of tough physical out-of-doors training, the rigid routines of military life, their own new role, and the obvious trust invested in them by their officers, all had their effect. The Legion's rank swelled weekly: the Recruiting Department of the British War Office supplied 35,000 names of aliens, and 35,000 envelopes. Ten officials wrote addresses; and Jabotinsky and his colleagues made one personal appearance after another to gradually less hostile Whitechapel crowds.

In the meantime, recruiting had begun in the United States and Canada. There, David Ben-Gurion and Yitshaq Ben-Zvi had started a campaign; recruits from the New World largely made up the 39th Royal Fusiliers. All told, by the end of World War I, there would be some 5,000 men under arms in the Jewish Legion, led by three lieutenant-colonels and some Jewish, some non-Jewish junior officers. Jabotinsky himself was one of twenty lieutenants.

Recruiting for the Jewish Legion in USA

Most important, in that part of Palestine already liberated by the British, hundreds of young Jewish men and women awaited the call to arms. Without knowing any of the details of the recruiting campaigns in England or America, plans were being laid in Pales-

A British tank in action during the attack on Gaza in Allenby's Palestinian campaign of 1917

Jerusalem falls to the British

tine for the establishment of a volunteer Jewish Legion, and a petition, signed by thousands, had already been given to the British, who, by this time, had crossed the Sinai Peninsula and were readying their crucial attack on Gaza. Six weeks after publication of the Balfour Declaration, Jerusalem fell to the British. Allenby, humbly entering the Old City on foot, through the Jaffa Gate, accepted the keys. In all the southern colonies the Jews were certain that now they would be allowed to take part in the final northward surge of the Allied war machine. The liberators had arrived; the future had opened up again; after all, the Zionist cause had been upheld by the greatest of all World Powers. They – the pioneers who had endured the Turkish regime and survived it; who had continued, despite nearly insurmountable obstacles, to maintain themselves in prime condition; who so craved the privilege of fighting for Eretz-Yisrael – surely now they would be allowed to do so. A happy, enthusiastic, weary Yishuv awaited the British.

52

The Turkish mayor of Jerusalem surrenders the city to two British sergeants on December 9, 1917. Left: Sgt. Sedgewick, right: Sgt. Hawcombe

The Legion embarks for the front

   In England, the Legion prepared to embark for the front. On 2 February 1918, it was ordered to London to march through the East End – from which so many of its men had come – before proceeding to Southampton. The Legionnaires were quartered overnight in the Tower of London; in the morning, in full kit, permitted as a special privilege to carry fixed bayonets, and preceded by a band of the Coldstream Guards, they bore the Union Jack and the Jewish flag through the City. The Lord Mayor, in his robes, took the salute from the Jewish soldiers. In Whitechapel, tens of thousands of Jews stood in the streets, fluttering miniature flags of their own, crying and singing; Colonel Patterson, from his horse, waved and smiled; in perfect unison, bayonets dead level, heads high, the 'tailors' marched into history. 'It was an occasion unique in British military annals', Patterson wrote.
   In Alexandria and in Cairo, the Legion received a rousing welcome. The British High Commissioner took the salute himself; and

53

Members of the Palestinian
contingent of the Jewish Legion
en route for Cairo, take leave
of their families at Jaffa

the entire Jewish population turned out to cheer the troops. But most encouraging, an emissary came from Tel Aviv to offer his blessings, to tell the Legionnaires that in Jerusalem, Tel Aviv, Jaffa, even in the north which was still in the hands of the Turks, the volunteers were waiting. There was no reason to expect that the British Military Administration would delay formation of a third regiment.

The Yishuv had learned about the Legion accidentally. Rachel Yanait Ben-Zvi, visiting the colony of Rishon Lezion, had picked up a Yiddish newspaper from New York. In a small story, under

an unimpressive headline, she read about the efforts being made by Ben-Zvi and Ben-Gurion to bring 'pioneers' to Palestine. Suddenly, she recalled early conversations with them, talks about participating in the war, about helping to overthrow the Turks; 'Pioneers', she understood, must mean soldiers. There had long been rumours about Jewish regiments, but nothing official, no definite word. Now, she knew it would happen soon, and the knowledge added impetus to the Yishuv's eagerness to fight.

Jabotinsky arrived in Palestine and confirmed the news. To the members of Hashomer, he seemed unduly interested in the political

The Jewish Legion encamped at El Arish, south of Gaza, 1918

55

implications of the Legion, what exactly it would mean in terms of the future, how it could best help to guarantee Jewish independence. The men and women of Hashomer were impatient with his rhetoric, they wanted information from him, the promise of action soon. Rachel Yanait made up her mind to meet General Allenby herself and in Jerusalem she spoke to him. She handed him the petition from the Yishuv, explained who she was, and why she was there. Also, she told him that the women of Hashomer wanted to fight with their men.

Colonel Margolin's 39th, with its majority of American and Canadian recruits, arrived in Egypt; now, only the Palestinians were missing. 'How odd,' said a high-ranking British officer, 'Why do these people push so to get into the army? The fourth year of the war, too; and so many of them!' The mood in GHQ was puzzling; there seemed to be considerable reluctance about mobilizing the Palestinians at all.

Finally, the long-awaited confirmation came from London. A battalion of Palestinian Jews would be formed. It was too late for it to participate in the conquest of the Galilee; the war against Turkey was over before the 40th Royal Fusiliers finished basic training. But the battalion, in which many of the leaders of the future Jewish State served, was to contribute not only to the occupation of Palestine by the British, but also, and perhaps even more significantly, to the crucial events that followed it. Having hoped for so long that they themselves would take part in the liberation of the north, the Palestinians were disappointed by the GHQ decree that they were to train in Egypt. Nonetheless, the leave-taking ceremony was memorable. Against the background of the small synagogue on Tel Aviv's main street, for many evoking earlier days and other rituals, a great scarlet and white banner spelled out the words 'In blood and fire Judea shall arise', and, as hundreds watched silently, Hashomer's standard was ceremonially presented to the flag-bearers of the 40th Royal Fusiliers.

Dr Weizmann, in Palestine with the recently appointed Zionist Commission which was charged with reporting to the British on the situation and drawing up plans for the future, addressed the recruits and, with tears in his eyes, bade them Godspeed. They were, he said, the fulfilment of the Yishuv's deepest yearning, full partners in the redemption of Zion from the Turks, soldiers of a Jewish battalion in the army of a mighty nation pledged to establish a Jewish National Home.

One of the Legion's medical officers writing home to London, described the arrival of the Legion's third battalion in camp.

'The Palestinians have come,' he wrote. 'Some seven hundred

Field-Marshall Viscount Allenby of Megiddo. Commander of the victorious British army in Palestine

opposite: This monumental sculpted lion looks out over the fields of northern Galilee at Tel Hai, commemorating its defence and fall, and the death of its commander, Joseph Trumpeldor

Unit of the Jewish Legion entrenched at Jericho on the River Jordan

oddments grouping themselves with perfect military precision into ranks and platoons, resplendent with rampant lions and crossed triangles. Never in your life have you seen such a crowd. They were in rags; the footgear was varied beyond belief; many had none, some had wrapped their feet in paper, others in rags, a few had boots. But their spirits were magnificent... Jews ready to do and die for their ideals. They may be the children of slaves, but they are of the blood of princes.'

In the meantime, the Legion's first two battalions fought in the great British offensive of the summer of 1918. By May, they had completed their training, and on 5 June, they left Egypt for the Holy Land. Colonel Patterson felt that the occasion should be marked in some way; he ordered a short prayer to be said, and trumpets to be sounded. Much later, he recalled that crossing by train into the Holy Land.

'All through the night, as we sped across the Sinai desert, we

could see the funnel of the engine belching forth a pillar of flame, and we were greatly reminded of the wanderings of the forefathers of these men in this very desert, who, in their night journeys, were always guided by a pillar of fire.'

The Jewish Legion spent its first days on the front in a valley between Jerusalem and Nablus; then, as the sweltering Palestinian summer began, it was ordered to the Jordan Valley north of the Dead Sea, the deepest spot on earth, where the heat, in August, is close to unendurable. Mostly flat, the Jordan Valley is slashed here and there by huge rocky ravines, some of them hundreds of yards wide. In one of these wadis, el Mellahah, on the extreme right flank of the northern front of the British Army in Palestine, with the Turks virtually on three sides of it, the Legion made its headquarters. Its task was two-fold: to be on the lookout for the expected Turkish attack, and, by fording the Jordan River, to block the Turks on the other side. It was both the weakest, and at that

Soldiers of the Jewish Legion guarding one of the bridges across the Jordan — known today as the Allenby Bridge

time, the most dangerous position in the entire British line. Had the Turks attacked as the British anticipated, it is probable that the Legion would have been in grave danger. But Turkish cannons constituted only one hazard; malaria, sunstroke and thirst gradually decimated the ranks. Daily, the sun beat down on the Legionnaires and the nights were suffocating. But by the end of September, the Legion had crossed the Jordan at the ford of Umm esh Shurt, marched across the valley to the mountains of what was later to become Transjordan and bivouacked at Gilead, where, at last, it rested.

The Legion crosses the Jordan   'It is a curious fact,' wrote Colonel Patterson, in his summing up of the campaign, 'that the whole movement of the British Army in Palestine, which swept the Turks out of the country, was actually pivoted on the sons of Israel who were once again fighting the enemy – not far from the spot where the Jews had crossed the Jordan under Joshua.'

Headed by General Allenby, commander of Britain's Egyptian Expeditionary Force from June 1917, the British had won two major victories on the Palestine front: one at Gaza, the other, nearly a year later, at Megiddo. There, at the biblical site of Armageddon, the British broke the Turkish lines and began to roll up the enemy force. Using mounted troops to consolidate his gains, Allenby surrounded the Turks, driving them northward. In October 1918, Damascus, Beirut and Aleppo fell to the British. Although the Jewish Legion at its peak numbered only 5,000 men, and constituted a tiny fraction of the vast EEF, the 38th and 39th Royal Fusiliers had indeed helped to chase the Turks out of Palestine.

The Turkish collapse was complete. Half-dead from exhaustion, thirsty, terrified, the Turkish Army disintegrated. On 31 October 1918, only a few weeks after the start of the British offensive, the Ottoman Empire acknowledged defeat.

Victory in Palestine   The Legion's participation in the World War had only been partial; it had come into being belatedly; a fourth battalion, made up of British and Americans, had, in fact, not even managed to train in time for overseas service. Many of the promises that had been made to the Legion originally had either not been carried out at all, or had been carried out so late that they had lost meaning; it was in fact a year after the cessation of hostilities that the much longed-for change of name was effected, and the three Jewish battalions were officially turned into one, called the First Judean Battalion. There were other, if less dramatic, instances of stalling and red-tape, but most of the men put these down to the inevitable and tortuous workings of bureaucracy. It was not quite as easy, however, for the Legionnaires to rationalize the often hostile atti-

60

tude displayed towards them by the headquarters of the EEF. The theme of anti-Semitism runs through most of the memoirs written by Legion officers after the war, and there was a constant battle between Colonel Patterson and GHQ about blatantly unfair treatment accorded the Legion. Nonetheless, when the war ended, the Legion was in a euphoric mood.

Whatever had gone wrong, whatever slights had been meted out, however galling the discrimination against it, the facts remained: the Allies had won the war, the Legion was in Palestine, and a new era was about to begin, a halcyon period in terms of the Zionist vision. It was, therefore, with a sense of considerable satisfaction that the officers and men of the Jewish Legion found themselves, in 1919, representing a quarter of all the infantry regiments still stationed in the country. At a time when the overwhelming majority of the British soldiers eagerly awaited demobilization, and complained bitterly about being sent to Syria or to Egypt, where serious unrest and anti-British riots had broken out, the Legionnaires regarded their garrison duty in Palestine as an end unto itself. It is true that many of the British contingent, Patterson's 'tailors', also wanted to go home; and that the Americans in the 38th and 39th Battalions, unable, and unwilling, to adjust to what they regarded as mistreatment at the hands of the Military Administration and some of their own NCO's, had taken part in a mutiny, which resulted in two court martials and stiff sentences of penal servitude, but on the whole, the Legionnaires were desperately anxious to remain on active service in Palestine. Many of the foreign volunteers planned to settle in Palestine; they visited the colonies, left food, arms and frequently their own clothing with the settlers, began to feel a sense of identification with the men and women who had endured so greatly and to whom they themselves meant so much.

The Palestinians, on the other hand, spent all of their free time worrying about the future of the country. Their tents were turned into offices in which they received endless delegations not only from other battalions but from all over the Yishuv. One of Corporal Ben-Gurion's officers calculated that in the first months of 1919, more mail was received by the 40th Battalion than by the entire GHQ. Colonel Margolin dealt with his Palestinians gently but firmly. Time after time, Ben-Gurion, Ben-Zvi, Berl Katznelson (one of the main spiritual leaders of the Yishuv's labour movement), and Levi Eshkol (who was to become third Prime Minister of the Jewish State) went AWOL in order to attend urgent conferences with the Zionist Commission, or to talk to Dr Weizmann. Margolin reprimanded, punished when necessary, but understood that in the

Berl Katznelson (1887–1944), although a member of the Jewish Legion, was more concerned with the post-war future of Zionism

tents at Sarafand some of his Legionnaires were designing the shape of the Jewish National Home-to-be.

The first serious warning that the Military Administration was not merely unfriendly but also contemplating a gradual backing-down from the Balfour Declaration came in the spring of that year. The situation in Palestine, though not to be compared with that in Egypt or in Syria, was uneasy. The Arabs, who had hauled away immense quantities of arms plundered from Turkish stores and dug-outs, were subject to considerable agitation from the rest of the Arab world, which was becoming resentful about the welter of pledges and counter-pledges made by the British and French – before and during the war – to the Jews, to the Arabs themselves, and to each other. Although the Arab Nationalist Movement was in its earliest infancy, and a number of Arab states were to be created out of the former Ottoman Empire, those Arab leaders, who had cooperated with the British in World War I, were in no mood to accept British or French control over them without a struggle.

The British Military Administration of Palestine, part of the overall Occupied Enemy Territory Administration, had, in fact, entered office in 1917 under difficult conditions. In its favour were the joy and gratitude of the Jews for the Balfour Declaration and Jewish relief at the overthrow of the Turks. Against it was the destitution of Palestine's population – little water, almost no food, no wood at all. The Turkish land registers were virtually non-existent, all livestock had been requisitioned, forests had been cut down for fuel. Currency was in a state of extreme confusion, and the official count of the languages spoken in the Holy Land reached forty! But more significantly, most of the high-ranking officials of the Military Administration found the Jews hard to deal with; unlike the Arabs, they seemed hard-headed, impervious to insult, and adamant about their rights. The first census taken in Palestine revealed that of the total population of 755,000, the Jews accounted for only 83,000. If the Arabs, feeling themselves betrayed, chose to make trouble, reasoned the Military Administration, it would be far more serious than any Jewish protest was likely to be.

This concern lest the Arabs overtly rebel led the British to make a decision, in the spring of 1919, which Colonel Patterson termed 'an unthinkable act of provocation'. That April, the Legionnaires were informed that for the duration of the Jewish holiday of Passover, Jerusalem would be 'out of bounds to all Jewish soldiers.' This edict, directed at troops of the British Army, at the men whose primary responsibility at that point was the defence of the railways which constituted Britain's lifeline in the area, was received with shocked foreboding both by the Legion and by the Yishuv. The storm of protest which arose caused the Home Government to remind the Military Administration in Palestine of the declared policy of His Majesty's Government, and for a while, it appeared as though the Legion would no longer be harassed.

GHQ'S attitude to the Legion, the restlessness of the Arabs, and the fact that it was by no means certain yet that the British would stay on permanently in Palestine led to a renewal of discussion about the question of Jewish self-defence. There were those in the Yishuv who argued that the British Army could be trusted to protect the Jewish population, and that the debate was no longer relevant. Others believed that the Legion, whose very presence in Palestine had helped to keep the Arabs quiet there, must be retained, and hundreds of the Legionnaires, particularly the Palestinians, favoured this idea. But a small segment of the Yishuv, notably Hashomer, pressed for reactivation of a Jewish self-defence unit, responsible only to its own leadership, and which, because neither alien nor beholden to any outside source, could be implicitly trusted whatever the circumstances. *The British Army, the Jews and Arabs*

While these discussions were going on throughout Jewish Palestine, news came of a massed Arab attack on four small northern settlements; the fall of these settlements and Trumpeldor's death in the defence of one of them, Tel Hai, lent force to the point of view of those who maintained that a Jewish self-defence organization was as urgently needed as ever. Trouble had been brewing in the north of Palestine ever since the end of the war. There was reason to believe that the Arabs would make a concerted effort to overthrow the French, who had occupied what were to become Syria and Lebanon. The four northernmost Jewish settlements – Tel Hai, Kfar Gileadi, (which was to have been called Bar Giora but was instead named for Israel Gileadi who had died in 1918), Hamarah and Metullah – were in a singularly vulnerable position; they were ill-armed, critically under-manned, and located in a hotly contested area, which turned into a battlefield between the French and the Arabs.

In the beginning of 1920, the Arabs began a series of sporadic attacks on the tiny colonies; Hamarah fell first, and its settlers moved to Metullah. One day, an Arab chieftain appeared in Metullah, demanding that his men be billeted there and that an Arab flag be flown over the settlement. The French, he said, must understand that they would never subdue the Arabs, and the Jews must help to make this clear to them. The colonists refused his demands, a refusal which enraged the Arabs, who promptly threatened to destroy the settlement. Hashomer sent out a call for rein- *Arabs attack isolated settlements*

The settlement of Tel Hai

forcements; thirty Legionnaires arrived in Metullah, and brought a nurse with medicines and surgical instruments.

Then the Arabs returned – this time with a new demand – to search Tel Hai and make quite sure no Frenchmen were hiding there. Anxious to prove the settlers' goodwill, Trumpeldor, despite grave reservations, let the Arabs enter the compound. It was, literally, a fatal mistake; once inside, the Arabs opened fire on the settlers and gave the signal for an attack by the Arab mob waiting outside. Tel Hai was overrun, and one of the first defenders to be mortally wounded was Trumpeldor himself, who died on the way to Kfar Gileadi. The settlement's casualties were severe, its arms supply had run out, the number of Arabs involved in the attack

64

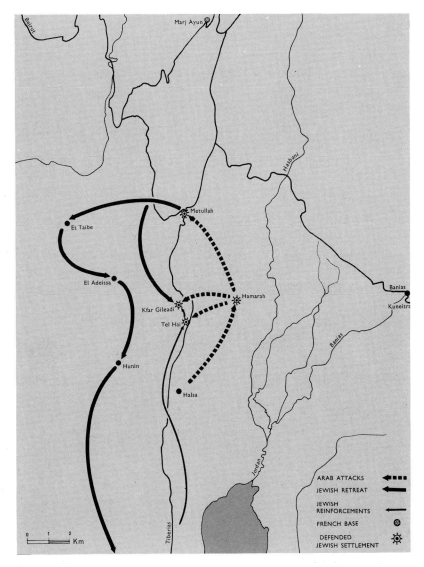

Marj Ayun

Beirut

Hasbani

Metullah

Et Taibe

El Adeissa

Banias

Kuneitra

Kfar Gileadi

Hamarah

Tel Hai

Banias

Hunin

Halsa

Jordan

Tiberias

ARAB ATTACKS
JEWISH RETREAT
JEWISH REINFORCEMENTS
FRENCH BASE
DEFENDED JEWISH SETTLEMENT

0 1 2 Km

Map of northern Galilee
showing the beleaguered Jewish
settlements

increased to hundreds. It was decided to abandon Tel Hai, and
to continue with the defence of Kfar Gileadi and Metullah. The
survivors loaded a cart with their few valuables, set fire to their
settlement, and walked away from it. Behind them, Tel Hai flamed.
In Metullah, an emergency ward was set up for the wounded, and
in Kfar Gileadi, the settlers buried their dead. Someone was sent
south to ask that Legionnaires and members of Hashomer rush
to the rescue.

Next morning, the attack was renewed; the target this time was
Kfar Gileadi; the Arabs had dragged up two French cannons with
which to shell it. The time had come to make a final decision about
evacuating the area. More than the current emergency was in-

A typical second-generation farming couple of Galilee on whom much of the responsibility for guarding the settlers' homes and crops fell. Naomi and Mordechai Paicovitch at Giv'at Benyamin

volved; the issue, it was felt, was a matter of national policy. Some of the settlers, and some of the defenders whom Trumpeldor had managed to recruit, felt that there was no point in hanging on; that to do so, in fact, was to spoil for trouble, and to become a party in a struggle between the Arabs and the French which, essentially, had nothing to do with the Yishuv. But many of those who spoke that day presented an entirely different line of argument; nothing must be abandoned they said; not one inch of land farmed by a Jewish worker must be given up; all of the settlements in Upper Galilee were in the balance, if not all of those in Palestine. 'We cannot claim what we can not or do not defend', said those who favoured digging in regardless of the cost in life. One of the most emotional pleas in favour of staying was made by a young Socialist, Yitshaq Tabenkin.

'There are no borders,' he declared. 'There is no problem here of local defence. If we fall in Galilee, we shall fall also in the desert. If we leave Tel Hai and Kfar Gileadi, history will record that this was our first retreat.'

The vote was close; tension, fear, perhaps above all, sheer fatigue influenced the decision. In wind and rain, the settlers abandoned their colonies and grimly made their way southwards. Tel Hai became a symbol of resistance; like Dunkirk many years later, it was to go down in history as a victory, even though it had ended in temporary defeat. Had it not been for those weeks of primitive defence against hordes of armed Arabs, much of the north would probably have been excluded from the Jewish National Home. As it was, the claim was staked; the intuitive reluctance of the men and women of Tel Hai to leave their settlement was to be wholly justified by future events. Tel Hai, whose defence is still marked yearly in Israel, was to bring several important developments in its wake: it redefined the advantages of a collective or cooperative society in terms of self-defence; it emphasized the need for a national defence organization; it fired the imagination of hundreds of immigrants-to-be, the pioneers of the Third Aliyah, and strengthened their determination to settle in Palestine.

Peace is restored in northern Galilee

Within a few months, the French quelled the Arab force in the north, took over in Syria and restored peace. When all was quiet, a convoy of carts, loaded this time with farm tools and seeds, made its way back to the ruined settlements. Tel Hai was never rebuilt, but the fields of Kfar Gileadi and Metullah were under cultivation again by the winter of 1920.

In his diary, Trumpeldor had written about the siege of the northern settlements: 'The hour of trial is near. A new generation stands ready on the border, prepared to give its life, and in the

66

interior of the country, the interminable negotiations go on ... as to whether to retain the defenders of the homeland or not.' The defenders to whom he referred were the Legionnaires and the men and women of Hashomer. Their presence in Tel Hai had not been enough to save it, but they had only been a handful. Tel Hai brought into focus again the importance of an available, mobile, armed and trained militia. The 'interminable negotiations', never theoretical in Palestine, were to acquire an entirely new dimension within only a few weeks of the fall of Tel Hai when serious rioting broke out in the city of Jerusalem, and the Jews found themselves both inadequately prepared and inadequately protected.

The multiplicity of faiths, and the fact that many Jewish, Christian and Moslem holidays tend to be celebrated at the same time, had long caused the Easter-Passover period in Palestine to be tense. The Turks had always maintained special troops in the Holy City during the weeks of the early spring. It was, therefore, natural for the Jews to prepare a plan for self-defence; it seemed likely that if anything untoward happened, the British would be able to cope with it, but those members of the Jerusalem Self-Defence Corps who had served in the Legion had reservations about the willingness of the British to act on behalf of the Jews, and those members of the Corps who came from the ranks of Hashomer believed, in principle, that the Jews should take care of themselves. Still, 4 April 1920 was typical of Palestine's short, lovely spring; the weather was crisp and sunny, and a pre-holiday mood prevailed in the city.

Anti-Jewish rioting breaks out in Jerusalem

That day, hundreds of Arabs poured into Jerusalem to celebrate Nebi Musa, a day dedicated to veneration of Moses, whom the Moslems consider a major prophet. As a British military band gaily led a long procession of Arabs through the Old City, the Military Governor and his entourage, from a balcony, watched with interest, and later followed the parade to the Dome of the Rock. There, the crowd paused to listen to a violent and inflammatory anti-Jewish harangue delivered by an Arab nationalist leader. The next day was the first day of the week-long Jewish Passover; the Old City was crowded with Jews on their way to the Wailing Wall. Suddenly, a mob of Arabs, brandishing daggers and placards about Arab independence, and screaming 'We shall drink Jewish blood' swept down upon the Jews, and within seconds the riot assumed dreadful proportions. Jews lay wounded and dead on the ancient cobblestones; homes and shops in the Jewish quarter were looted and burned; stones hurtled through the air. The Arabs, uncontrolled and uncontrollable knew no bounds. Even the few British soldiers who happened to be in the Old City were injured and one was killed. The responsibility for maintaining law and order had,

67

Sir Herbert (later Viscount) Samuel. A Jew and first High Commissioner of Palestine

Imprisonment of Jabotinsky

inexplicably, been handed over entirely to Arab policemen; these now either removed themselves from the path of danger, or joined the rioters.

The Jewish Self-Defence group had made a critical error; it had posted its men outside the Old City, many of them on roofs which overlooked the Jewish Quarter. By the time they understood that the Arabs were running amok, there was no way of coming to the rescue of the Jews. The British had sealed the Old City; no one could get in and no one could get out. Inside the walls, Jews were being murdered and raped; outside, the British busied themselves with arresting the members of the Self-Defence Corps; among them Jabotinsky, who had been forced to leave the Legion some time before for having complained directly and not through official channels to General Allenby about the attitude of the Military Administration.

The Jews, shaken by the British refusal to open up the Old City, petitioned the Military Governor to turn its defence over to the British Army, to forbid further demonstrations and to remove the Arab policemen. Above all, they asked that some official standing be granted the Jewish defenders. Eventually, the Military Government acceded to one of these requests; the Army was sent into the Old City, and when this did not end the three-day pogrom, martial law was declared. Those members of the Legion who had tried to come to the aid of the Jews were rounded up and disarmed, in full sight of armed Arab crowds, and Jabotinsky and his men were arrested. The charge against them horrified the Yishuv; the Ottoman penal code had furnished the phraseology: twenty members of the Self-Defence Corps were accused of 'banditry, instigating the people of the Ottoman Empire to mutual hatred, pillage, rapine, devastation of the country and homicide in divers places.'

A British military court, stating that it did not consider itself bound by any rules of procedure, sentenced Jabotinsky to fifteen years of penal servitude, and the other sentences were almost as severe. Jabotinsky, manacled between two Arab rapists, and nineteen of his fellow-defenders were marched through Jerusalem. The Yishuv declared the day of their conviction as a day of fast and protest. When the train bearing the new convicts reached Lydda, thousands of Jews met it, waving farewell, promising not to forget. A little apart from the others, Colonel Margolin and four hundred of his Legionnaires stood, respectfully at attention, as the train moved on, taking the prisoners to an Egyptian jail, from which, after weeks, they were finally transferred to Palestine's central prison, the Citadel in Acre.

Many miles away, in a flower-bedecked villa called Paradise, in

Zeev Jabotinsky exercising in the courtyard of Acre Jail, 1920. He was sentenced to 15 years imprisonment but was soon reprieved

San Remo, Italy, on that same day, the principal Allied powers confirmed the Balfour Declaration and decided that Britain should be awarded the League of Nations Mandate over Palestine.

In 1920, the Military Administration concluded its final term of office, and a civil administration took its place. In a gesture of goodwill and in an obvious attempt to clear the air and restore the faith of the Yishuv in its intentions, the British Government appointed a distinguished British Jew, Sir Herbert Samuel, to serve as Palestine's first High Commissioner. Sir Herbert, who had been one of the most influential supporters of the Balfour Declaration, arrived in Jerusalem in the summer of 1920. He was received with overwhelming joy by the entire Yishuv; his appointment was felt to be the beginning of a new chapter, the dawn of true cooperation between the British and the Jews, and a wholly auspicious prelude to the British Mandate over Palestine, which was formally awarded in 1923.

The first years of the Palestine Government were marked by an intensification of Jewish trust in the ability, and desire, of the Mandatory Power to control the unease in Zion, and to put an end to Arab rioting. Although it would be an exaggeration to say that the Yishuv permitted itself to relax for long, or that it had become complacent about security, in the main, and in terms of the population as a whole, the situation seemed, slowly but surely, to be approaching normalcy. Those, however, whose specific concern re-

The British Mandate over Palestine

69

Dov Hos (1894–1940), shown here in Jewish Legion uniform, was a founder-member of Haganah and a member of its high command. He was instrumental in creating the rudiments of an airforce. The airfield of Tel Aviv today is named after him

mained the question of defence were less optimistic, and continued, despite months of surface serenity in Palestine, to try to make the Yishuv as conscious of defence problems as possible.

Hashomer was officially disbanded; in its place – according to a resolution adopted by the Histadrut (General Federation of Labour) – arose a steering committee, charged with establishing a broadly-based self-defence organization, which would become known as the *Haganah* (Hebrew for self-defence). Hashomer had little faith in the efficiency of such a non-selective body; looking back on its own past, it warned of the dangers of excessive democracy in matters of defence. It would be far better, its members insisted, to retain the pattern of Bar Giora and Hashomer, to rely on the dedication and mobility of small secret task forces, and on an underground élite. But the majority opinion in councils of the Yishuv was opposed to this philosophy. Times had changed, said Eliahu Golomb, Dov Hos, and others in the steering committee; it was no longer a matter of defending an outpost here, or a settlement there; of standing guard in a vineyard, or of patrolling a kibbutz on horseback. Not the few, but the many were needed now; not so much the valour of individuals, but rather the total commitment of an entire population.

The fledgling Haganah began to operate simultaneously in many directions. Since every major Arab riot in Palestine was accompanied by a British decision to halt Jewish immigration temporarily, the Haganah took upon itself the responsibility of seeing to it that Jews continued to arrive in Palestine. The first of the thousands of so-called illegal immigrants whom the Haganah was to bring to the Holy Land in the course of the next thirty years consisted of a group of young Jews from Crimea, on their way to Palestine when the Jerusalem riots erupted in 1920. The Haganah made connections in Lebanon with smugglers who were prepared, at a price, to help transport the Crimeans to Palestine. Late one afternoon, the immigrants boarded a small boat which brought them to Haifa after a four-day journey. From Haifa, they were sent to one of the Jewish settlements where, dressed like the farmers themselves, they blended into the background and were safe from detection. The use of the collective settlements as way-stations for 'illegal' immigrants was to become an important Haganah tradition in the years ahead.

The Crimeans, sturdy and good-natured, were to form one of the elements in the Yishuv which, in the summer of 1920, joined the *Gdud Ha'avoda*, the 'Labour and Defence Battalion', named for Joseph Trumpeldor. The Battalion was an expression of principles first enunciated by Hashomer, but it included many sectors of the Yishuv and contributed substantially to the absorption of the hundreds of new immigrants who began to stream into Palestine in the 1920's. Among the groups most prominent in the Labour Battalion were graduates of Jewish Palestine's only high school, a Tel Aviv landmark, named for Herzl, which was to play a unique role in the country's history. From this school came many of the Palestinian Jews who served in the Turkish army and who later went into the Legion. In many respects, the *Herzlia Gymnasia* was a proving ground for the Yishuv's intelligentsia; in its high-ceilinged rooms studied many of the founder-members of the youth pioneering movement, the future leaders of the Haganah and of the Israel Defence Forces-to-be, and of the entire Jewish community of Palestine.

The Labour Battalion also included newcomers from Lithuania, Poland and Russia; young Socialists who feared that they would find no place for themselves in post-revolutionary Eastern Europe and who had been displaced and rejected in the wave of anti-Semitism which flooded Russia during the Civil War. Other members of the Battalion were ex-Legionnaires, undecided about their future, still hoping that the now-demobilized Legion would be reactivated, or that some kind of Jewish Army would take its place. Before and after work hours, the Battalion prepared itself to be used as a military reserve force for the Yishuv. It went on route marches, did strenuous physical training and target practice. It was organized in squads, each with its own leaders; and it added to, and enriched, military and social traditions already shaped by Hashomer and the Jewish Legion.

The Battalion's chief source of work was the network of roads which the new Palestine Government now set about building throughout the country; the workers lived in tents by the roadside and ran their little canvas communities as cooperative settlements. Those who did not get jobs in road construction found work as stevedores, fishermen and in quarries. Trumpeldor had predicted that 'after the war, the Jewish people, liberated and independent, will want to defend itself. To do this, an army will have to be created; several battalions of disciplined, well-trained soldiers, coming from the ranks of the Jewish workers.' The Labour Battalion felt itself to be the embodiment of Trumpeldor's prophesy; at night, in their tents, the workers planned the future of the Yishuv's defence, composed ardent, sentimental songs and poems about their link with the land, accompanying themselves on mouth organs and listened hungrily to stories about Tel Hai. A kind of Battalion costume emerged: the Labour Battalion is easily recognized in photographs of the period: the men capped or in sombreros, wear-

Eliahu Golomb (1893–1945), one of the founders of Haganah, had also been actively engaged in recruiting for the Jewish Legion. From 1931 he was commander of Haganah

ing khaki shorts, cotton shirts, sandals and the wide military-looking coats which many of the new immigrants had brought with them from Europe. These were not particularly becoming clothes, but they were eminently practical, and even more importantly, they connoted an affiliation with working men everywhere, defining the distance between the Labour Battalion and the 'capitalist' immigrants in Tel Aviv who were setting up small factories and shops.

The first Haganah course for instructors

From the ranks of the Labour Battalion the Haganah chose the first candidates for an instructors' course, which included three of the young Crimeans. Headed by Yitshaq Sadeh, burly Commander-in-Chief of the Battalion — à Russian Jew who had become an expert quarrier — the course was held partly in the Herzliya Gymnasium, partly on the sand dunes outside Tel Aviv. It consisted of thirty men, almost all veterans either of World War I or of the Russian Civil War. After several weeks in Tel Aviv, the course moved to Kfar Gileadi. The men and women of Kfar Gileadi, former members of Hashomer, found it hard to take the young instructors seriously. They were disdainful of the effort to inculcate military bearing, scoffed at the idea of training people to stand to attention, and muttered about the pointlessness of trying to establish a formal military unit. Squads and platoons, they said, would never replace individual action. Not entirely lovingly, they dubbed the instructors 'little clowns' (*comedianchikes*), a nickname which time did not eradicate. But the 'little clowns' became the Haganah's first officers.

The Haganah and weapons acquisition

The problem, however, which most concerned the Haganah in the immediate post war–years, and which was to continue to dog it for decades, was the dearth of arms. One of the first actions undertaken by the Yishuv even before the Haganah committee was established, was an attempt to acquire weapons and ammunition from the stores of the major powers. The arms stores of Jewish Palestine in the early 1920's were almost empty. Most of the smaller settlements dotted throughout the country could count on a rifle for every three men, although some were able to produce a rifle per man, plus one or two hundred bullets. Tel Aviv had the grand total of fifty pistols of varying calibres, a stock of small home-made bombs, constructed by filling tins with gelignite and nails, and a few rifles to its credit. Since all defence activities were essentially passive, most of the settlements relied on elementary fortifications, involving trenches, sandbags and barbed-wire fences.

It was obviously necessary to find arms; with the disbandment of the Jewish Legion, which had managed to turn over most of its personal weapons to the Jewish settlers, a small 'purchasing mission' was despatched to Europe. Arms dealers in Vienna and

72

A clandestine weapons workshop in Tel Aviv, 1929. Such workshops functioned under great difficulty as discovery would have crippled the provision of munitions for Haganah's meagre supply of weapons

in other centres of the former Austro-Hungarian Empire had set up lively arms trading centres, and although the Allies were trying to eliminate these stores, there were still more than enough arms to go around. The funds at the Yishuv's disposal were meagre, but arms were bought and transferred to Palestine. Sometimes the weapons were concealed in suitcases with false bottoms, in ice-boxes, in beehives, and even in hollowed-out millstones; from Europe, these unwieldy receptacles were shipped to Beirut and on to Kfar Gileadi where they were distributed. When ten machine guns were acquired, they were dismantled and sent to Palestine inside steam rollers and cement mixers.

A special armoury was elaborately constructed in Kfar Gileadi; it was deep underground and had secret entrances and an emergency exit. It took a year to complete, and all the work was done at night so that even the members of Kfar Gileadi should not know of its existence. One of the men who helped construct the armoury described part of the process: 'We knew we would have to insulate it against dampness, and waterproof the walls with some special plaster. We found a man who had done this kind of work before; one night, we blindfolded him, carried him to the site on a stretcher, let him down by ropes, and listened while he gave us a lesson in plastering.'

The concealed armoury at Kfar Gileadi

Like the men who built the armoury, the leaders of the Haganah in the years after the Great War were amateurs, novice smugglers of arms and of Jews. But out of the Jewish Legion and the Labour Battalion, from the ordeals of Jerusalem and Tel Hai, sprang a paramilitary organization upon which, though its founders could not have known it, the Yishuv was soon to depend for its very existence.

3 Haganah Takes Root

Palestine in ferment — Sadeh and Wingate — The White Paper and Peel — Restraint or retaliation? — Haganah expands

For the Jews of Palestine, the 1930's were marked by a number of major events which were to determine the scope, character and the very future of the Yishuv, and lead not only to the consolidation of the Haganah as a *national* instrument of self-defence – rather than a decentralized and localized militia – but also, and far more significantly, force it, in the end, to abandon a static and passive military posture in favour of a policy of activism and initiative. Three crucial circumstances formed the background to the Arab riots of 1936-9, any one of which, operating separately, would have profoundly affected the fate of the 400,000 Jews in Palestine, and all three of which, operating simultaneously, resulted in the creation of an underground movement able, when the time came, to assume the immense burden of the struggle for independence.

Without question, the single most critical factor was the rise of Nazism. British policy-making circles were, in any case, inclined by then to doubt the advisability of establishing a Jewish National Home in Palestine, and frightened by Mussolini's conquest of Ethiopia, Hitler's march into the Rhineland and the Spanish Civil War, they arrived, easily and with some finality, at an anti-Zionist assessment of the situation in the Middle East. Secondly, the Arabs, disunited on all other fronts, appeared to be – and were, to a considerable extent – united in their determination to oppose further Jewish progress in Palestine. The fact that the Arabs constituted seventy percent of the population of Palestine, and that their favours were greatly sought after by the Axis powers, made it even easier for the British to think in terms of shedding their responsibility for the Yishuv. *Realpolitik*, more specifically the oil wells of the Arab countries, and, which was to become gradually more important, of course, the Suez Canal, lent whatever additional force was needed to the British argument in favour of appeasement of the Arabs: the mood of Munich was not limited to the European

The spectre of Nazism in Europe

opposite: A girl member of the Haganah on guard duty at one of the 'Stockade and Tower' settlements (see pages 92–93)

75

continent, nor was Neville Chamberlain's way of thinking restricted to 10 Downing Street.

Lastly, the Yishuv itself began, albeit slowly and painfully, to appreciate the possible extent and implications of Nazi Germany's official anti-Semitism, to realize more clearly than ever before that its destiny might soon lie in its own hands, and that its survival – based on its ability to defend itself, to continue Jewish immigration and to increase Jewish settlement on the land – was not to be taken for granted. In the course of the three years of rioting, during which 2,287 Arabs, 520 Jews, and 140 Britons were killed, the British, the Arabs and the Jews were all to arrive at a final formulation of their respective positions.

Renewed Arab rioting

The conflagration of 1936 had been preceded by savage Arab rioting in 1929. As before, (1920 and 1921), the 1929 Arab assault on the isolated Jewish quarter of Jerusalem, the slaughter and mutilation of fifty-nine Jews – men, women and children – in Hebron, Safed and Motza, and the wave of murder and looting which spread like an awful infection throughout much of the country and ravaged a number of Jewish villages, had found the Haganah too ill-equipped and too poorly organized to play a really effective role. However, without its presence, the slaughter would undoubtedly have been far greater, although one hundred Jews were killed. The British eventually restored peace, but did so in such a halting way that the Arabs had taken heart and been reinforced in their conviction that the Palestine Government was most unlikely to hasten to the aid of the Jews at any future time, or even to punish Arab miscreants severely.

The Mufti of Jerusalem and incitement

The atrocities of 1929 had been directed by a remarkable Arab nationalist, Haj Amin el Husseini, the Mufti of Jerusalem; a soft-voiced, blue-eyed, ruddy-bearded, well-groomed Moslem spokesman known to have been largely responsible also for the 1920 riots in Jerusalem. Shrewd, worldly and possessed of a hypnotic Rasputin-like personality, he was subsequently appointed as head of the Supreme Moslem Council by Sir Herbert Samuel. Although in 1929 there had been no doubt at all as to his direct involvement in the riots, a British Commission of Enquiry, charged with assessing the cause of the outbreak, had chosen to ascribe them to the rise in the rate of Jewish immigration rather than to the political venom of the Mufti or his henchmen. Officially exonerated, more popular than ever among the Arabs of Palestine, and recognized leader of the country's Moslem malcontents, in 1936 the Mufti readied himself to assume direction of another Arab campaign of violence.

By 1936, the Yishuv, despite sporadic Arab attacks, had pros-

76

pered. Hundreds of orange groves were under cultivation, entire forests had been planted, the disaster that had befallen German Jewry had brought to Palestine a new type of settler; industrious and unromantic, the German Jewish refugees came to Palestine not only with their capital, but with know-how and a sobriety of approach. They invested in new businesses, established cooperative villages of their own, became expert poultry farmers and fashioned a tidy, attractive way of life for themselves, one which the Middle East had never known before. The Arabs chose to represent this as an additional threat. They were not the revolutionaries of Hashomer, eager to be accepted by their Arab neighbours and drawn to the trappings of the Arab way of life. They were an entirely new element.

German Jewish refugees arrive

In fact, however, although the Arab masses were not aware of this, many of the 60,000 German Jewish refugees who arrived in Palestine in the thirties were extremely anxious to establish a dialogue with them, and from the ranks of the German Jews came several of the most eloquent advocates of Arab-Jewish cooperation and amity. The Mufti, however, continued to travel around Palestine, shrilly warning the Arabs that they were about to be 'displaced' by this onslaught of Europeans, and blurring over the fact that the standard of living had risen for everyone, and that hundreds of Arab families had become impressively wealthy as the result of exorbitant prices paid to them by the Jews for land. The anti-Jewish propaganda blaring from the powerful transmitters of Radio Bari in Fascist Italy, and beamed at Palestine, served to emphasize his dire message.

Accustomed to tension, preoccupied by the far-off crisis in Europe and by their own intense activity, the Jews of Palestine were not aware of any particular significance in the darkening clouds of the spring of 1936, though it was punctuated by various incidents, including several fatal attacks on Jews. It is still not clear who gave the signal for the riots of 1936 to start in Jaffa. The trouble was certainly due, in part, to the hundreds of 'illegal' Arab immigrants who had poured into Palestine in 1935 from the mountains of Hauran in Syria. Strangers in a strange land, unemployed at winter's end (the end also of the citrus season) and ripe for incitement, they were loudest in the cry, 'Death to the Jews', and on 19 April 1936, milling through the narrow streets of Jaffa, they responded enthusiastically to an unknown starter's gun.

The shadow of Fascism falls across Palestine

At all events, Jaffa became a backdrop for murder that day. A rumour spread that three Haurani Arabs and an Arab woman had been killed in Tel Aviv; the Arabs, enraged and ready for bloodshed, turned on the Jewish shopkeepers and clerks who worked

British police and Arab rioters
in the streets of Jaffa in April,
1936. Waves of Arab rioters,
usually incited to hatred by
their leaders, swept through
Jewish quarters of many towns,
leaving death and destruction
in their wake

The Mufti of Jerusalem,
Haj Amin el Husseini, Chairman
of the Arab Higher Committee.
He was a noted Nazi sympa-
thizer and was largely responsible for the murder of the
Jewish population of Bosnia

and lived in Jaffa. Some Jews found shelter in government offices; others hid in police stations; and a few moderate Arabs even
opened their homes to Jews. But the mob was not to be stilled;
the British took no action; the main connecting roads between Jaffa
and Tel Aviv were blocked; in all, nine Jews were stabbed to death
and shot that day.

Next morning, the long cortege wound its way through Tel Aviv
for the mass funeral; and the riots which had started in Jaffa spilled
over to outlying areas. By nightfall, sixteen more Jews had been
murdered, while six Arabs had been shot in belated police action.
A wave of terror spread through the entire country. Unlike the
outrages of 1929, it was obviously inspired by more than the desire
for booty, or wanton blood-thirstiness; a controlling hand was
clearly at the helm and there was every reason to believe that it
was the Mufti's.

At the end of the first twenty-four hours of rioting, the Arab
Higher Committee, headed by Haj Amin el Husseini, declared a
General Strike. Its terms were simple: no Arab anywhere in Palestine would go to work until all Jewish immigration ceased, all
transfer of land ended, a boycott proclaimed against the Jews, and
a government established whose local parliament would be elected
by the people. Correctly read, it was a demand to end the vision
of a Jewish National Home; the Mufti's real aim was to force the
British to annul their commitment to the Jews as expressed in the
Balfour Declaration and ratified by the League of Nations in the
form of the British Mandate over Palestine. The declaration was
accompanied by an ultimatum: The Jews and the Government of
Palestine were given until 15 May to make up their minds. If the
conditions laid down by the Arab Higher Committee were not met
by that date, a revolt would break out; terror and sabotage would
become the order of the day, for as long as necessary.

The Arab peasants went on working in their fields, but in the
towns and larger villages, the Arab leadership dealt ruthlessly with
all strike-breakers, and it was not unreasonable to assume that within a week or two the country would be totally immobilized.

The Palestine Government refused to give way to the threat, and
the Jews proceeded to fill the ensuing economic vacuum. When
the Arabs paralysed the Jaffa port, the Jews opened a jetty in
Tel Aviv, portent of a future harbour; when striking Arab bus
drivers left the country's transport in chaos, Jewish bus drivers,
at great personal risk, took over their places; when Arab produce
no longer reached the market, the Jewish villages and kibbutzim
met the challenge. But the economic penalties were not as menacing
as the Arab attempt to terrorize the land. When 15 May came and

went, and the gauntlet flung in the face of the Government remained not picked up, a methodical reign of murder, arson and destruction took the place of Arab non-cooperation. That year witnessed the uprooting of 200,000 trees, 380 attacks on trains and buses, and 1,996 attacks on Jews, 80 of whom died.

In addition to accelerating its agricultural and industrial output and its transport facilities, the Yishuv, in the dangerous months of the summer of 1936, reached a complicated, collective decision; it ordered the Haganah to limit itself to direct self-defence against Arab attacks and to refrain completely from any form of counter-terror. This policy had its roots in an overwhelming revulsion against the idea of punishing the innocent. Of course, as we shall see, there were small groups within the Jewish community who believed that counter-terror might end the Arab riots, and who claimed that the language of force was the only one clearly understood by the Arab terrorists. These groups did, in fact, carry out various 'wildcat' operations, but far from frightening or deterring the Arab leadership, they furnished fresh excuses for retaliation.

Havlagah (the Hebrew word for self-restraint) was motivated also by various practical considerations: to begin with, the Zionist leadership was anxious to disprove any possible British insinuation that a civil war was in progress in Palestine, or that the attacks by Arabs on Jews were Arab-Jewish riots. 'The Arabs', said Ben-Gurion, 'will be forgiven one day: whatever they have done will be forgotten. But this is not true for us!' Then, it was hoped that imposition of this iron discipline by the leadership of the Yishuv would prevent the British from curtailing Jewish immigration this time – as had happened several times before; in fact, whenever the Jews had participated too actively in their own defence. And immigration – the bringing to the shores of Palestine those who were now homeless in Europe – was regarded, it must be remembered, by all the Jews of Palestine not simply as a priority, but, literally, as an irreversible obligation. Finally, it was imperative not to hand the British any easy rationalization for limiting their aid to legal Jewish self-defence.

Besides this, in general the Zionist leadership tended to place as much emphasis on the political battles being waged between themselves and the Colonial Office in London, as on the actual situation in Palestine. It was in London, after all, not in Jerusalem, that weighty decisions were made and White Papers published. Havlagah was basically a policy of not combating terrorism by senseless and non-discriminatory counter-terrorism. Nevertheless the Jews continued to defend themselves, to amass 'illegal' arms and develop their military organization and to bring refugees into

The Yishuv embarks on a policy of 'self-restraint' — Havlagah

Political battles with the British

the country regardless of legal restrictions, to settle on the land, and to recruit as many volunteers as possible for the ranks of the auxiliary forces attached to the British Army and the Palestine Police. Thousands of Jews bore arms, but these arms, with very few exceptions, were used exclusively for defensive purposes.

That tiny minority which was unable to accept the galling limitation and regarding it as perilous, duly splintered away from the Haganah and formed its own military organization which, unfettered by any considerations of consensus, threw bombs wantonly, raided Arab villages, and invoked the law of retaliation. But, as far as most of the Yishuv was concerned, Havlagah remained binding throughout the three years. Within the Haganah High Command, of course, the debates pro and con Havlagah continued, as the months of rioting went on; but the will of the majority prevailed. The moral and practical arguments marshalled in favour of self-restraint won out; the beginnings of statehood are discernible in the Haganah's deference to the orders of the national institutions, and in its understanding of the need for elected national discipline. But beyond the high moral content of Havlagah, apart from the fear of creating endless blood feuds with the Arabs, regardless of the inherent and profound Jewish abhorrence of random killing, there was also the ineluctable fact that, in 1936, the Haganah was unprepared for much more than defence. When conditions changed, when the competence of the Haganah increased, two men – one, that gifted, stocky Russian Jew, Yitshaq Sadeh; and the other, an equally gifted, eccentric British officer, Orde Wingate – would seize the day and lead the underground, at last, into active self-defence.

In the meantime, there were several legal channels open to the Jews, and all of these were exploited. By the end of May, the situation worsened. Nails and glass scattered on the roads by Arabs to halt Jewish transport gave way to daring armed attacks; armour-plated buses kept open the main arteries of the country and escorts were given to trucks which worked for British concerns. Nightly, tracks were loosened on the railroads, and settlement after settlement helplessly watched its crops go up in flames or saw its plantations ruined. The Haganah underwent a much-needed reorganization; in the cities, including Tel Aviv where its HQ was located, young men and women went on guard duty each night in the outlying districts, passed first-aid courses, and stood ready to defend the city from attack. Teenagers were mobilized in high schools to act as couriers or serve in a rudimentary signal corps.

But outside the all-Jewish city, which the Arabs did not dare to attack in force, conditions were far more difficult. The British,

A Jewish Noter, or guard, Zvi Ben Gershon on duty in 1938

unable to defend the settlements properly, increased the allocation of legal weapons to the Jews, and averted their gaze from the unwelcome sight of 'illegal' arms. The sealed armouries which the British had given to many settlements after the riots of 1929 were now broken open; although the arms inside often proved either obsolete or useless, they were better than nothing. Since military rifles could not be legally issued to the Jews, other than according to an inflexible quota, the government gave out licenses for hunting rifles and finally it began to enlist Jews for auxiliary services.

The 3,000 Jews who carried legal arms in Palestine by the end of 1936 and who formed an intrinsic part of the country's defensive network during the riots were, almost to a man, members of the Haganah; it was their experience, deepened and extended, which was soon to bring about the establishment of Jewish forces capable of meeting the enemy face to face. Possibly the British understood that this development was inevitable; certainly they knew that by creating the various categories of the supernumerary Jewish Settlement Police, they were opening the way to the semi-legalization of the Haganah which was to last, in one way or another, for a decade. But they had little alternative; the troops at their disposal seemed incapable of tackling the Arab bands. Mechanized, loaded down with heavy equipment, unused to the climate or the terrain, the British troops were unable to suppress the Arab terrorists, unable even to give chase to them as they disappeared into the hills they knew so well, unable to discover the places in which men and arms were hidden.

At least the Jews were familiar with the country and anxious to serve in any way possible: this being the case, the British, their prestige at its lowest ebb, listened with more than usual attentiveness when the Jewish Agency suggested that a number of Jews be

Jews join the Palestine Police

83

A group of notrim — Jewish Settlement Police — at Kfar Tabor in 1937 (top, second left, Yigal Allon)

mobilized to strengthen the ranks of the Palestine Police and to free policemen from routine desk jobs and standard watch duty. The Agency spokesmen explained that *they* would provide the volunteers and pointed out that the Police Regulations of the Palestine Government, issued in 1926, provided for 'supernumerary police', and for a lesser breed called '*ghafirs*'. The supernumerary police were entitled to possession of a military rifle, to clothing and wages; the ghafirs (relics of Turkish days when notables and important institutions were allowed to maintain private guards) were given light arms, policeman-like uniforms and were paid by their employers. Also, explained the Jewish Agency representatives, it was permissible, under emergency regulations, for unpaid volunteers to be co-opted, given armbands or uniforms and issued arms in their capacity as 'special constables'. All of these categories of special police were encompassed in the Hebrew word '*notrim*' (guards).

The Notrim   The first of the notrim appeared on the scene in 1936. They did not make much of a show; some of them wore ill-fitting work clothes and, like cinema ushers, sported armbands to identify themselves. Others in khaki, wore flowing Arab headgear or Turkish-style 'kolpak' hats with the word 'ghafir' on them. Their weapons were confined to ordinary rifles and they were not issued with machine guns or even hand-grenades, which had to be acquired illegally. The notrim were a substitute for a real militia, a surrogate for a Jewish army. But, like Hashomer and the Legionnaires before them, the notrim, and in particular the Jewish Settlement Police,

84

A mixed group of Haganah members and notrim man a barricade against Arab rioters in the Jewish Quarter of the Old City of Jerusalem

widened the mainstream of Jewish self-defence. In the years that followed, they coped bravely with the problem of divided loyalty, did their best to follow government orders and still give invaluable cover to the Haganah, providing it with arms and ammunition. Not clandestine themselves, they were indispensable to, and barely indivisible from, the underground. By the autumn of 1936, although only about 750 notrim were on the government's payroll, there were 1,800 others, financed by the Jewish settlement authorities, permitted to stand watch in orange groves, fields and vineyards.

But they were not the only Jews to help guard the settlements: the Haganah enlisted volunteers from the cities, and sent them to the Jewish villages and kibbutzim. The contact between the urban youngsters and their rural contemporaries boosted the morale of both groups, and revived what had been, for the past few years, a waning sense of identification. Now the boys and girls from the cities became acquainted with those who lived in isolated settlements and joined them in debate as to the necessity to move from passive resistance to active self-defence. The national council of the Kibbutz Hameuchad movement meeting at the end of 1936 at Yagur, inspired by men like Yitshaq Tabenkin, Eliahu Golomb, Israel Galili and Yehoshua Globerman, adopted a resolution which marked a turning-point in national policy, demanding from the Yishuv leadership and the Haganah High Command the right to 'burst through the fences', in the phrase they formulated, and to seize military initiative.

Resistance to the restrictions of Havlagah

85

Two of the leading proponents of self-defence were Israel Galili (*above*), today a member of Israel's cabinet, and Shaul Avigur, (*below*)

At least, said these young people in tens of settlements throughout Palestine, we must try to put the fires out, make some attempt to repel the Arab attacks, get out from under the fence. In one or two places, they took arms, jumped on to lorries and trundled through the orange groves. Elsewhere, small groups of Haganah volunteers, on their own initiative, made their way to the hills and when the Arabs began to shoot, they replied with grenades. Gradually, the static pattern altered and broke. In Jerusalem, Yitshaq Sadeh, who had left public life when the 'Labour Battalion' was disbanded, and who now placed himself at the Haganah's disposal, did something concrete about his intuitive and extreme opposition to this passivity. Possessed of limitless personal courage and endowed with a rare quality of leadership, Sadeh was one of the few high-ranking members of the Haganah able, at all times, to project his own unconventional insights into the real meaning of self-defence. He was to become a foremost figure in the annals of the Jewish liberation movement in Palestine, the father of the Field Companies which were created at the height of the riots, and later of the *Palmach*, the shock troops of the Haganah. Other men led the Haganah ideologically; Eliahu Golomb was its uncrowned leader for many years, its mentor and its prime philosopher. Israel Galili, a member of the High Command, who was to become Commander-in-Chief of the Haganah, was, together with Golomb and Shaul Avigur, among the most outspoken and influential proponents of active self-defence. But it was Sadeh – that bespectacled, warm, crumpled, ordinary-looking bon-vivant-cum-poet, that great lover of country, of women, and of the implacable logic of history, who, in 1936, symbolized most vividly the fighting spirit of the underground, and who discovered and taught war to a group of teenagers destined, within only a few years, to lead the army of Israel.

For weeks, the small Jewish settlements in the hills around Jerusalem had been exposed to ruthless Arab attack. Throughout the spring, Haganah volunteers obediently guarded them from behind sandbags and inside dug-outs. Some of the volunteers were fairly good marksmen, all of them were young and strong, and most of them chafed miserably under their enforced immobility. Night after night, they lay on their stomachs, peering through the sights of their guns, hearing the Arab war cries, and longing to give chase. Although they did not yet realise it themselves, in effect they were waiting to be organized and trained for battle. When Sadeh came to them, they were more than ready for him. He began with two of the group. Armed with grenades and revolvers, he started to plan ambushes at night. He worked out and implemented unpre-

cedented surprise attacks on the raiding Arabs – from the rear, in pitch dark; and after a while, he formed small mobile patrols. Instead of concentrating his young men in one place, dooming them to stationary positions, to debilitating boredom and to frustration. Sadeh fanned out, looked for action, and got it. His first full-fledged mobile patrol (*Noddedet* in Hebrew) was made up of about seventy boys. From some mysterious source, Sadeh found a kind of uniform for them: they wore khaki shirts and shorts, and he provided them with sun helmets. He trained them as he profoundly believed soldiers should be trained; he took them on tough route marches at night, sharpening their sense of direction, familiarizing them with the terrain, with the sounds and sights of night. He told them, as Orde Wingate was to tell his men two years later, that the night must no longer be the sole domain of the Arabs. Jews, too, must move freely in it, bend it to their own needs, live in it comfortably.

For days on end, Sadeh's boys sat drinking in his every word. He told them stories they had heard before, but to which they had never listened. His tales about Hashomer, Trumpeldor, the World War, the Civil War in Russia and about the Labour Battalion acquired new relevance, and they felt themselves links in a long and won-

At Kibbutz Hanita in 1938. Left to right: Moshe Dayan, Yitshaq Sadeh, Yigal Allon

above: Lieutenant-General Sir Arthur Wauchope, High Commissioner of Palestine
below: General Sir John Dill, Commander of the British forces in Palestine

opposite: Palestine under the British Mandate

derful chain. He gave them a sense of self-reliance, of being warriors in a stalwart company, stout fellows like Sadeh himself. His effect and influence on them was incalculable, and he changed their lives.

After a few weeks, he took them farther afield, on ambushes closer to Arab villages. The British soldiers in the area, despondent, encumbered and lost in the hills, got to know Sadeh and his boys, and a silent pact sprang up between them. The Palestinians served as advance patrols for the soldiers-in-uniform, scouted for them and led the way through the mountain paths. Each night brought its own lesson: how to whisper, how to dress, how to drop to the ground and take cover, how to listen – and what to listen for. A new world opened up – a world of excitement and dignity, of honour and participation, and Sadeh's boys, for the first time, began to understand that they, too, like their parents, would have to fight for the land – or be destroyed.

Elsewhere in Palestine, the Arabs had their way. No one was safe anywhere; here, a sniper felled a farmer; there, a car exploded on a mine. The terror, unleashed, was aimed at the Jews, at the British, at the Arabs themselves. Their resources drained, scared and rebellious, thousands of Palestinian Arabs refused to cooperate with the armed bands. The toll had been enormous; they had provided food, money and men, and there seemed no end in sight to the General Strike. But the assassins brooked no refusal: they killed Arab peasants, Arab merchants, and finally they threatened the powerful well-to-do moderate Arab families who had also started to balk at the reign of terror. In August, 1936, a supreme Arab military commander came from across the border. Fawzi el Kaukji, born in Syria, an ex-Turkish officer who had studied in a military school in Iraq, now assumed the cloak of leader of the Arab rebellion, and boasted that 10,000 men were under his command.

The Palestine Government wrung its hands: the High Commissioner, a mild-mannered Scot, Lieut. General Arthur Grenfell Wauchope, delicate, canny and civilized, perfectly represented the British dilemma. He encouraged the Jews in their cultural activities, praised the quality of Tel Aviv's newly formed Palestine Philharmonic Orchestra, opened exhibitions and cut ribbons, and, above all, let into the country as many Jewish refugees from Germany as he could. But although the Palestine Government had drawn into the country more than the equivalent of a division, the Arabs still moved around with impunity.

'As long as they didn't actually walk around with rifles on their shoulders and didn't get caught by low-flying aircraft, they were all right', commented one of General Dill's staff officers, soon to

LEBANON

Dafna
Dan

SYRIA

Hanita
Nahariya   Eylon
Shavei Tzion
Acre   Safed
Ein Hamifratz
Haifa   Usha'
Kfar Hamaccabi   Mishmar   Tiberias
Hashlosha
Nazareth   Bnei   Sha'ar Hagolan
Ein Hashofet   Brit   Massada
Ma'ayan Zvi   Afula   Gesher
Zichron Yaakov   Daliya   Sde   Beit Yosef
Nir David   Nahum   Hamadiya
Kfar Glickson   Jenin   Sde   Ma'oz Haim
Hadera   Eliahu   Tirat Zvi
Netanya
Beit   Nablus
Yehoshua
Herzlia
Tel Aviv
Jaffa   Petach Tikvah
Rishon Le Zion   Lydda
Ramallah   Ramalla
Rehovot   Jericho
Kfar Menahem   Ma'ale   Jerusalem
Hahamisha
Bethlehem

Hebron

Gaza

Mediterranean Sea

Jordan

Dead Sea

TRANS JORDAN

Beersheba
Gevulot
Revivim

EGYPT

JEWISH SETTLEMENT
ARAB SETTLEMENT
MIXED SETTLEMENT
HOMA U'MIGDAL SETTLEMENT

20   40
km.

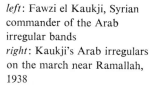

left: Fawzi el Kaukji, Syrian commander of the Arab irregular bands
right: Kaukji's Arab irregulars on the march near Ramallah, 1938

be brought to Palestine to try to end the terror. Acidly, the same British officer added, 'The performance of the Palestine Government looked like that of a figure in a dressing gown and slippers, pathetically padding along in the dusty wake of the Arab Higher Committee'. The British patrols went out daily in the heat of the sun, and did their best, under confused direction and against great odds, to assert themselves. But the Palestine Government seemed to have no real desire to stop the sub-war or to re-establish British authority. It did everything slowly and ineffectually; it took months to bring captured rebels to trial; Arab internees, languidly rounded up, were sent to a camp near the Egyptian border where they were treated as guests of the government rather than as prisoners; martial law was considered, but instead statutory martial law was applied and weeks went by while the regulations were drawn up. In the meantime, an exhausted, irritated garrison was unable to guarantee security on the roads, safety in trains, or reasonably assure any citizen of the country that he or she was immune to murder by the Arab gangs which held sway.

In September, tempers flared in London. The ineffectuality of the Palestine Government came in for heavy and bitter criticism, and the British lion, stung at last, roared. General Dill, heading reinforcements which brought the total Palestine garrison up to 30,000, arrived to restore order. He worked quickly, sensibly and skillfully, like the expert soldier he was. Within a month, the terror faded, the Arab General Strike was called off and Kaukji had escaped across the border. The first round of the riots had ended;

British forces blow up the house of a suspected Arab terrorist, in 1936

the victory, however belated and however partial, went to the British. Dill had largely broken the pattern of violence by super-imposing upon it his own pattern; collective fines for villages suspected of harbouring terrorists, the demolition of houses in which weapons were found; night-long curfews and the immediate imprisonment of any Arabs unfortunate enough to fall into the dragnets which combed Palestine. The riots did not end entirely, but a tentative peace settled over the country.

The British announced the formation of another Royal Commission to inquire into the causes of the riots and propose a solution to what had now become known in England as the 'Palestine Problem'. In the interim, the Haganah took stock. It had changed a great deal in the fifteen years of its existence. It was beginning to function like a truly national defence organization; it had survived the periodic peeling-away from the main body of groups which opposed Havlagah; through the Jewish Settlement Police, and the other notrim, it had acquired a substantial and fairly well-trained potential reserve force. But its shortcomings had been stressed by the six months of the riots, and now the time had come to make accounts and plan for the future.

The Royal Commission on Palestine

The general feeling was that, although neither the Mandatory Government nor the Colonial Office could be absolved of their responsibilities for the maintenance of law and order in Palestine, they were certainly not to be relied upon exclusively. It was imperative that the Yishuv organize itself militarily to defend Jewish property, Jewish lives and Jewish honour against Arab aggression.

91

Haganah acquired its first planes in the 1930's and thus laid the foundations of the Israel Airforce

A conclusion arrived at during this same period of soul-searching was that the notrim, who should be as well-equipped and prepared as possible, must serve as a cover for a clandestine force which would be insulated from British counter-measures and answerable only to the Yishuv itself. Finally, these forces should be readied for a possible wide-scale confrontation with united Arab forces which might enjoy a considerable degree of mobility through the neutrality of the Mandatory authorities and the British garrisons.

At a meeting in Tel Aviv, the Haganah commander pointed out that a greater enemy than the Arabs was formulating war aims, directed not against a few hundred thousand Jews in Palestine, but against the entire Jewish people. In 1936, however, not even the Jews of Palestine could have foreseen the true nature of the German final solution, nor, foreseeing it, could they have done much about it.

That meeting and a round of other such meetings bore fruit. A number of far-reaching conclusions were reached, and the Haganah's structure re-examined. The Haganah was already a quasi-army, controlled by the Yishuv's elected institutions which acted essentially as a quasi-government. At the top of the underground's organizational pyramid was a secret committee of civilians, who had been appointed by the executive branch of the Jewish Agency, and who represented various (and almost all) streams of life within the Yishuv. This committee was known as the National High Command (*Mifkada Artzit*) and its chairman was a *de facto* Minister of Defence. This committee appointed a General Staff (headed by the General Chief of Staff), made up of branches: logistics, planning, training, education, operations and manpower. In addition to tightening-up the organization, the country was divided into defence regions – north, centre, and south, with a special command for the Jerusalem district. Each of these regions had its own armoury, and each had its own headquarters. At the same time, the beginnings of a military industry were established; some full-time Haganah workers were employed, and the principle of entirely voluntary work was sacrificed on the altar of efficiency. Although the Haganah had, by then, some 25,000 members, the number was considered inadequate, and a recruiting campaign was quietly undertaken. Another year was to pass before the reorganization of the Haganah was finally completed, but the last month of 1936 saw the start of one of its most dramatic and most meaningful contributions.

Known as Operation Stockade and Tower (*Homa u'Migdal* in Hebrew), the settlement by the Yishuv of strategically placed points in areas of Palestine, such as the northern Galilee, the western Galilee and the Jordan Valley, where Jewish settlement was dis-

couraged or prohibited was the first major expression of the determination of the Jews of Palestine to possess the land. As such, it
entered the legends of the nation, became the subject of books and
songs, and lifted the spirits of those for whom the compulsory
inactivity of the past year had been so demoralizing. In order to
confront the Arab High Command and the Palestine Government
with a *fait accompli*, and for vital reasons of security, the operation
required that the two essential components of any Jewish settlement in Palestine, namely the wall around it and its watchtower,
be set up at once.

Accordingly, the stockade and watchtower were prefabricated;
the stockade was constructed of wooden boards, filled like a giant
sandwich with crushed rock and gravel; the tower, some thirty six
feet high, was topped by the inevitable searchlight. The assembling
of both on the site was accomplished, as a rule, in less than twelve
hours and became the occasion for enthusiastic volunteering. Between 1936 and 1938, thirty six such settlements arose on some
21,000 acres of land. The first was Kfar Hittin in the lower Galilee,
the second Nir David in the western part of the Beisan Valley,
not far from the Jordan River. On 7 December 1936, the word
went out: a call for volunteers. From all over Palestine, men and
women arrived with hoes, pitchforks, spades and food. A convoy
of trucks and tractors, each loaded with prefabricated parts, marked and numbered according to a blueprint, set out for the area.
Kfar Hittin was duly established in a tangle of thorns and scrub;
by sunset, its tower was up; so was the wall, and those men whose
names appeared on the work roster for guard duty that night were
already at their posts.

'There is no room to swing a cat in Palestine,' Lord Passfield,
British Colonial Secretary, had told Dr Weizmann in 1929 in order

'Stockade and Tower' settlements sprung up virtually overnight all over Palestine. Sha'ar
Hagolan, built in 1937, was a
typical example

*British restrictions on
immigration and land
purchase*

93

Lord Peel, who was
Chairman of the Royal Commission on Palestine, died in
1937 shortly after the publication of the Commission's
recommendations

to justify British restriction of Jewish immigration and land purchase. Operation Tower and Stockade in 1936 was part of the
Yishuv's reply to Lord Passfield's evaluation of the country's ab-
sorptive capacity. Before the riots were to end, many more settlements were founded, some under conditions which were, in fact,
those of a 'constructive' war, many in the remotest and most hazardous parts of the country.

That winter, the new Royal Commission arrived. Six British gen-
tlemen, under the chairmanship of Lord Peel, former Secretary of
State for India, conscientiously toured the length and breadth of
Palestine under heavy guard, held thirty-six protracted meetings
with key personalities (thirty-one of these meetings were open to
the public) and gathered testimony and opinion as to possible and
lasting ways of solving the problem of the much-promised land.
The Arabs refused both to testify before or to cooperate with the
Commission, although the Royal Air Force was dutifully sent up
to shower Arab villages with leaflets assuring the inhabitants that
the members of the Royal Commission were free of Jewish connections or blood. The Commission remained in Palestine until the
summer and then returned to England to consider all that it had
heard and seen, and to begin work on the 404 page report which
it issued in July 1937.

Although its publication was preceded by a general feeling in
Palestine that it would be just another in the series of British on-
the-one-hand and on-the-other reports, and although the Jews in
particular had no reason to assume that it would favour the Zionist case, the Peel Report created a sensation. Written with ele-
gance and clarity, it was highly appreciative of the Zionist position,
accepted the Jewish contention that the Arabs had gained greatly
in the economic sphere, criticized the behaviour of the Palestine
Government – and advised that the Mandate was unworkable.
Economics, declared the Report, had nothing to do with the case;
there could be no compromise in the forseeable future between the
two conflicting nationalisms.

*The report of the
Peel Commission*

The Report proposed that the country be divided; that a Jewish
and an Arab State be created in Palestine with an international
enclave for Jerusalem and a corridor from it to the coast. The
Arabs rejected the solution at once and absolutely. The Jews, after
much heartsearching, announced themselves prepared to examine
it. Although the total area of the proposed Jewish State reduced
the original Jewish National Home from some 45,000 or 50,000
square miles to a trivial 2,000 square miles, and thus raised serious
doubts as to the viability of such a truncated entity, the Zionist
leadership, with some notable abstentions, eventually accepted the

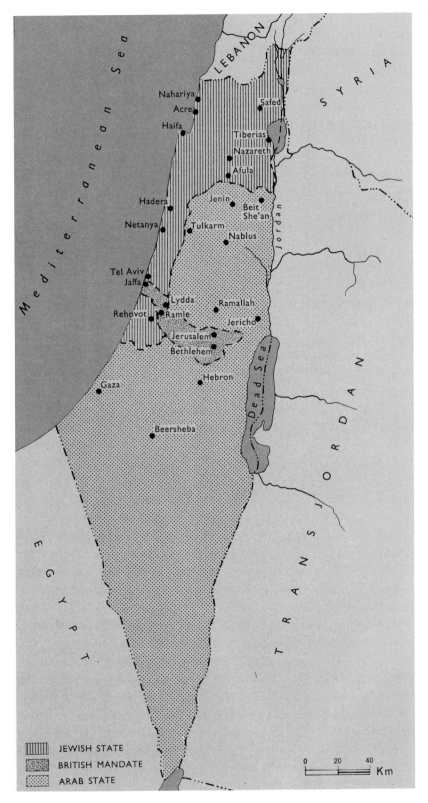

The Royal Commission on
Palestine headed by Lord Peel,
and known as the Peel Commission, recommended that
Palestine be divided into a
Jewish and an Arab state,
leaving Jerusalem as an international enclave. Although
accepted with little enthusiasm
by the Jews, the plan was
violently rejected by the Arabs

JEWISH STATE
BRITISH MANDATE
ARAB STATE

0   20   40
Km

substance of the plan. At least, said its advocates, it would permit the Jews of Europe to enter a Jewish State freely and immediately.

The Arab response to this was predictable: riots broke out all over Palestine again, and this time they escalated. Since the Peel Report indicated that the British were prepared to give up the Mandate, it now seemed possible that they would do so soon, in the face of the renewed and widespread Arab terror. The Haganah drew a long breath and asked itself what would happen if circumstances should indeed force the British to leave. A top-secret plan was drawn up for the Jewish occupation of Palestine. It took for granted that the confrontation between the Jews and the Arabs would not be joined by a third party and that neither side would have access to cannons or planes. Four hundred thousand Jews, according to the Haganah's grim estimate, could prevail. A defensive line of fortifications, encompassing all of the Jewish settlements, could be drawn and held; it would be connected to the main concentration of the Jewish population by use of armoured cars. All told, the area to be held involved some 1,789 square miles and was projected as being about 283 miles long; it would contain almost the entire Yishuv, including 118,000 Jews with combat experience. Behind this line – envisaged as a barbed wire fence with advance and rear defence positions consisting of pillboxes and trenches – the Jews would create a fully-autonomous island for themselves.

The plan further stated that this defensive line would take only two weeks to build, and could be guarded by a unit of battalion strength: 900 men would stand watch, night and day, with another 400 as a mobile reserve. The Haganah blueprints were meticulously detailed: they stipulated that thirty-five Haganah members would be needed to defend each group of one thousand Jews. In all 45,000 soldiers would be required: 10,000 as a standing army; 3,200 for the defence of Jerusalem, and 30,000 infantrymen. A second plan (Plan B) envisaged the occupation by the Jews of all of the Galilee, and the annexation of Jerusalem by the rest of the 'state'. This further move would require a total of 50,000 soldiers, 17,000 of whom would form a garrison.

In order to implement Plan A, it would be necessary to mobilize about 43,000 men and women; it was suggested that all Jewish boys from the age of fifteen to nineteen (about 15,000) be trained forthwith. As for equipment, the Haganah High Command decided that some 28,000 rifles would have to be secured somehow, although its armouries still only included about 6,000. Other equipment – tents, the barbed wire, trucks, etc., – would have to be bought or made. But all this, said the authors of the plan,

96

was secondary to the patience and will of the people. 'If only one out of every three men in the Yishuv are ready to do their duty, it will be enough.' The plan was considered, gravely weighed and finally abandoned as being too static, and essentially obsolete in concept. It is interesting that the Haganah in 1937, unlike the French government of the same period, rejected the idea of a Palestinian Maginot Line as being costly and impractical.

But whatever would happen as the result of the riots, whatever the final British decision, the Haganah set about deepening and extending its own strategic and geo-strategic thinking, began to think in terms of compulsory military training for the Yishuv and, for the first time, paid serious attention to problems of quarter-mastering and deployment of transport. Defence in depth, a military organization based on clear-cut military units, would have now

above: young Haganah members learn to strip a light machine gun
below: Haganah members of the 'Dolphin Sports Club' learn to handle small boats

A unit of Yitshaq Sadeh's Fosh (field companies) passes through the Arab village of Yasur, near Be'er Tuviya

to replace individual, amateurish defence plans for each and every settlement. Military schools, aircraft, expert tactical advice and money would all be needed – regardless of the immediate British response to the situation.

The structure and grasp of the Haganah began to change; a change made possible partly by the British decision to crack down, once and for all, and terminate the intolerable rule of the Arab gangs. The time had come, also, when Yitshaq Sadeh was allowed, at last, to put into effect his deeply-held conviction that Jews assert themselves militarily. Lastly, Captain Orde Charles Wingate, moody, talented and consumed by his love of Zion, appeared on the Palestine scene. 1937 and 1938 saw the turn of the tide; although the riots were not to wane until 1939, the die was already cast and the outcome certain.

In line with its new approach, the Haganah High Command now empowered Yitshaq Sadeh to establish a permanently mobilized force responsible, in the first place, to him as its chief officer, and then directly to the GHQ in Tel Aviv. With characteristic gusto, Sadeh set about handpicking those who were to serve in his small army. He selected them from the rank and file of the notrim; from the daring young men who manned the Haganah's so-called 'Flying Columns' – the grotesque, steel-plated pick-up trucks which lumbered along Palestine's roads, escorting Jewish workers to fields and factories and sometimes even conducting illicit ambushes against Arab raiders; and from the Jewish Settlement Police, whose task was to defend the countryside and whose NCO's had passed special courses run by tough British sergeants.

The Fosh   From all these, Sadeh chose the strongest, the most intelligent

98

and the most dedicated. The first of the Haganah's fully operational
units, the *Fosh* (Plugot Sadeh, the Hebrew for 'Field Companies'),
called for physical prowess, for enterprise and for a strong sense
of comradeship. No more suitable a commander could have been
found than Sadeh. As is true of all warriors who have ever become
part of a nation's saga, he himself, in his person, demonstrated
these attributes to an astounding degree. Despite the fact that he
had a grizzled beard and was much older than the boys he recrui-
ted, he was their hero. He had mastered many crafts and trades in
his life. He had been a journalist, a playwright, a quarry manager,
a wrestler and a farmer, but, above all else, he was a military leader.
Sadeh's men loved and honoured him; they called him *Hazaken*,
the Old Man, and from him they learned to become military
leaders themselves.

The Fosh became a mobile force, empowered to act throughout the country, in cooperation with the regional commands. It
acquired its own headquarters in a house on Tel Aviv's Rothschild Boulevard; there, Sadeh organized a quartermasters unit, a
topographical unit, and an educational corps. He created a small
Arabic-speaking intelligence service, and established a group of
orthodox volunteers, earlocks, skullcaps and all. He financed the
Fosh partly through the 'Coffer Hayishuv', a national arms levy
to which most of the Jews of Palestine contributed monthly, and
partly from the salaries of the notrim. Money was always a problem; the men of the Fosh had to make do without proper uniforms, without sufficient equipment, often without adequate battle
rations. But the difficulties and the obstacles paled before real
action; and by March 1938 the Fosh already boasted a thousand

The British authorities decided to make an example of members of the dissident organization Irgun Zvai Leumi. The British Military Tribunal found Shlomo Ben Yosef guilty and hanged him — for 'illegal possession of arms'

men, organized in thirteen regional groups, and had five hundred more ready for training. The more conservative Haganah leaders grumbled that Sadeh had taken their best men; Zionist politicians complained that by openly confronting the Arabs and even retaliating against their attacks, the Fosh was endangering the existence of Jewish legal defence; there were even accusations within the GHQ that the Fosh constituted a potential élite, and was politically undesirable, to say nothing of the fact that it imperilled any chance of a reasonable relationship with the Arabs. Eliahu Golomb listened to the objections, smoothed ruffled feathers, and continued to give Sadeh full backing.

Some of the young men and women who had left the Haganah to form their own defence organization, and who, in revolt against established policy, had created the right-wing *Irgun Zvai Leumi* (National Military Organization) – and were responsible for much near-terrorist actions against the Arabs up until 1938 – now reunited with Haganah ranks. But one of these IZL reprisal actions was to shatter the newly-heightened mood of the Yishuv, and to have important political consequences.

In the Upper Galilee, near the Jewish village of Rosh Pinah – one of the first to be founded in Palestine – a group of young men belonging to the IZL nightly stood guard under the overall leadership of the Haganah district commander. It was a compromise arrangement arrived at in many places and for the most part it worked. As everywhere in those days, in Rosh Pinah, too, there was much heated discussion about the pros and cons of Havlagah and these particular young men were greatly out of sympathy with the

100

whole idea and philosophy of self-restraint. In March 1938, a car on its way from Haifa to Safed was attacked by Arabs near Rosh Pinah: four of the ten passengers were killed, including two women and a child. The police duly arrived, gave chase, and killed four of the Arabs. But the young men in Rosh Pinah vowed that they would seek revenge.

Some three weeks later, they took pistols and grenades, and fired at the first car to pass by. They hit nothing, not even the car, but their trial, for 'illegal possession of arms', turned into a *cause célèbre*. The Palestinian government – in particular, the unpopular pro-Arab new High Commissioner, Sir Harold Macmichael, former Governor of Tanganyika – saw in the episode a chance to put the Jews in their place and to create the impression that irresponsible elements existed in the Jewish community as well. The sentences were made public in June: one of the boys was declared 'not responsible' for his actions, the other two were sentenced to death. Eventually, one of these death sentences was commuted to life imprisonment, but Shlomo Ben Yosef was to hang. The High Commissioner, under Palestine law, constituted the last court of appeal, but he remained adamant, uninfluenced by appeals for clemency from Jerusalem, London and Washington. On 20 June 1938, singing the Zionist anthem *Hatikvah* ('The Hope'), and walking to the gallows with a dignity which belied his years and the circumstances, Shlomo Ben Yosef was executed.

A British soldier searches a Jew suspected of carrying arms, Jerusalem, 1938

The IZL mourned him with a wave of violent retaliatory acts, including the use of time bombs made of oil cans or milk tins. 'Ben Yosef is the first casualty of our war of liberation against the hostile administration', announced the IZL; from that date on and for years to come, it regarded itself in a state of war with the Palestine government.

But while the IZL struck out at the Arabs at random, striking down its unknown victims in Haifa and Jerusalem, a carefully planned, thoroughly prepared method of retaliation was being taught to the forces of the Haganah by Captain Orde Wingate. Of all the extraordinary personalities – and there have been many – to flare on the Palestine horizon, Orde Wingate was one of the most striking. Born in India to a pious British military family (his parents belonged to the Plymouth Brethren), and steeped throughout his English childhood in Bible lore and Puritanism, he was a cousin of the one-time High Commissioner of Egypt, Sir Reginald Wingate; related to Lawrence of Arabia; and a professional Arabist who had seen service in the Sudan before he was sent to Palestine. Like Lawrence, Wingate was short, slight, and had deep glowing eyes which bespoke fanaticism. Posted to Palestine in 1936, within

'The Friend'

101

Captain Orde Charles Wingate
(1903–1944). Founder of the
Special Night Squads and convinced friend of Zionism. He
was killed as a Brigadier-
General while commanding the
legendary 'chindits' during the
Burma Campaign of World
War II

opposite: A unit of Wingate's
Special Night Squads conducting a search in an Arab village
in the Galilee

a few weeks he developed what was to become an abiding passion for Zionism. Of this conversion, he wrote: 'When I came to Palestine, I found a whole people who had been looked down upon and made to feel unwanted for scores of generations, and yet at the end of it, they were undefeated and were building their country anew. I felt I belonged to such a people'. In the beginning, the Jews who met him tended to regard the young British intelligence officer with suspicion, but Wingate persisted in trying to win their friendship. His personal habits, however, were no help: he was unkempt; given to fits of deep depression and impatient with conventions such as wearing clothes when relaxing. His manners were abominable and he was given to great bouts of onion-eating. But his unquestionable sincerity about Zionism, his ardour, his familiarity with the Bible – and his doggedness – gradually dispelled the scepticism he had initially aroused.

He journeyed around Palestine, and wrote long letters to his cousin Sir Reginald Wingate in England, reporting on his impressions. In one such letter, he wrote: 'I have seen the young Jews in the kibbutzim. I tell you that they will provide a soldiery better than ours. We have only to train it.'

He talked in this fashion to his superior officers and to high government officials; to whomever he met, compulsively he presented his argument for arming the Jews, and to the Jewish Agency he offered himself as the commander of a legal Jewish Defence Force, if such should ever be created. Within a short time, he had gained the total confidence of the Jews. They started to confide in him, and soon he came to be known as '*Hayedid*', the Friend, and as such he was referred to by the Yishuv for the rest of his life.

Wingate proposed to the British that Special Night Squads be formed, part Jewish, part British; properly armed and trained, he was sure that such units, operating on Arab-held territory, could break the back of the Arab terrorists, and he persuaded Sir Archibald Wavell, who had taken General Dill's place as Commander-in-Chief of the British troops in Palestine, to let him try to organize them. Having received Wavell's blessings, he proceeded to talk to the Haganah High Command. At first, the Haganah was reluctant to enter into such close cooperation with the British against the Arabs, but Wingate was insistent and convincing and, in the end, the Haganah leaders agreed. Wingate picked his headquarters and his men with great care. He spent the weeks prior to the formation of the Special Night Squads, reconnoitring alone, without a guard, clutching two rifles, a Hebrew dictionary, and a letter written by Eliahu Golomb. One of the places which most impressed him was the small settlement of Hanita on the Lebanese border. There, on

102

An all-Jewish unit of the
Special Night Squads, at
Kibbutz Hanita

21 March 1938, four hundred men and women, travelling in fifty
trucks, had helped to put up a tower and stockade overnight.
Before dawn, the Arabs had attacked and two of the Jews were
killed. The attacks continued for weeks, but the ninety settlers
refused to evacuate Hanita. They felt that the borders of the Jewish
State that might arise depended on their endurance – and they stuck
it out. Wingate arrived in Hanita about a month after its establishment. He talked to the settlers about what he called 'mobile
ambushes' which would appear out of nowhere, terrify the Arab
villagers and stop them from helping the terrorists; he explained
that it was wrong to leave the initiative to the enemy, and that
surprise was a weapon to be respected. Some of the Hanita settlers
had served under Sadeh and they understood Wingate at once. He
talked in the same way in a number of settlements and then chose
one, Ein Harod, which had been founded in 1921 by the Labour
Battalion, as his headquarters.

Yitshaq Sadeh had met Wingate at Kibbutz Ein Harod and
between them these two unlikely soldiers succeeded in making the
SNS operational within a month. Wingate paid great attention to
detail; he was prepared to spend hours talking about footgear,
arguing against conventional military attitudes, such as restricted
drinking of water on the march, of which he disapproved. 'Use
every possible opportunity to drink and to rest,' he preached. His
British NCO's trained the Haganah squadsmen in the use of light
arms and nightfighting, and Wingate gave them a course in horse-
manship. One of his unrealized and characteristic dreams was the
formation of a cavalry unit led by a rider who would blow, like
an Old Testament warrior, on a ram's horn trumpet. Bugles were
suggested instead, but, eventually disconsolate, Wingate abandoned
the fantasy. He spoke to the Jews as if he were one of them. 'The
Arabs think the night is theirs,' he said, that 'only they can fight
us in the dark. The British lock themselves up in their barracks
at night. But we, the Jews, we will teach them to fear the night
more than the day.'

Wingate's doctrine   He advocated the use of grenades and bayonets and extolled the
merits of hand-to-hand fighting. He was delighted by the kibbutz-
im and praised them as being ideal encampments in which his
detachments could be absorbed by day, inexpensively maintained
and kept secret from the Arabs. He preached the doctrine of finding
'bottlenecks' through which the Arab bands would have to pass
and where ambushes could be successfully laid for them. Above
all, Wingate reiterated, secrecy and surprise mattered more and
would always matter more than numbers or equipment. His strategy came from his own imagination, rather than from manuals;

104

years later his inventiveness and understanding of the terrain involved stood him in good stead in Ethiopia and in Burma; and were to provide the Haganah shock troops, the Palmach, with their most fundamental characteristic. In point of fact, much of what Wingate taught the SNS, Sadeh had taught his boys earlier; but Wingate was a British officer and his words had tremendous impact. Many of the men who gathered at Ein Harod, in the settlement's ramshackle unplastered amphitheatre on 13 September 1938, for the Jewish Sergeants' Course which Wingate organized, remembered the occasion for the rest of their lives. Wingate began in Hebrew: 'We are here', he said sternly, 'to found a Jewish Army'. Then, in English, he gave his scheduled lecture on the obligations of command. It was hard for the Squadsmen to concentrate. He had put into words what all of them felt, but what none of them had ever heard a stranger say before.

A mixed unit of Jewish and British members of the Special Night Squads leaving on a mission

The Squadsmen, in their blue shirts, broadbrimmed Australian hats and rubber-soled shoes, fought their best-known engagement at an Arab village called Dabburiyah (named for Deborah the Prophetess) beneath Mount Tabor. Despite a number of mishaps, and Wingate's own wounds, they inflicted severe casualties on the Arab gangs and forced them to run. It was the first major SNS action – and successful. The SNS went on dozens of forays and ambushes; and assumed much of the responsibility for defending the Iraq Petroleum Pipeline; and helped to guard the Teggart Wall, that long defensive fortification which the British constructed on the northern frontier in an attempt to stop the Arab bands from entering Palestine from Syria and Lebanon. The Teggart Wall was built by a thousand Jewish workers in all of three months; three hundred members were sworn in as notrim to defend them, and the SNS and the Fosh made possible continuation of the work, despite the incessant and punitive Arab attacks.

The British disband the SNS

Wingate opened another course for NCO's in Ein Harod; he had high hopes of having close to two thousand men in Jewish units attached to the British Army within a few weeks; in the event of a World War, they would defend the Holy Land. But the British balked: Wingate's reputation as a friend of the Jews, and his undeniable eccentricity, had annoyed too many of his superior officers, and the Palestine government was anxious to be rid of him. The SNS was to be disbanded. The proud NCO's-to-be were told by the government that they would only be ordinary notrim after all. The last day of the course came: Wingate spoke to his dejected Squadsmen for the last time. 'Tomorrow', he told them, 'you will be privates in the British Army, instead of sergeants. But the dream of a Jewish Army has not ended; it is only postponed. I wish for

Jews demonstrate in Jerusalem against the British White Paper of May, 1939

all of us that the vision of the people of Israel, free in their homeland, will come true soon.' He said 'Shalom', and promised to come back, as a refugee if necessary.

Wingate left Palestine in 1939. In his files, the date of his departure was duly noted; also the words: 'A good soldier but a poor security risk. Not to be trusted. The interests of the Jews are more important to him than those of his own country. He must not be allowed to return to Palestine.' Years later, long after Wingate won fame as a leader of irregulars fighting the Italians in Ethiopia and died, in 1944, in an air crash in Burma; long after the Jewish State had been established, Yitshaq Sadeh summed up the experience of the Special Night Squads. 'Eventually,' he said, 'we would have done by ourselves what Wingate did, but we would have done it on a smaller scale, and without his talent. We were following parallel paths until he came and became our leader.' It was both a fair assessment and a generous one.

In 1939, the Haganah underwent another development, one which underlined the new determination to achieve professionalism, to create a significant reserve force, and to provide military training for a larger number of people. Against the will of the Fosh leadership, the Field Companies were disbanded, and in their place, the Haganah High Command established what it called the *Hish* (the acrononym of the Hebrew *Chail Sadeh*, the Field Force). Unlike the Fosh, the Hish was not permanently mobilized, nor did it have a unified command. Its units, essentially infantry units, were under the various regional commands; the Hish functioned as a sort of territorial home guard, able to go into action at a few hours notice, and trained on weekends and holidays.

That year spelled the official end of the Arab riots. The time had come to check the score. Although the toll of life and property was high, almost unendurably so, the Yishuv had emerged stronger than it had been in 1936; not a single Jewish settlement had been abandoned or had fallen in the face of Arab attacks. Even more importantly, the Jews, through Operation Stockade and Tower, had penetrated into areas of Palestine which were of crucial strategic value; settlements had been established near the Lebanese, Syrian and Transjordanian borders, others in lower Galilee. Above all else, by 1939 the Yishuv was clearly an important military factor in the Middle East, one that would have to be reckoned with in the future, and the Haganah was well on its way to becoming one of the largest and most competent underground forces in the world. But, the Arabs, defeated in the field, had won the political war, after all.

In the spring of 1939, half a year before the outbreak of World

War II, the Yishuv's attention was focused not on the embers of the Arab riots, but rather on the talks which were in progress at St. James' Palace in London. The British, despairing of unravelling the Palestine imbroglio, had summoned the Jews and the Arabs to talks in England. The Arabs had refused to sit at the same table with the Jews, and the talks were held with each group separately. Since the British had recently proven themselves highly vulnerable to Nazi blackmail, it was logical to expect that they might give way before Arab threats – and indeed, they did. The Jews were committed, in any case, to a profoundly anti-Nazi position. The Jewish population of Palestine that year (including the 86,000 Jewish immigrants who had come since 1936, many 'illegally') still amounted to less than half a million. Other than an appeal to the conscience of the British on the grounds that curtailment of Jewish immigration meant dooming hundreds of thousands of European Jews to degradation and death, the representatives of the Yishuv could say little on their own behalf. As in Czechoslovakia, appeasement prevailed in Palestine too. The British were eager to close the Palestine chapter as quickly as possible, and it did not matter that, by doing so, they slammed shut the gates of the one country in the world to which Jewish refugees could come as of right, rather than sufferance.

On 17 May 1939, the Chamberlain government published its White Paper on Palestine. It referred to a Palestinian state to be created within ten years and to be based on a constitution guaranteeing the rights of minorities. The projected state would be divided into Arab and Jewish cantons; Jewish immigration would be limited to 75,000 immigrants during the forthcoming five years and then stopped altogether – thus making the Jews a permanent third of the population. Jewish land purchases would be prohibited entirely – except in some five percent of the country. When the ten years were up, Palestine would emerge as an Arab state with a Jewish ghetto; meanwhile, the British would act as caretakers.

The Jews, shattered by the betrayal, rejected the White Paper entirely. The Arabs agreed to look into it, on condition that the Jewish minority would not be allowed to hinder implementation of the Palestinian state, and asked that a definite date be fixed for the cessation of all Jewish immigration. In Palestine, demonstrations and hunger-strikes marked the Jewish protest, but the Yishuv, dazed at first, slowly began to come to terms with the realization that the Jewish National Home had been shelved by the British forever, that Palestine was to be closed to refugees, and that there was no alternative left other than to defy the British bans, and fight the White Paper.

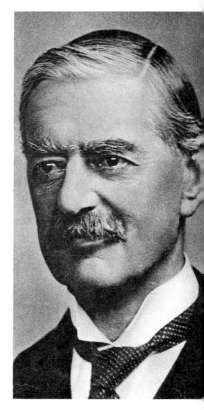

Neville Chamberlain, Prime Minister of Great Britain, acted as Chairman of the meetings at St. James Palace. His task was complicated by the refusal of the Arabs to sit at the same table with the Jews

4 Palestine at War

Birth of the Palmach — With and against the British — The Holocaust in Europe — Palestinians behind the enemy line — The Jewish Brigade

The struggle of the Yishuv against the White Paper and all it represented started in 1939, and continued throughout World War II, but it was overshadowed, influenced and often checked by the over-riding demands of the war against Nazism. The situation – physical and psychological – of the Jews of Palestine was unenviable; the Mandatory Power had declared war against the Zionist Movement, and undaunted by the proclaimed Nazi plan to annihilate the Jews of Europe, the British resolutely turned away from the shores of Palestine those Jewish refugees fortunate enough to have escaped from Nazi concentration camps. Even the looming danger, by 1941, of an Axis conquest of Palestine; the enemy victories in Europe and in the Western Desert; the surrender of France and the subsequent Vichy French control of Syria and Lebanon, did not weaken the British determination to enforce the restrictions of the White Paper.

1939 and 1940 were the years of the so-called Phony War in Europe, but the false calm prevailing in London and Paris in no way reflected itself in Palestine. It became abundantly clear to the Yishuv that the British would not only stop all attempts at additional settlement and immigration but would actively try to put paid to all activities of the Haganah by means of arms confiscation and arrest of its members. In November 1940, two ships arrived in Haifa; they were virtually cockleshells – unseaworthy, crowded, and deserving of their grim label: 'floating coffins'. Together, they bore some one thousand refugees, among them many women and children. The Palestine government, true to its word, transferred the refugees to a larger ship, the s.s. *Patria*, announcing that they would forthwith be transported to exile on the island of Mauritius in the Indian Ocean.

The efforts and petitions of the Yishuv were in vain; there seemed no way to postpone or prevent the expulsion of the refugees. The

Palestine on the eve of World War II

opposite: A group of uniforms of different periods.
above: A noter — Jewish Settlement Police, c. 1936; Palmach, 1947; Women's Auxiliary Airforce, c. 1942; Zion Mule Corps, 1915.
below: Special Night Squads, 1938; Hashomer, c. 1900; Jewish Brigade, 1944; Jewish officer in the Turkish Army, c. 1914

Haganah, concerned not only with the plight of the people aboard the *Patria*, but also with encouraging the Jews in Nazi-held Europe and demonstrating that active resistance to the British decree was possible, decided to damage the ship. By the time it was repaired perhaps the British would reconsider their verdict, understanding at last that the Jews of Palestine would never submit to the policies of the White Paper. On 25 November 1940, the *Patria* exploded in Haifa harbour; 257 of the would-be immigrants aboard went down with her. One of the Haganah men responsible for the action wrote later: 'We couldn't understand how so large a hole could have been blown into the iron walls of so big a ship by so small a bomb. We had every reason to suppose that the *Patria* was in good shape. It turned out, however, that she had been grossly neglected, so that a small charge of explosives was enough to wreak fatal damage.'

The s.s. 'Patria'

Desperate attempts to reach Palestine

The disaster of the *Patria* marked the start of the life-and-death battle for immigration which typified the years before the establishment of the State of Israel, and which was, indeed, to be largely responsible for it. Within a few months of the *Patria* disaster, another 1,600 refugees arrived in Palestine aboard the s.s. *Atlantic*; dragged off to a British detention camp in the north of Palestine, they were later forcibly placed aboard a British vessel which duly took them to Mauritius; there over one hundred were to die of disease. In 1941 the s.s. *Salvador* sank at sea; those refugees aboard her who were saved arrived in Palestine aboard another ship, the s.s. *Darien*. The Yishuv was sure that this time the British would relent, that the sight of the miserable, ailing and terrified survivors would melt the heart even of this most adamant officialdom. But, however tragic their situation, the immigrants on the *Darien* lacked the necessary official certificates which would have bestowed legality upon them, and they too were pulled off the ship and imprisoned.

The s.s. 'Struma'

Most indelible of all was the episode of the s.s. *Struma* which arrived, desperately seeking haven, in Constantinople in the winter of 1941. It seemed likely that the Turks would permit her 760 refugees to disembark; many were children, all had escaped Nazi Europe through a devious, perilous route which had left them exhausted and sick. But the long arm of the British government reached out to Turkey; the British warned the Turks not to give way and warned the refugees that they would not be allowed to proceed to Palestine, or to land there even if they managed to arrive. Lacking any alternative, trapped in a man-made limbo, and helpless, the refugees decided to make for Palestine after all. Near the Straits of Bosphorus, the *Struma* hit a mine and all but two of

110

the refugees were killed. A new word entered the vocabulary of the Yishuv; it was both a poignant noun and a battle cry. Ordinary immigrants had been known as *olim*, those who 'ascended' to the Holy Land. The 'illegal' immigrants who now battered against Palestine's barred gates were called *ma'apilim*, a Hebrew word for those who ascend against great odds, like mountain climbers striving to reach the peak.

The year was 1941; the second year of the World War. In the Middle East, it appeared as if nothing could avert the onslaught of the Axis. In the Western Desert, a huge concentration of enemy power prepared to roll against Egypt; in Vichy-held Syria and Lebanon, the *Luftwaffe* was firmly entrenched and further away, in much of North Africa, the Vichy French held sway. The Axis plan was clear: Syria and Lebanon would be used as takeoff points for the conquest of the entire Middle East; the pincers would close in on Palestine from Egypt in the south and from the two Levant states in the north. The Germans, with good reason, were optimistic about a speedy victory in Palestine; many Arabs were open supporters of the Axis; in scores of Arab villages and mosques throughout Palestine, there was constant open talk of Axis conquest and colourful cheerful conjecture about dividing up the spoils of the destroyed Jewish community. The Mufti of Jerusalem, Haj Amin el Husseini was already ensconced in Berlin, readying himself to join the victorious Nazi army as soon as it rolled into and over Palestine. Airborne Nazi agents were dropped near Jericho to organize the Arabs for receiving the German troops, and one of the leaders of the 1936 Arab riots returned to Palestine from Iraq to command the armed bands which were to sabotage Allied installations when the hour neared. The British were defeated in Libya, and from Syria and Lebanon, German planes took off to aid the pro-Nazi revolt of Raschid Ali in Iraq. Mussolini had declared himself the true Defender of the Moslem Faith, and Hitler was loudly proclaimed its redeemer. Little wonder, then, that the Nazis were sanguine about the Middle East.

German successes in 1941

It is difficult, in the face of this catalogue of onrushing catastrophe, to understand, even in retrospect, the extent to which the British were still obsessed by the relatively minor problem of battling the Jews' determination to save Jewish lives. But, undeterred by the ominous war situation, the Palestine government permitted itself no pause in the hunting down of the wretched refugees. Also, and with equal fervour, it continued to look for and to confiscate 'illegal' weapons, to detain and arrest Haganah members. The government justified its stand simply: it was in Palestine, it said, to maintain law and order. No one would be allowed, regardless of

The British attitude to the Palestine problem

Some of the Members of
the Haganah High Command
at Kibbutz Mishmar Ha'emek,
1942

1. Yitshaq Sadeh
2. Israel Galili
3. Yehuda Arazi
4. Yigael Yadin
5. Yitshaq Dubno
6. Yaakov Dori
7. Alex Zur
8. Moshe Sneh
9. Eliahu Golomb

external threats facing the country, to bring in arms from abroad, or to arm in secret. A private army spelled treason to the government; no illegal organizations would be tolerated, and Jews caught possessing rifles or hand grenades would not be considered as part of a *defence* organization – in any case, such an organization was against the law, and unnecessary. As to the war effort, the British Colonial Office made clear that it was, at best, indifferent, and at worst, actively hostile to any suggestion involving the direct use of Palestinian Jews on the battle fronts.

The Yishuv, embittered by the British stand, unalterably committed to the fight against Nazism, and now forced to witness the deteriorating military situation all around it, searched for a formula which would reconcile the need to try to cooperate, whatever the cost, with the British in their battle against the Germans and still make clear that its own struggle against the White Paper would continue in full force. David Ben-Gurion, Chairman of the Jewish Agency, finally and tersely defined the Jewish position: 'We shall fight the war as if there were no White Paper,' he said, 'and we shall fight the White Paper as if there were no war.'

The Haganah High Command met in secret conclave to review its situation and prospects; neither of which were reassuring. The Fosh had been disbanded; the Zionist leadership was conducting

112

Haj Muhammed Amin el Husseini, the Mufti of Jerusalem, wasted no time in aligning himself with the Nazi leaders

a successful campaign to persuade the British to let the Jews of Palestine volunteer for the British Army with the result that the best of the Haganah's forces were already outside the borders of Palestine; the notrim and the Jewish Settlement Police, although made up mostly of Haganah members and profoundly loyal to the underground, were nevertheless under British command and could not, therefore, be regarded entirely as a potential independent Jewish fighting formation. There remained the tens of thousands of ordinary citizens, who were, in one degree or another, under Haganah orders, and who served it whenever and wherever called upon to do so, but they were certainly not sufficiently well-trained and equipped to function, in the event of a British defeat and subsequent evacuation, as a holding force against the Nazis.

There was, clearly, an urgent need to create military forces which would be directly and exclusively under Haganah command, and which could be relied upon to stave off or to slow down the Nazi conquest of Palestine. The Haganah, contemplating the feasibility of establishing such a force, now found itself locked in dispute with the Zionist leadership, which was not disposed to permit any alternate form of recruiting in the Yishuv.

The argument presented *against* the creation of a real militia for the Yishuv was cogent, and hard to refute: the British decision to

Haganah considers ways of protecting the Yishuv from the Nazis

113

Moshe Sharett, head of the
Political Department of the
Jewish Agency, visits Palestinian
troops in the British Army,
Italy, 1943

allow the Jews to volunteer for the British Army had been reluctant and limited. The story of World War I seemed to be repeating itself: if the Jews were allowed to participate in the war, as official partners, they would undoubtedly demand, and feel themselves morally entitled to, some recompense as 'allies'. This recompense would certainly relate to the abrogation, or at the very least, to a toning-down of the White Paper, and the British were not enthusiastic about this. Also, they had reservations about arming and training thousands of young Palestinian Jews. Who knew against whom these arms would ultimately be used? The whole idea of providing the Yishuv with a 'free' military education was repugnant to the British, and they assessed the Jewish clamour to join the Army with considerable suspicion. There was, the British knew, also the strong additional motive force of Jewish hopes that Jewish soldiers, in British uniforms, would be able, one day, to make contact with the Jews of Europe, and help to bring to Palestine as many Jews as possible. Finally, the British still remembered the Jewish Legion of World War I, and still recalled the trouble it had caused.

The Jewish Agency had coped with all these arguments skillfully and had leaped all of the hurdles placed in the way of Jewish recruitment; when the British announced that the Jews (130,000 registered for military service within a few weeks of the outbreak of war) could only volunteer on a parity basis with the Arabs, the leadership of the Yishuv had bided its time, knowing that the Arabs were not anxious to fight the Axis. The pace of Arab enlistment into the British ranks had been snail-like, and the principle of parity eventually crumbled before the onrush of events in the Middle East. In the end, parity was abandoned, and the Jews permitted to enlist, more or less, freely. The British adopted a policy of keeping the Jews from combat units and using them mainly as drivers, in the ordnance and service corps, and the medical corps. Consequently, the Jewish Agency hastened to soothe ruffled feelings and to explain, again and again, that what mattered most was for the Yishuv to fight the Germans, and not where or how this would be accomplished. The point was equally to participate in the war against Hitler, and *to be seen to participate*. Moshe Sharett, the able, multi-lingual head of the Jewish Agency's Political Department, though pressing for establishment of a Jewish Brigade, made clear to the Yishuv that the moral implication of the existence of Jewish units in the British Army – even though they were known as 'Palestinians' rather than as Jews, and, for the most part, treated as 'natives' – was of overwhelming moral and political significance.

For all these reasons, said prominent Zionist leaders, it would

114

Palestinians flocked to recruiting centres to join the Jewish Brigade of the British Army. They also joined the Royal Navy, (a unit seen here is training in 1943). The knowledge and background they gained were to stand them in good stead when the Israel Defence Forces came into being

A Palestinian officer in the ATS

Haganah's strength as the Nazis draw nearer to Palestine

The establishment of the Palmach

be foolhardy to start siphoning-off young men and women for an underground force; it would halt the flow of Jewish recruits into the British Army, it would antagonize the Palestine government even more, and in any case, if the British Army *was* forced to retreat from the Middle East, a few hundred, or even a few thousand Jews could not possibly resist the Nazi might. The main military effort of the Yishuv should and must remain an integral part of the Allied war effort. But the Haganah High Command – Eliahu Golomb, Israel Galili, Shaul Avigur, Moshe Sneh, Yitshaq Sadeh, Yohanan Rattner and others – who looked over and beyond the edge of the immediate future – presented their conclusions with equal conviction. Without denigrating the importance of volunteering into the British Army, they questioned the wisdom of putting all of the Yishuv's military resources into one basket, a basket held by provenly hostile hands. They returned to the question of the no-longer improbable British defeat and evacuation: Palestine, the Jewish settlements and towns, would be left to the mercies of the Arabs and the Axis, with only a handful of inadequately trained and sparsely armed Haganah members to defend them.

True, in 1941, the Haganah did not present an encouraging picture: its best instructors and hundreds of its fighters had enlisted; the training of its 'reserves' was restricted, for the most part, to evenings, Saturdays and holidays, and was very much of a 'spare-time' activity. The 'professional' soldiers at its disposal were only a few hundred hard-core, full-time Haganah members, veterans of the *Fosh* and of the Special Night Squads, who were awaiting a decision and who, in the event of a negative decision regarding creation of a fully mobilized and properly trained force, would also enlist in the Army. In short, the Yishuv would be, literally, defenceless before a combined and ruthless Arab-German attack. What the dark hour called for, said the Haganah High Command, was an independent, mobile, permanently mobilized task force, subject only to Haganah authority, and so equipped that it could effectively go into action against the enemy in any part of the country.

No one, in the course of all these debates and discussions, talked about a Jewish Army in the service of a Jewish State; no one postulated that this was the real meaning of the Haganah demand. The men who called for this force – and the men who questioned its usefulness – were united in their forebodings about the future; their minds were riveted on the possibility of a Nazi invasion of Palestine. The question was survival, not sovereignty; but the decision taken in Tel Aviv on 14 May 1941, which established the *Palmach* (*Plugot Mahatz* or 'striking companies' of the Haganah) was a decisive step towards the birth – seven years later to the

116

day – of the Israel Defence Forces. It was a bold decision, boldly taken, on the eve of what well might have been the most crucial period in the brief history of the Yishuv – a period which was already, though few knew this, the most dreadful in the long history of the Jewish people.

The Palmach had two primary aims: the defence of the Yishuv against the Arab bands which would inevitably harass the Jewish towns and settlements and engage in local rioting as soon as the British retreated from Palestine; and the defence of the country against the Axis invaders. It was to go into direct action in the event of local outbreaks, to undertake defence of the weakest part of the lines of defence, to give the Yishuv time to mobilize for the emergency, and then to form a concentrated task force for offensive warfare. If and when the British lines broke, and the Germans and Italians, aided by the Arabs, entered Palestine, the Palmach was to attack the enemy whenever possible, disrupt enemy communications, conduct sabotage, destroy Axis airfields and place itself at the disposal of the Allied armies preparing for evacuation. It would, therefore, be trained, in the first instance, in guerilla tactics; taught to attack in small units, to become expert at demolition and sabotage, and to engage in a variety of intelligence activities for which, in the eyes of the Haganah High Command, the Yishuv was uniquely suitable. The nucleus of a separate command was accordingly formed; Yitshaq Sadeh was named Palmach Commander, and it was decided that the largest single operational unit within the new force would be a company; six companies were to be established as soon as possible.

With his usual zest for action, Sadeh took over at once. It was still not clear whether the Palmach would be fully or only partially mobilized; or even how it would be financed, but Sadeh did not wait for the details to be determined. He set about looking for, and finding, the proper men and women. The selection of recruits, conducted in total secrecy, as were all the steps leading to the formation of the Palmach, was rigorous in the extreme. Candidates were interviewed personally by the new company commanders, whom Sadeh himself had selected. There, no attempt was made to paint a rosy picture: prospective recruits were told that the new fighting arm would probably involve full-time mobilization commando training, and few tangible rewards. There would be no uniforms, minimal pocket money, and no public applause of the kind which the volunteers to the British Army had received. In fact, there would be very few compensations at all, other than the satisfaction of guarding the Land, protecting the people, and hitting back when and if the invasion would take place.

Yitshaq Sadeh (1890–1952) charismatic Russian-born founder and first commander of the Palmach

Yitshaq Sadeh organizes the Palmach

117

While Sadeh and his company commanders were organizing the Palmach, the military situation worsened; the British began to realize that the enemy would swallow the entire Middle East unless they took the initiative and embarked on an offensive. Anxious to avoid open and prolonged warfare between the Vichy French and themselves, the British decided to attack Syria and Lebanon quickly. To do so, they needed a special force which could move easily across Palestine's northern borders and which would be made up of men familiar with the terrain, who spoke the necessary languages and could undertake sabotage from land and sea. On their doorstep, the British military authorities now found the infant Palmach, with its experienced Fosh veterans and its flamboyant leader. The idea of an alliance between the Haganah and the British Army suddenly became appealing, and in London, the light cast by the only completely reliable pro-Allied beacon in the entire area, the Yishuv, shone dazzlingly in British eyes.

Negotiations commenced; the British, happily, refrained from suggesting that the Palmach become part of the British military establishment. Although all of the planned operations against the Vichy French would be financed by the British Army, the force was not ready for 'active service'; it was only a few weeks old. Then, might not acceptance of the British offer set a hazardous precedent by placing the Yishuv's one and only force under British command – even temporarily? Besides, how temporary would the alliance really be? Also, there was the matter of secrecy; it was imperative that the Palmach be clandestine if it were to accomplish its stated aims and defend the Yishuv. The British met this objection by agreeing not to demand either the real names or the addresses of Palmach members. They also agreed that the personal expenses of all Palmachniks involved in the projected operations against Syria and Lebanon would be paid through the Jewish Agency. In the end, the desire to participate in the security of the country won out against all counsels of prudence and the Haganah accepted the British proposal; an acceptance made the easier because the partnership was with the British Army rather than the Palestine government or with the hated Palestine Police.

The most junior and least-known of all the Allies in the war against the Nazis entered action for the first time in the summer of 1941; one hundred Palmach men in all. The first mission was given to a group of Arabic-speaking Palmachniks, charged with crossing the Palestine-Syria border at night and penetrating various Syrian and Lebanese towns where they could effectively help the Free French in psychological warfare aimed at 'softening up' the population and readying it for an eventual Free French takeover.

Some of the crew of the 'Sea Lion' which made an ill-fated attempt to carry out sabotage operations against the Vichy French. Twenty-three Palmach members and an accompanying British liaison officer were lost without trace

At the same time, a series of sabotage operations were drawn up, timed to coincide with an Allied attack on the two Vichy-dominated Arab lands, and twenty-three of the most hardened and gifted Palmach members were picked to prepare and implement plans for an attack on the oil refineries near Tripoli, in Lebanon, from which Vichy French and German planes were fuelled. The amphibious operation was intended not only to cripple the refineries but also to warn the Axis.

The loss of the '23'

But the mission was ill-fated; the motorboat with the twenty-three Palmachniks and a British liaison officer never reached Tripoli; neither it nor its crew were ever heard of again. The Palmach was bereft, in a single day, of its most promising men. Yitshaq Sadeh, summing up the loss of his boys, wrote: 'If the operation had succeeded, it would have proven the rare ability of our men, their talent and courage, and the efficiency of our small units. But since it ended as it did, we had to find other ways of proving our worth, and the opportunity to do so was at hand; within a few weeks, we drew up and submitted to the British a number of other suggestions.'

Sadeh's list was long, and useful: the Haganah High Command proposed a variety of operations to the British, some of these had to do with the gathering of information about strategic points in Syria and Lebanon, others were focused on sabotage: the destruction of communication and transportation networks, the cutting of telephone lines and blowing-up of bridges and it offered advance patrols which would find roads on which the Allied armies might travel fast and arrive in Syria and Lebanon unexpectedly. The British accepted Sadeh's list with alacrity, and a week before the actual operations were to take place, the Palmach began to scout the northern border, crossing into Syria and Lebanon nightly, now and then taking a friendly Arab or Druze scout with them. On 8 June, the first operations began; mixed squads, some made up of Palestinian Jews and of Australians, others entirely Jewish, went into action.

Palmach in action with the British

The Haganah units proved themselves as Sadeh predicted they would; the Palmach men turned out to be excellent scouts, cool-headed and ingenious saboteurs, and effective night-fighters. All that they had learned in the days of the Noddedet and the Fosh, everything that Wingate had preached so fervently at Ein Harod, all of the experience accumulated with such difficulty over the past five years, now came into use. The Australians were deeply impressed and made their admiration obvious; Sadeh, elated by the success, pressed the Haganah High Command to provide the Palmach with its own camps and to continue its training. As long as the Middle East was in danger, he said, the British would need the Palmach, and the chance to see action should not be lost. That summer, two Palmach 'bases' were created, one in a eucalyptus grove in Kibbutz Ginosar on the shores of the Sea of Galilee, the other in the heart of a forest near Kibbutz Beit Oren on the Western Carmel. They were camps in name only; the Haganah was not even able to provide tents, and the men slept under trees, on straw mats. There were none of the usual appurtenances of army life, no army cooks, no orderlies, no quartermaster. Despite the shortage of funds, and the incongruous conditions, Sadeh was determined to return the Palmach to underground conditions, to remind it collectively that it was a Jewish force, and to wean it away from what he thought might be the weakening effect of co-operative action with regular army forces. But Syria and Lebanon were now under Allied control and the leadership of the Yishuv, never very enthusiastic about the Palmach, reconsidered its status. There was a renewed campaign for enlistment into the British Army; the Palmach camps, if they were to be made permanent, would be very costly and funds were short. The more conservative argument won out; the Palmach was informed that its two tiny camps were to be broken up and that its members were to go home, pending some final decision.

The British disband the Palmach

Disappointed, bewildered and angry, the Palmachniks reluctantly obeyed orders; Sadeh tried to cheer them up. Training would continue, he told them, even if only for a few days once a month. A compromise solution was found; the Palmach companies remained partially mobilized from the summer of 1941 until the summer of 1942. Six days a month, each Palmach member reported for duty, did target practice and went on route marches. It was a far cry from the tightly-knit permanently-mobilized task force that Sadeh had envisaged, but he was insistent on keeping the group together and creating in it, despite the unlikely circumstances, a binding sense of unity and comradeship. Early in 1942, the fortunes of the Allies in the Middle East took a sharp turn for the worse. The Axis advanced in the Western Desert; Greece and Crete fell; the British drew up a plan for evacuation which included retreat from Egypt, from Palestine, from Syria, Lebanon and Iraq – as far, in fact, as the very borders of India – if the worst came to worst.

The Axis continues to advance eastwards

Once again, the British GHQ, surveying the area in search of a possible holding force, remembered the Haganah. If the retreat was indeed inevitable, at least the Haganah could be depended upon to harry the Germans and the Italians while the Allies readied themselves to recapture the Middle East. However long the interim might be, there was no likelihood whatsoever that the Yishuv would collaborate with the Nazis, or that a puppet government which included the Jews of Palestine would be set up. The Palmach, competent, eager for action and dedicated, could be counted upon, as the British already knew, to carry out complex espionage and sabotage operations against any occupying power.

Without reference to the political situation, or to the refugee ships which were still being chased and fired upon by British coast guard patrols; without, in fact, any commitment regarding the future, the British now made a second proposal to the Haganah: they offered to support three hundred Palmach members who would be given intensive training as saboteurs and scouts, at the expense of the British Army. Since the Palmachniks would serve without any pay, the British allocation to cover their expenses could be – and was – stretched by the Haganah to cover the needs of twice that number, without the knowledge of the British. The offer was accepted at once, and by June 1942, a full-scale course in sabotage and demolition was underway in a Palmach camp located in a forest near Mishmar Ha'emek, a kibbutz in the Valley of Jezreel. Most of the senior instructors were old-time commanders, and a few British officers were seconded to them; partly for liaison purposes, partly as instructors in some of the more esoteric paramilitary arts. In addition to the Mishmar Ha'emek camp, a large apartment was now rented in Haifa (on Massada Street), which served as official Palmach headquarters.

The British enlist the support of the Palmach again

The basic Palmach doctrine, inherent in its past and later to flower in the Israel Defence Forces, provided the military philo-

121

Yeruham Cohen, commander of the Palmach's, 'Arabic Unit', directed intelligence activities in Vichy-occupied Syria during World War II

sophy which underlay the training at Mishmar Ha'emek. 'We must learn to fight with whatever is available rather than with what is theoretically desirable,' said Yitshaq Sadeh, and in the woods at Mishmar Ha'emek he put the Palmachniks through their paces. They learnt to function both in small groups, and as individual saboteurs; they studied topography, tracking, scouting; became expert map-readers and facile exponents of the latest techniques of demolition. They practised, and perfected, 'hit-and-run' sabotage, and learned to work with equal ease by day and by night.

Three language-based groups of Palmach fighters came into existence at Mishmar Ha'emek: one was an Arabic-speaking unit designed to operate among the Arab population of Palestine and the neighbouring countries. Unlike other resistance movements, the Haganah knew that it would not be able to count on the assistance of a basically friendly and covertly supportive population – and plans were made for this Arabic-speaking unit to mingle freely, and undetected, as pro-Allied agents chiefly among the Arabs of Palestine. A 'German Platoon', made up of German and Austrian immigrants was also formed; these Jews who were fluent in German, including various German and Austrian dialects, proficient in the use of German arms, and familiar with the refinements of German folklore, slang, music and literature, would operate beyond the borders of Palestine when the Allies withdrew, and plans were even drawn up for their deployment in the Western Desert. Also, there was a special platoon composed of Palmachniks from the Balkans. But the real emphasis at Mishmar Ha'emek was on Palestine itself: on its highways and byways, its hills, valleys, its mountains, wadis and woods, all of which could be used for cover, or as vantage points for attack. The Jews of Palestine, in the person of the boys and girls of the Palmach at Mishmar Ha'emek, prepared, in short, to meet the Nazi invaders on their own ground – and to hold it, come what may.

Subsidiary courses were also given in the use of enemy arms. Guerilla warfare against the Nazis would have to be conducted in the absence of regular or even adequate supplies of arms or ammunition. The Palmach learned to shoot with anything likely to come to hand: British, Canadian, Turkish, French, Polish, Greek, German and Italian weapons were all meticulously studied, as were the kind of arms most likely to be employed by Arab irregulars. 'Cold' weapons – truncheons, knives, and even fists, were not forgotten, and finally, the Palmach was prepared, morally and physically, to endure Nazi torture, and the protracted investigations which would undoubtedly precede and follow it.

The 'Carmel Plan'   It was in this understated but sober anticipation of a last-ditch

122

stand that one of the more spectacular preparations for a possible Nazi invasion of Palestine was made by the Palmach HQ, with the approval of the Haganah High Command. In many respects the 'Carmel Plan', analysed today, acquires both depth and significance which at the time, were not apparent. To the Palmach commanders, in particular to Yitshaq Sadeh and Professor Yochanan Rattner, of the Technion (the Technological Institute) in Haifa, who were its parents, it represented merely the logical, and perhaps the only possible, method of forestalling the otherwise inevitable slaughter of the Yishuv, either by the Nazis, by their Arab followers, or by both together.

Essentially, the Carmel Plan, curiously enough, anticipated the creation of conditions almost identical with those which were later to endow Tobruk and Sevastopol with staying power, to permit the beleaguered outposts to hold out until the tide of war turned, and the enemy was overthrown at their gates. The map of Palestine provided the key to the Plan: the greater Haifa area, around the Carmel mountain range and its foothills, up to the Western Galilee and the Valley of Zebulon, is large, fertile and protected; hard to attack, easy to defend, and open to supply from the sea. Into this hilly region of some thirty-nine miles, the Haganah proposed that the entire Jewish community of Palestine be moved; there to live out the months, or years, of Nazi conquest; there to hole up, to resist and to maintain a state of siege. The Plan, like the early Haganah blueprint for resistance, was highly detailed. The population, involving hundreds of thousands of Jews, was to be governed by a Jewish military administration; it was to be provisioned by planes, by submarines and through its own agricultural resources; it would defend itself by using the abandoned arsenals of the retreating Allied forces, and establish a complete medical, educational and cultural network, as well as a variety of miniature industries and workshops. According to Sadeh and Rattner's calculations, a well-organized and strongly motivated population could survive an invasion, and perhaps even force back the invaders. Topography, and the will to live were on the side of the Yishuv, said Sadeh. But the Carmel Plan was more than a static scheme for survival. Its authors envisaged the enclave as a giant emplacement from which the enemy could be *attacked*, and the Plan included the establishment of bases from which night raids could be carried out, and from which enemy lines of communication and supply could be disrupted and destroyed. It was also hoped that the Carmel fortress could be used as a bridgehead for an Allied landing, were a counter-invasion to take place.

It is doubtful whether the British, who immediately approved

Professor Yochanan Rattner of the Haganah High Command and a teacher at the Haifa Institute for Technology - the Technion, was one of the co-authors of the Carmel Plan, conceived as a last-ditch effort to prevent Jewish Palestine from being over-run by the Axis. In 1949 he was Israel's military attaché in Moscow

the Carmel Plan, knew much, or indeed anything, about the epic of Massada which had taken place in the Holy Land two thousand years earlier, but, for the Haganah, the analogy was inevitable: at Massada, a fortress in the Judean Desert, 960 Jews had held out for three years against the Roman Tenth Legion. Their siege finally broken, the defenders of Massada killed themselves rather than surrender to the Romans. The saga of Massada was known to almost all of the Jews in Palestine, and to the Palmach in particular. Regular route marches to Massada were part of the Palmach training programme, and its members knew by heart the short, gallant words of defiance which the leader of the Massada rebels, Eliezer Ben Yair, had left, in 73 AD, as his testament to future generations.

The historic connection between Massada and the Carmel Plan was, therefore, fully understood by the Yishuv; the Plan, like Massada, was a way, perhaps the only way that would remain, of preserving at least a remnant of the population of the Jewish National Home; of ensuring minimal national continuity; of dying, if need be, with dignity and with a sense of purpose.

El Alamein – the German tide is turned back

The Plan was never carried out. At El Alamein the German military machine was put to flight and Palestine was saved from Nazi conquest. But the Carmel Plan, like the ill-fated expedition to Tripoli, had not been a waste of time or effort. Through it, the Haganah added a new dimension to its military thinking and broadened its military concepts. The very need to study the structure, strategy and tactics of the German army provided the Haganah with clearer understanding of what a European regular army entailed, wherein lay its strength and its weakness, and opened up new possibilities of guerilla warfare. As the prospects of their withdrawal from the Middle East faded, the British, not unnaturally, lost interest again in their new partners; and in the Yishuv, the old debate commenced again as to whether it was more important to increase the number of Palestinian Jews in British uniform, or to reinforce and augment an all-Jewish fighting force. The debate

Conflicting training methods between the British and the Palmach

was not theoretical; different, often diametrically opposed methods were involved. Infantry training in the British Army was orderly and schematic, while the Palmach stressed individual ability and collective flexibility. Where British instructors taught their men that enemy positions could be softened by heavy artillery barrages or from the air, the Palmach, lacking either possibility, emphasized the use of darkness and explosives. Where British army tacticians thought in terms of formal and inflexible arrangements such as infantry, artillery, engineers, etc., the Palmach regarded itself as a single multi-purpose force. Palmach section commanders were not trained as NCOs but as officers; they were taught to make decisions

124

alone – each soldier and his weapon was considered as the basic unit of the force. Unconventional tactics were advocated, and the Palmach was drilled to anticipate unconventionality from the enemy.

The 'German Squad' of the Palmach on a training march. This unit served in the Western Desert and was specially trained for the eventuality of German occupation of Palestine

The main principle of Palmach training was active defence: i.e. initiative, and preemptive attack whether by day or night. The Palmachniks were educated to think and to function in terms of utmost flexibility and to accommodate themselves to the needs of the hour; to expand or to contract in size and depth as required. Lastly, the Palmach was developed as a task force composed of various elements, each one of which – or all of which together – were to be used as indicated by each respective situation as it arose.

The Palmach as a flexible fighting force

In due course, the battalion was introduced as a tactical unit. Palmach officers were schooled to think in terms of battalion strength; four companies headed by a battalion commander. This was, perhaps, the first time that an underground movement anywhere had reached such a degree of military sophistication, and it marked a new maturity in the Haganah's development.

Early in 1943, the British sensed victory in the air. The shaky partnership in Palestine began to dissolve. The camps at Mishmar

Yaakov Dori, Haganah Chief of Staff, became the first Chief of Staff of the Israel Army and later, president of the Israel Institute of Technology, Haifa

Ha'emek and on the Carmel were disbanded. The British started to press for lists containing the real names and addresses of those whom, in more perilous days, they had been eager to train on the basis of *noms de guerre* alone. The 'German Platoon' and the 'Arabic Platoon' dwindled. The alliance finally ended in a spirit of considerable ill-will, engendered by the British Army's abrupt appropriation of the Haganah arms which had previously been used in the joint effort at Mishmar Ha'emek, and for which the British had agreed to pay token rent. Now, the arms were confiscated; the claim being that they had, after all, been paid for by the British. The Haganah argued that rent did not entail possession, but the British were adamant. Palmach troops stood by, disbelieving, as British soldiers piled the precious Jewish arms on to lorries and drove away with them. Within a few nights, the inevitable return match took place. The Palmach broke into the British arsenal to which the weapons had been consigned, took back the Haganah arms, and departed, without as much as disturbing the British sentries. The break was permanent and complete. The months of working and training together had not appreciably lessened British hostility or suspicion; the Haganah, in general, and the Palmach in particular, were relegated to semi-enemy status once more. Yitshaq Sadeh made clear to the Palmach what lay ahead. 'The Allied victory', he told the force, 'will be our victory, the victory over the most terrible of all our enemies, but it will not be the *ultimate* victory. That will come only when we have won our war of national liberation – a war which may well start when this World War ends.'

By 1943, the Palmach numbered over a thousand. There were some 22,000 Palestinian Jews serving in various capacities in the British Army, and these were now joined by new recruits, many of them men who had been in the Palmach and were impatient for action. It appeared as though the Palmach was doomed for dissolution; unless some means, however scanty, of supporting it could be found, it would be forced out of existence. The Haganah High Command – Eliahu Golomb, Shaul Avigur, Israel Galili, Moshe Sneh, who became Commander in Chief, and Yaakov Dori, the Chief of Staff – wracked their minds, and pockets, in search of a solution. But the saving idea came from Yitshaq Tabenkin; Tabenkin, one of the leaders of the Second Aliyah, a founder of Ein-Harod and one of the spiritual leaders of the kibbutz movement, had come to the rescue before. Now, his suggestion saved the Palmach from disintegration.

Farmer-soldiers of the Palmach

Let the Palmach earn its own living, proposed Tabenkin. If its members will agree to become part-time farmers, the kibbutzim

126

can be persuaded, in return, to provide them with bed, board, and not least importantly, with cover. If each established kibbutz takes in one or two Palmach platoons, and provides them with accomodation in exchange for fourteen work days a month, then the remaining sixteen days of each month can be used for military training. The Palmachniks were less than overjoyed: they had already volunteered once, for secret military service. Were these services really so little valued by the Zionist leadership, they asked, that the Palmach had to support itself? Those for whom the proffered pill was too bitter to swallow left the underground and enlisted in the British Army. But the rest – the majority – stayed on, grumbling and hurt, but willing, since they saw no alternative, to use ploughshare and sword simultaneously. In the end, it was in the kibbutz way of life that they found attitudes and ideals which suited their own, and these became deeply imprinted into the Palmach's own tradition.

Yitshaq Tabenkin, veteran leader of one of the largest kibbutz movements and its spiritual head, made the revolutionary suggestion that the Palmach blend in with the kibbutzim, thus adopting perfect cover for its military activities

Just as other underground movements, Tito's Partisans and the French Maquis, hid out in woods and thickets, so the Palmach used the kibbutz movement as its 'forest'. Its soldiers looked, dressed, and for half of their military service, actually functioned as fully-fledged members of cooperative settlements; stables, milking sheds and orchards partly replaced the barracks of more conventional armies. It became a point of pride for the Palmach boys and girls to undertake the hardest, most thankless and least pleasant jobs to be done on the kibbutz. Here and there, arguments arose about the work roster; now and then a Palmachnik, exhausted, lost his temper over a row of beetroots or an intransigent cow. Nonetheless, the concept of the farmer-soldier and of the citizen-warrior deepened and took hold. Just as in Tel Aviv and Haifa, office workers, at a moment's notice, turned into Haganah sentries, and teachers metamorphosed, with a telephone call, into clandestine wireless operators, so the Palmachniks accustomed themselves to the idea that, when necessary, they could fill a dual role in the embattled society to which they belonged. Their strictly functional approach to national service – without any ameliorating spit and polish – and their mastery of the ability to work and to fight with equal vigour were attributes which the Israel Defence Forces were to inherit directly from the Palmach.

In the kibbutzim the Palmach fashioned its own way of life and acquired a distinct collective personality. The Palmach *kumsitz* (get-together) around a bonfire at night – with the brass *finjan*, an Arab-style beaked coffeepot, being passed from hand to hand – became an institution. So did the songs written for and about the Palmach by its own troubadors which were often sung till dawn.

Around the bonfire

127

The Palmachniks, in their faded, torn clothes and their old boots, penniless and anonymous, became the subjects of a unique mythology. The word *Palmachnik* itself acquired special meaning: it came to stand for a voluntary, committed élite, for a band of young men and women deeply tied to the land, and capable of undertaking its defence. In 1947 and 1948, in the months of Israel's War of Independence, this mythology was dramatically substantiated.

Girls in the Palmach

From the start girls were taken into the Palmach for active duty. In the beginning, they were given the same commando training as their male companions and did the same courses. But both the Palmach and the Haganah High Command worried about the possible aftermath of intensive combat training for women. The girls, for their part, stormed at any proposed discrimination, arguing that it ran counter to the spirit of the new society being built in Palestine to restrict women to domestic chores, particularly since they had proven their competence as marksmen and sappers. In the end, the wiser counsel prevailed: the girls were still trained for combat, but placed in units of their own so that they would not compete physically with men. Whenever possible they were trained for defensive warfare only; Palmach women soldiers were used extensively as wireless operators, front-line nurses, scouts and quartermasters, though many also fought, and died, in battle.

Glider training under cover of amateur aero clubs laid the groundwork for Palavir – the Palmach air unit – which in turn became the fledgling Israel Airforce

The presence of women in combat units blurred and decreased the harshness of military life; it lent substance to the Palmach concept of an armed force free of militarism; and it precluded the brutalization of young men thrown into an all-male society for months on end. The mobilization of daughters, sisters, sweethearts and often wives turned the Palmach into a true people's army; it followed that when the Israel Defence Forces was created in 1948, girls were drafted for national service – as they still are. In this respect, too, the Palmach served as a template for the army-to-be.

With the stability afforded it by its new quarters, the Palmach began, consciously, to prepare for the day when it would be called upon, as Sadeh and his followers were so sure it would be, to function as a national liberation army, serving the Zionist movement. As soon as World War II ended, a full-scale Jewish immigration from European shores would have to be launched; although foreign ships and foreign sailors could be hired, self-reliance was an integral part of the Palmach philosophy. If it were to transport the survivors of the Nazi camps – and in 1943 no one imagined that their number would be so pitiably small – the Yishuv would need its own naval captains, ships' officers, engineers and crews. Accordingly, a Naval Officers' Course was launched in 1942, and every Palmach recruit was given elementary amphibious training.

Women played an essential role in the Haganah and Palmach – a tradition continued in the Israel Army today

Palyam (an abbreviation of the Hebrew words for 'seaborne Palmach') consisted basically of four courses: naval sabotage, naval transport, the use of landing craft and frogmen and unconventional techniques of naval warfare with small craft. When the time came – and it was not far off – Palyam, together with hundreds of Palestinian Jews who had served in the British army and navy and other Allied forces, played a crucial role in the rescue of thousands of Jews from the DP camps of post-war Europe.

Also in an effort of genuine pioneering Palmach took to the air, albeit on a small scale. In the summer of 1943 the Haganah High Command approved a plan for the training of glider and small light aircraft pilots. The conditions for training were lamentable: a few antiquated gliders, and some not much younger Piper Cubs. In addition to the meagre resources at the Palmach's disposal, this training was further handicapped by the Palestine Administration's control over all Palestine's airfields. The courses, however, were adjusted to the paucity of means, and the entire venture was given the cover of an amateur aero club which the British agreed to license. The activities of the 'Club' were conducted in great earnest: the young pilots were taught reconnaissance, aerial photography, navigation, mathematics and physics, and learned to use their aircraft in combat against ground targets. Since it was unlikely that this air arm in-the-making would ever have to fight the RAF itself, the Palmach's secret pilots and navigators consoled themselves that although their planes and gliders were primitive, so also were the Arabs against whom they might one day be employed. That handful of week-end fliers, however, were to be among the forerunners, the unglamorous, and sometimes even ludicrous initiators of an airforce which, within twenty-five years, would be lauded as one of the most effective in the world.

Despite these activities, there were, of course, Palmach members who looked longingly at their friends and relatives in trim British army uniforms and who were impatient to bear arms openly. Every now and then, a Palmachnik rebelled against the drab combination of anonymity and agriculture and 'defected' to the nearest army recruiting centre. But the overall number of Palmach troops increased steadily throughout 1943 and 1944.

Perhaps the most significant, and certainly the most dramatic, World War II Palmach activity involved the training and dispatching of Palestinian parachutists behind enemy lines in the Balkans, and northern Italy. Part of the folklore of modern Israel, the story of these parachutists, like that of Tel Hai, is the saga of a largely unsuccessful endeavour which served to inspire and encourage thousands, and which, for this very reason, turned – in the course

German storm-troopers
systematically destroyed the
Jewish ghetto of Warsaw,
house by house, and with it its
tenacious and gallant resistance
fighters

of time – into an inspiring story of triumph over great odds.

Although the details and the dimensions of the disaster that
befell the Jews of Nazi-held Europe were still not known, its contours were visible. The leadership of the Yishuv, and, specifically,
of the Haganah – chiefly in the person of Eliahu Golomb – was
convinced that the mass of European Jewry could be activated into
self-defence; that guerilla activities on the part of Jews if properly
organized and carried out, could tie up some fraction, however
marginal, of the German Army for days, if not weeks – thus con-
tributing to the serious harassment of the Axis. That Golomb and
his colleagues were right was to be proven beyond any doubt years
later when the first stories were made public about the doomed
fighters of the Warsaw Ghetto who accumulated arms, closed the

The Warsaw Ghetto

131

ghetto gates, and for thirty-six days battled German infantry and artillery units. Inevitably, the ghetto was razed and all those in it killed, but for 900-odd hours, German tanks and planes had been diverted from other action.

The Jewish Agency attempts to find ways of aiding the Jews of Europe

The Political Department of the Jewish Agency bombarded the Allies with proposals for making contact with the Jews of Europe, for arming them, teaching them sabotage techniques and helping them to escape. 'We knew', Eliahu Golomb later told the Palmach, 'that if we could only penetrate enemy territory and send our boys into the heart of Europe, they would form concentrations of Jewish youth, especially of young Zionists, and organize them into fighting units. We were certain we could create cadres of Jews who would resist the Nazis, and upon whom, whatever their ultimate fate, would be bestowed the privilege of dying in combat.'

The plans presented to the authorities ranged all the way from dropping Palestinian Jews into Poland so that arms might be smuggled into the ghettos, to supplying the ghettos with arms by submarine. All the suggestions were carefully worked out, and all were informed by a quality of vividness which interested and tempted various branches of British Intelligence. One of the most fervent advocates of the Haganah approach was Orde Wingate who had originally, and characteristically, believed that World War II would end at Armageddon, as foretold in the Bible. He envisaged himself as the captain of a Jewish host which would meet and vanquish the enemy on the windswept plain of Palestine's Megiddo, the ancient Armageddon. But after the breakthrough of El Alamein, he changed his mind: 'He was ready then', reported Golomb, 'to lead the Jews against the Germans in Europe. Wingate discussed the idea with high-ranking British and American officers, and told us that these conversations would, he thought, bear fruit.' But Wingate was wrong; the men in whose hands such decisions lay decided against the proposal.

Palestinian parachutists behind enemy lines

For a long time, the British continued to veto what they regarded as likely to be an unduly expensive and not necessarily successful programme. Again and again, the bogey of Jewish post-war demands was brought up, and scheme after scheme subsequently turned down. By the summer of 1943, however, the need for pro-Allied saboteurs and for reliable liaison with the partisan movements in the Balkans and in northern Italy was great; the British, half-heartedly, gave in to the Jewish Agency's pressure. Retaining the basic sense of the Haganah's plans, they whittled down the proportions. The Haganah had proposed the dispatch of hundreds of parachutists behind the lines: in 1943, the British finally agreed that thirty-two Palestinian Jews, of a total of two hundred and fifty

132

Thirty-two Palestinian volunteers – men and women – parachuted into several German-occupied Balkan countries and provided the Allies with valuable information. Their exploits have become part of the folklore of modern Israel
above, *left*: Peretz Goldstein
right: Raphael Reiss
bottom, *left*: Abba Berdichev
right: Zvi Ben-Yaakov
who were captured and executed by the Gestapo

volunteers – the majority of them members of the Palmach and three of them girls – should be trained to jump into Axis-held territory.

The operations were to serve a dual purpose: the parachutists were to aid Allied prisoners, mostly captured airmen, to escape; to conduct sabotage activities; to maintain communications with the partisans. But also (and for all of them, this was by far the most important part of their mission) they were allowed to establish contact with the Jewish underground movements, to encourage the Jews to make desperate last-minute efforts to leave those Balkan countries which were not yet wholly in the grip of the Nazis, and to help those who could to get away to the forests. Few in number, too late to be really effective, the Palestinian parachutists, nonetheless, pierced *Festung Europa*. Emissaries of the Yishuv, they brought a message of hope to those who, for years, had been hopeless; by their very presence in the heart of a sealed continent, they demonstrated that they cared enough about the Jews of Europe to leave their farms and settlements and go out into the dreadful night. Although the Nazi Final Solution was to be accomplished almost in its entirety, and six million Jews were to

Palestinian secret agents in a plane en route for their drop behind German lines

134

be murdered in the Holocaust, the thirty-two parachutists from Palestine, like flames dropping from the sky, made small pools of illumination in the dark; and by the flickering light they gave, hundreds of thousands of Jews knew that they would not perish alone and that somewhere other Jews had heard their cry and had ventured towards them.

In Cairo, the British set up a special camp to train the parachutists, and in Haifa the Jewish Agency established a remarkable office which gathered minute pieces of information about conditions in the various countries into which the Haganah agents would be dropped. Interrogating scores of newly-arrived immigrants for weeks, the Haifa Office painstakingly put together complete, and astonishingly accurate, mosaics of contemporary life in Bucharest and Budapest, in Novi Sad and Timisoara, and in dozens of small Balkan towns and villages. By the time the parachutists had completed their training in Egypt, they knew as much about the land of their destination as though they had only left it a week ago. They knew what people were wearing; when shops opened and closed; what trains arrived and departed and how much the fares cost. They knew how military installations were

Palestinian agents together with partisans in German-occupied Yugoslavia

above: Hannah Szenes
below: Haviva Reik
The two girl parachutists from
Palestine both of whom were
captured by the Gestapo and
killed

guarded, and by whom; which Jewish families would risk their lives to take them in; what films were playing at local cinemas, and the names and addresses of political personalities and public figures.

Nine of the parachutists were dropped into Rumania, three into Hungary, two into Bulgaria, three into Italy, five into Slovakia, two into Austria and eight into Yugoslavia. They were all natives of the countries to which they were now sent, all spoke the required languages and dialects, all still had relatives there. Of the thirty-two, seven did not come back. They died with the Jews they tried to save, in the death camp of Dachau, in the courtyard of a Hungarian prison, in execution chambers in Slovakia and Germany. Brave in life, they became national heroes in death; the subjects of books, songs and plays; ultimate proof that the Yishuv had responded, somehow, while the rest of the world had averted its gaze and chosen not to believe the ungraspable truth of what was happening in Europe until it was far too late for any action.

Today, the best-known of the parachutists is Hannah Szenes, the dark-eyed gifted girl whose father was a popular Hungarian dramatist, and who had come to Palestine alone, as a pioneer, in 1939. It had been hard for her to part from her family, but she finished a course at an agricultural school and then joined a young kibbutz, Sdot Yam, near Caesarea. There she worked – and wrote. Hannah Szenes left a rich literary legacy behind her; a diary in which she recorded her love for the land and her deep sense of a special personal destiny. Also, she wrote poetry; most of her poems are short and lyrical, and at least one of them is taught in all of Israel's schools. She wrote it in June 1944, on the night she crossed the border from Yugoslavia to Hungary where she was caught, imprisoned, tortured, and then – while her mother waited nearby to see her – shot.

It is a poem about sacrifice, courage and the exaltation of martyrdom. As such, it says much about the twenty-three-year-old Hannah Szenes and the spirit in which she invoked and accepted her mission. It is all of four lines long.

'Blessed is the match that is consumed in kindling flame,
   Blessed is the flame that burns in the secret fastness of the heart,
   Blessed is the heart with strength to stop its beating for honour's
      sake,
   Blessed is that match that is consumed in kindling flame.'

But most of the parachutists were not poets; nor were they hungry for self-immolation. Haviva Reik, of Kibbutz Ma'anit, the other woman parachutist to be killed, openly longed to return safely, to marry and have children. She had joined the Palmach

136

in the days of El Alamein: she had told friends then that 'it is
easy for me to go. I have no family, no children yet.' Withdrawn,
calm, stoic, Haviva confessed before she jumped in September 1944
that a family was still what she wanted most. In Slovakia, she
helped to organize a Jewish underground unit, and established a
transit camp for escaping Russian prisoners of war and Allied
airmen. After a month, she was captured with two other parachutists from Palestine. In November, all three were executed; after
the war, their bodies were found in a mass grave in Slovakia.

Enzo Sereni was the oldest of the group, and perhaps the most
admired. Ebullient, charming, warm-hearted and possessed of deep
convictions, among them pacifism, he was forty when he died
in a German extermination centre. Sereni was born and raised in
Italy; his father was personal physician to the King, his uncle a
nationally-recognized lawyer; Enzo grew up in a rarified intellectual atmosphere; inevitably, he became an amateur sociologist and
developed a lasting interest in philosophy. In his twenties, he im-
migrated to Palestine, where he became active in the labour movement of the Yishuv, and was among the founders of a large
kibbutz, Givat Brenner. When World War II broke out, Enzo was
among the first Palestinian Jews to volunteer for service; he served

137

Brigadier Ernest Frank Benjamin, Commander of the Jewish Brigade Group of the British Army, Egypt, 1945

opposite: A signaller of the Jewish Brigade in action in a communications trench, Italy, 1944

the Allies in many ways and in many places. He went back to Italy as an anti-Fascist saboteur, edited and published an anti-Fascist Italian newspaper in Egypt which was read by thousands of Italian prisoners of war, and in May 1944 as one of the Haganah parachutists, he dropped into Italy. There, he hoped he would be able to rescue at least some of the 50,000 Italian Jews and 30,000 Jewish refugees from other countries now in deadly peril as a result of the Nazi invasion. But he was caught at once, imprisoned by the S.S. and transported, with other Jews, to Dachau. Sometime between 17 and 20 November, Enzo Sereni was killed by the Nazis. He had talked and written much about death. Ironically, before he jumped, he reassured his colleagues that 'only those die who wish to die,' and once he wrote: 'If we want to live, we must be ready to die, and to kill, to go out towards the looming dangers... even in death, there are the seeds of life.'

The parachutists entered action too late: within a few months of the airborne operations, another major hope of the Yishuv materialized belatedly. On 20 September 1944, the British finally permitted the formation of a Jewish Brigade Group, made up of five thousand Palestinian Jews. Carrying its own standard, the Brigade was in time to see action in Italy in the spring of 1945.

Had it been formed earlier, and with fewer restrictions, it might have prevented much of the accumulated bitterness of the Jews of Palestine towards the British, buoyed up and reinforced the lingering hopes of the Jews of Europe that succour was at hand, functioned as a prime sign and symbol of the Jewish stand against the Nazis. As it was, the Jewish Brigade, though it comported itself with distinction in various battles on the Italian front, was robbed of any real wartime purpose, and destined, instead, to play a significant role in the cataclysmic events that shook Palestine in the immediate postwar period. Nonetheless, however tardily brought into being, the Brigade was an independent fighting force, equipped with its own staff, services, and supporting arms, and it became a training ground where hundreds of Palestinian officers and NCOs, for the first time, learned logistics, organization and tactics on a brigade scale.

Yitshaq Sadeh had once posed a pertinent question: 'The American soldier bears the American rifle. The Soviet soldier carries Soviet arms. But who will bear arms for the Jews?' he had asked. To a large extent, the sum total of Palestinian Jewry's hard-won military experience in World War II answered that query. Thousands of young men served and fought in the Middle East and in Europe, in the Western Desert, in France and in Italy, in the ranks of the British Eighth Army and in the Jewish Brigade Group – and

Palestinians of the Jewish Brigade Group, winter, Italy, 1944

Brigade soldiers guard a dejected group of German prisoners (note the shoulder flash of the Jewish Brigade Group)

all that they learnt, they brought back home to Palestine with them. Although the British were ungenerous in the extreme in terms of the publicity given to the Palestinians' participation in World War II, their record, in fact, was both long and distinguished. From October 1939 (one month after the outbreak of war) until war's end, the small Yishuv (which numbered only some 600,000 by 1945) gave 32,000 volunteers to the British Army. These served in *all* capacities on *all* the Allied fronts, and included 450 officers (of whom fifty were women) and over 200 doctors.

Palestinian participation in the war effort

In view of the British insistence upon keeping this participation as little known as possible, a partial breakdown of the numbers and duties of these volunteers is of interest. The record reveals that there were 4,800 Palestinian infantrymen, 3,300 Royal Engineers, 4,400 members of transport units, 1,250 members of the Royal Ordnance Corps, 1,100 members of the service corps, 650 artillerymen, 2,000 members of the Royal Air Force, 1,100 sailors and 4,000 women who served in the ATS and the WAAF. In addition, some 3,400 Palestinian boys served, heroically though not

140

A unit of the Jewish Brigade
Group saluting the Zionist flag
in a victory march-past,
Antwerp, Belgium, 1945

happily, in the lowly ranks of the British Army's Pioneer Corps
where, as 'natives', they undertook what was essentially back-
breaking manual labour.

At first, the Palestinians were, in no way, identifiably Jewish,
but eventually the British permitted the units from the Yishuv to
wear shoulder flashes with the Shield of David and the word
'Palestine' on them. When the time came for a call to arms in
Palestine, in the struggle which heralded and gave birth to the
Jewish State, the veterans of the British Army and of the Jewish
Brigade were invaluable; together with the Palmach and Hish, they
formed the nucleus of the Israel Defence Forces, bringing to the
infant Jewish Army all of their formal training and their considerable know-how. But first, immediately with the end of hostilities, they were to become involved – as was the entire Yishuv – in
a draining, complex and possibly unprecedented effort to organize
the mass escape of the Jewish survivors of Nazi Europe to Palestine, and simultaneously, the first major preparations for full-scale
military defiance, at last, of the British White Paper.

141

5 The Struggle against Britain

'Illegal' immigration — The underground railway — Arms procurement — Home weapons industry — British reprisals — UNSCOP

In the summer of 1945, with the end of World War II, a series of confrontations took place in various parts of Europe which were ultimately to change the history of the Middle East, and which were to result in the creation of a Jewish State, within only three years. One such meeting came about that June, in a pleasant town called Tarvisio which lies at the junction of Italy, Austria and Yugoslavia; there, a unit of the Jewish Brigade Group was camped. The Jewish Brigade, which existed for a total of twenty-one months, and in which there were soldiers born in fifty-three countries, had served on various Allied fronts. Wherever it went, it concerned itself also with the local Jewish populations, brought the Jewish communities hope of better things to come, spoke of the possibility of immigration to Palestine with the dawn of the new era that would surely follow the war, encouraged the Jews to learn Hebrew and talked to them about the history of the Yishuv and the principles and rewards of pioneering. Even in Malta, where there were only a few hundreds Jews, the Jewish soldiers had attracted considerable attention and had altered the quality of Jewish life. The word 'Palestine' on their shoulder flashes, the Shield of David on their trucks, their Hebrew conversation, and the material help which they gave so unstintingly to Jews wherever they camped, served to lend to the brigade an aura entirely its own, an aura which deepened as the Allied forces penetrated into Europe.

In Tarvisio, for the first time, the boys of the Brigade met Jews from the very heart of Europe: four young men who appeared on 4 June at Brigade headquarters. They had made their way, they said, from Poland, Rumania, Hungary and Czechoslovakia; they had heard about the Jewish units and they had come to find out if what they had heard was true; if there were indeed fighting Jews from Palestine who had participated in the war against the

Palestinians and the Jewish remnant in Europe

opposite: 'Illegal' immigrants make their way across sand dunes. The long journey from Nazi Europe and the DP camps to Palestine was over — for these refugees at least

143

Soldiers of the Jewish Brigade Group in Italy, 1945, with a few of the 'remnant' children – survivors of the Holocaust

Nazis and who had given shelter, food and clothing to all the Jews they had met on their way. They were strange messengers these four, as if from another planet, and they disappeared almost as suddenly as they had arrived. But with them they took back the story of the Brigade and of the Jewish boys in the transport and other units of the British Army, who came from the cities and farms, the kibbutzim and villages of Palestine. And then, the Jews began to come to Tarvisio. They came in hundreds from all over Europe – by train, truck and on foot – to see and touch the Jewish soldiers and to ask for help in finding their way to Palestine.

The trickle becomes a flood

144

Awareness of Palestine became the only source of hope for the hopeless – the pitiful survivors of the Nazi Holocaust. Six million had been killed and the only desire of much of the remnant was to get out of Europe and reach the one country that would welcome them. The trickle started in June 1945; by the end of the year it had become a flood of people moving towards the collection centres organized by the Palestinian envoys and towards the ports of embarkation

One night that June, thirty-five trucks arrived in Tarvisio bearing 1,100 would-be immigrants and all that night the officers and men of the Brigade cared for them, and listened to them. The story was always the same: the Jews of Europe had vanished. Only one out of every six had survived the Holocaust. Now, the remnant of the six million was leaving the newly-liberated camps, driven by the need to know what and who was left. But there was no one to meet them; their families, friends, homes and property were gone and there was nothing to wait for in a continent which had become a Jewish cemetery. So they started to wander, to walk in the direc-

Clement (later Lord) Attlee became Prime Minister of Britain in 1945 after the British electorate, by a massive majority, rejected the leadership of Winston Churchill. Attlee's Government bolted the gates of Palestine to the refugees from Europe

tion of the one place in which they knew that Jews still lived. Always, they walked south, towards the southern ports, in a trickle which turned into a stream, and then became a river. And as they walked, they looked for the Jewish Brigade, for other Jewish units, and for the Palestinian soldiers.

That summer, the Labour Party came to power in Britain; for years, at Party Conferences and in one solemn statement after another, the Zionist cause had been upheld and the White Paper bitterly condemned. It was natural, therefore, that in Palestine the Jewish community confidently expected Britain's new Prime Minister, Clement Attlee, and his Foreign Secretary Ernest Bevin, to abrogate the ban against unlimited Jewish immigration to Palestine. The Labour Party's success at the polls seemed, in itself, an augury: whatever the past had held, whatever the relationship between the Yishuv and the Palestine Administration had been, regardless of the ingrained pro-Arab attitudes of the British Foreign and Colonial Offices, the Jews of Palestine, not unreasonably, believed that now everything would change. Not only because the government had changed, but also because – in the face of the newly-revealed facts about Auschwitz and Bergen Belsen, Theresienstadt and Treblinka – it seemed impossible that Palestine would remain barred to the survivors of Hitler's Europe. Accordingly, the Yishuv, in which there was hardly a family that had not lost relatives in Europe, prepared itself to take in the homeless, the hopeless and the bereaved. However, Israel Galili cautioned the Yishuv on behalf of the Haganah High Command that the time was not yet ripe for enthusiasm and only time would tell if the new government would prove more loyal to its promises than its predecessor.

Indeed Ernest Bevin's first speeches on the subject of Palestine made clear, beyond a shadow of doubt, that, in this respect at least, the British Government's policy had not changed at all. To Whitehall's traditional anti-Zionism and conservatism, there was now added a new and harsh note of anti-Semitism. The British Government, Bevin truculently declared, would effect no change whatsoever in the White Paper, all of the Labour Party's past promises and pledges notwithstanding. Those Jews legally entitled, under the provisions of the White Paper, to enter Palestine could do so; while the others, neatly disposed of as 'displaced persons', would have to find themselves a place in Europe again. If they tried hard enough, surely they could be reabsorbed into its economic and social life; at all events, the British Government's order of priorities did not include any swift or dramatic life-saving edicts.

Even to the most hopeful and pro-British elements in the Yishuv,

146

it was now apparent that the Jewish population of Palestine, and, in fact, the Zionist movement, stood before a crucial decision: either the Yishuv would turn its back on the refugees, already clogging the roads of Europe in their search for a haven, or else it must embark on a struggle against the White Paper, a struggle to be known in Hebrew as the *ma'avak*, which would inevitably lead to an armed conflict. It was a grim decision to make but the response of the Yishuv was unequivocal. If throughout the war, the Allies had failed to do enough (or some said, to do anything) to rescue the Jews of Europe – even when, in part, as in the Balkans, this might still have been feasible – it was now intolerable and, in effect, impossible for the Yishuv to agree to consider the difficult position of the crumbling British Empire. If the British government still clung to the myth of Arab strength in the Middle East, and still paid nervous heed to Arab threats of massive unrest in the area should any alteration be made in the status of the White Paper, the Jews, on the other hand, had their own impelling order of priorities: first and foremost, the remnant must be delivered out of Europe and brought to Palestine.

Ernest Bevin, Foreign Secretary of the Attlee Government, was the leader of the policy to keep the European refugees out of Palestine

That summer the Jews of Palestine faced their future squarely and drew the necessary conclusions: there was no alternative other than to decide to resist the White Paper – and to resist it on four fronts, at one and the same time. Of these fronts, by far the most urgent, was immigration. But also, the Yishuv determined to continue to defy the British ban against Jewish settlement in those zones prohibited by the White Paper. Simultaneously, it undertook, through its underground organizations, primarily through the Haganah, to attack and destroy governmental, military or naval strategic objectives, particularly those involved in the struggle against the so-called illegal immigration. And, finally, there was the internal front itself; the strengthening of the authority of the elected national institutions of the Zionist Organization and the Jewish community as a semi-official government; their transformation, in fact, into an independent body able to direct the Jewish drive to sovereignty and to organize and control that armed force upon which the final outcome of the ma'avak would certainly depend. It was a decision unique in the annals of resistance movements; the Jewish underground in Palestine, backed by a population of only half a million Jews, sombrely committed itself in 1945 to a titanic struggle not only against a powerful and hostile government – French, Greek and Yugoslav partisans had done this during the war – but also, and far more meaningfully – to the doubling of its own numbers in a country still not under its control.

The Yishuv strengthens its political control of Palestine

Between the summer of 1945 and the end of 1947, some 71,000

147

immigrants were brought to Palestine 'illegally'. It was not a sensational number as such, but it involved a remarkable effort of coordination, resourcefulness, persistence and sheer stamina. Each one of those 71,000 Jews – men, women, children, and sometimes even babies – had to be transported, in dead secrecy, from the DP camps of Europe to embarkation points from which they could sail to Palestine. Their lives had to be organized in some sort of tenable day-to-day routine until the moment of embarkation came, and they had to be prepared not only for the perilous voyage which lay ahead, but also for the hazards of a new life in a new land. Their embarkation had to be planned, and implemented, under conditions which were often physically unbearable, and which included a constant lack of funds, inadequate vessels, and the dodging of the skilled and ruthless surveillance of British agents. And once in Palestine, they had to be assimilated immediately into protective surroundings which would make it difficult, if not impossible, for the British to find them. All of this intricate network was controlled by a few dozen Palestinian Jews; volunteers, whose military and naval experience had been, at best, sporadic.

The sheer weight of the details upon which the success of each single voyage depended would have discouraged any less committed group. Each party of refugees had to be moved, concealed under tarpaulin, in military vehicles, which stood a chance of getting past European frontier checkposts, and taken to secret transit stations from which, in convoys, they were later driven to the ports of sailing; each voyage meant that documents, blankets, provisions had to be obtained in suitable amounts without attracting undue attention; each convoy had to be made self-sufficient in terms of spare parts and fuel; each ship had to be bought or chartered, repaired, disguised, turned into a floating dormitory, and manned; and each ship had to find its way, past British radar, planes and eventually the might of the British navy, to Palestine, there to be met by the Haganah landing parties at exactly the right beach at exactly the specified time. All told, in the thirty-odd months of the ma'avak, some seventy ships, bearing Jews, left Europe and arrived in Palestine.

The underground railroad which directed this activity was called the *Bricha* (Escape). It was initiated by the remnant of the Zionist Youth movements, and run by an organization known as the *Mossad*, ('Inslitution'), created by the Haganah for carrying out the wide-scale 'illegal' immigration known in Hebrew as the '*Ha'apala*'. The Mossad had come into being before the end of the war; it was the inspiration largely of Eliahu Golomb and

Shaul Avigur, although, tragically, Golomb died before the first ship left Europe. But it was in his home in Tel Aviv, in that flat which was open for everyone, with its creaky old chairs and innumerable glasses of tea, that the first seeds of the Mossad were planted in 1942. That spring, forty men and women of the Haganah – carefully selected by Golomb, Avigur, who was to head the Mossad, Yehuda Braginsky, and David Nameri (who had been Sadeh's deputy), – attended a secret course held on the grounds of Mikveh Israel, Palestine's first agricultural school, established in 1870, not far from Tel Aviv. In Mikveh's lush botanical gardens, the members of the course discussed ways and means of helping to rescue Jews from the countries of their persecution; studied the demography, the history and the geography of those countries through which Jews might be able to escape and took refresher courses in driving, map-reading, coding and marksmanship. At the same time in Sdot Yam at Caesarea, a 'naval' base of the Palyam was set up, which was to become a centre for training personnel that later manned the ships of the ma'apilim.

In the meantime, there was overland immigration from the Arab countries to be dealt with; the plight of the Jews in the Moslem states which neighboured Palestine was serious; in Iraq, following the pro-Nazi putsch of 1941, there had been violent anti-Jewish pogroms, and in other Moslem lands as well there was a climate of fear and repression. In the years to come, the *bricha* from Europe was to be accompanied, at certain stages, by publicity, but the overland immigration from the ghettos of the Arab countries to Palestine was clandestine from start to finish. As was true of the European operations which got underway in 1945, the underground railway which terminated in Palestine's northern kibbutzim (at Hulata, Kfar Gileadi, Ayelet Hashachar, Dan and Dafna) was run in the face of a complex of installations and heavily guarded checkposts with which the British hoped to catch the Haganah red-handed. As was true later in Europe, this illicit aliyah also depended greatly, in its initial phases, on Jewish soldiers; on the Palestinians stationed in Egypt, Syria, Lebanon, Iraq and Iran whose transport frequently included refugees hidden in the back of army trucks and who encouraged and aided the fleeing Jews.

Special Haganah staging posts were set up, at intervals, along the northern borders of Palestine; to these way-stations came the organized convoys of Jews, grouped mostly in families; from there, at dusk, at the appointed hour, guided mostly by Arabic-speaking Palmachniks, sometimes by Arabs in the pay of the Haganah, carrying their belongings and their children with them, the immigrants walked to the very borders of Syria or Lebanon, where

Operational plans are drawn up for the underground railroad

Immigration from Arab lands

149

Misha, a young kibbutznik, was taken off his kibbutz and sent to Italy where he helped to organize the Mossad operations

armed members of the Haganah waited to take them across the frontier. These were literally walks in the face of death; on one side lurked Syrian and Lebanese border patrols – to say nothing of Arab brigands who tried to force the immigrants to pay a so-called transit tax; on the other, the British. But the Jews had limitless faith in their escorts, and much courage; in small exhausted processions, in the pitch dark, on foot, they crossed into the Holy Land and, still walking, came to the Jewish settlements where, at last, they rested.

The overland immigration, in some ways the most difficult and tiring of all the Haganah operations, served substantially to sharpen further the 'night senses' of the Palmach in whose devoted and agile hands it was entrusted. Scores of men received expert training on the vital northeastern frontier of the country, learned to solve complicated logistic problems on the spot, and, at the same time, accustomed themselves to the investment of time, thought and patience, to the solid groundwork on details which, of necessity, preceded each separate crossing. Only about 8,000 Jews entered Palestine through these secret exits from the Arab lands, but the education which the Haganah forces acquired in the course of these years was invaluable, as was the clandestine training in self-defence cells, which Haganah operators, working undercover from the Atlantic to the Persian Gulf, gave to thousands of Jews living in fear of their lives in ghettos in Arab countries.

Various members of the Mikveh Israel course served terms of duty in the Moslem lands. One of these, Misha a young kibbutznik, had worked with the Mossad in Teheran and Basra, and had then returned to his kibbutz. One day, a phone call summoned him to Shaul Avigur in Tel Aviv; the signal had come; he was to leave for Europe to work in the cause of Ha'apalah. It seemed to him that he had no qualifications for the job; he knew nothing about shipping, nor even the necessary European languages. There must be better candidates, he said to Avigur. But Avigur waved aside the kibbutznik's demurrers: he had, said Avigur, the only important attribute for the essential and dangerous work, and that was his proven ability to improvise, to keep his wits about him, to think fast and clearly. Avigur gave the young farmer a hundred Palestinian pounds and informed him that he was on his own, that he would have to make his own way to Europe, and once there, figure out by himself what should be done to organize the escape of Jews. The top command of the Jewish Brigade was prepared to help, Avigur added, but Misha and the colleague who was to accompany him would have to attend to all the details themselves.

150

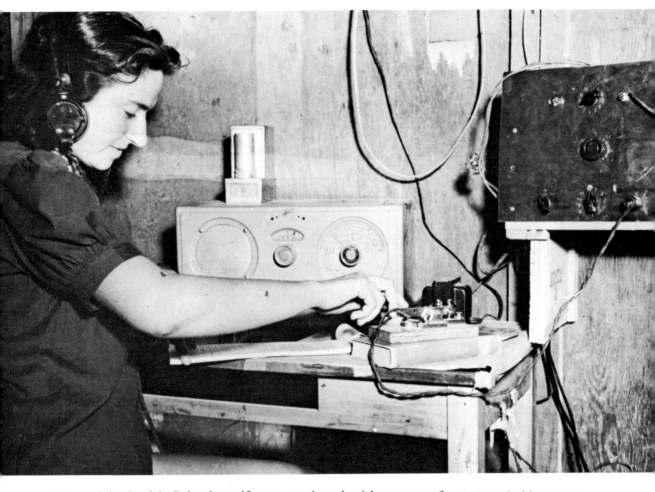

A Haganah girl operates a secret Mossad transmitter at Bari, Italy

Dressed in Jewish Brigade uniforms, equipped with papers of privates returning to their Brigade base in Egypt from home leave in Palestine, the two members of the Mossad sailed with the Brigade in the spring of 1945, aboard a British troop transport. To make room for them, a Brigade officer quietly saw to it that two bona-fide Brigade soldiers were left behind in Egypt. In the south of Italy, helped by Italian partisans and Palestinian Jews in British transport companies, the two Mossad workers established escape routes from Rumania through Yugoslavia, and when Florence and Pisa were liberated by the Allies, they readied themselves for the start of the bricha. Using secret transmitters built by a group of Palestinians (a group which later, and under most difficult conditions, equipped all the Mossad ships with radios) they set up a communications system with Palestine.

The next move was to inform the Jews of their presence. They found loudspeakers, and in Bologna and other liberated towns, they called upon the Jews to leave their hiding places and make

One of the many non-Palestinian Jews who joined the efforts of the Mossad was an Italian tanker captain, Enrico Levy. Captain Levy settled in Israel, becoming Director of the new port of Ashdod

ready to go to Palestine. In a small Italian port the Mossad agents located a small, still unfinished thirty-five ton fishing craft and bought it; whiskey, bribes and a certain amount of judicious 'borrowing' provided them with the wood and spare parts needed to put the boat into working condition. It was now May, 1945; the Brigade was on the Italian-Austrian front, and Jews were beginning to come from everywhere for help. But who would captain the first ship? An Italian Jew, a tanker captain, called Enrico Levy, offered to help out. He made no attempt to disguise his scepticism about the venture, but he was fascinated by the staying power and ingenuity of the two Palestinians, and he went to work fulltime for them. Living on canned food and biscuits donated by the Brigade, holding on to their still unspent precious hundred pounds, and relying, for identification, on papers they had forged in the back of a car adroitly turned into a mobile forger's 'studio', the trio attended to the final preparations: a motor had to be bought for the fishing boat, water had to be obtained, and the minimum of food.

Enrico Levy was sure that the small boat would never sail the Mediterranean, but he kept his promise. A crew was assembled: two Palmachniks, a refugee sailor, a wireless operator. Thirty-five Jewish refugees made ready to depart: the fishing boat had originally been named the *Sirius*, but the Mossad team dubbed her the s.s. *Dallin* (Eliahu Golomb's pen name). She was a trail blazer, the first of that strange fleet of Mossad ships which plied the Mediterranean from 1945 until the day in May 1948 when the State of Israel was founded. The *Dallin*, making her way through mine-seeded seas, reached Palestine eight days later, in August 1945, and anchored at Sdot Yam. On the shore, under Nameri's command, the Haganah established an outpost from which communication with the ship was maintained, and a semi-circle of armed Palmachniks stood guard. All possible precautions had been taken, including the setting up of a minute first-aid station on the beach. When the *Dallin* berthed before dawn, the Palmachniks carried or guided the immigrants to shore, where trucks were lined up to take them, along secret by-paths, to the nearest kibbutz. That same night, the 'nutshell', as the men of the Mossad affectionately called her, returned to Italy, taking with her other Mossad emissaries.

In the first few months after the end of the war, over a thousand Jews were brought to Palestine in the *Dallin* and other such flimsy craft; a year later, their number had increased to nearly 22,000 and by 1947, it had risen to over 40,000. Mossad teams began to arrive in Italy in force; some came by boat on 'return trips',

152

others by plane, and many disguised as soldiers. Their work would have been impossible in those first months had it not been for the Jewish troops who supplied them with rations and blankets, placed their transport at the Mossad's disposal and established centres where the Jews, wandering between central Europe and the harbours of the Mediterranean, could assemble. Sometimes the countries through which the DPs passed were friendly, sometimes not. Here, a customs official looked the other way; there, money changed hands. The escape routes were charted slowly, by a process of trial and error. The Palmach on behalf of the Mossad, took over the actual handling of the boats, provided most of the Mossad's radio operators and sailors, and was in charge of most of the voyages, although the crews themselves at first were largely foreign.

Yehuda Arazi, one of the commanders of the Mossad operations in Europe. Before that, he had been one of the Haganah men responsible for setting up the Shai — the clandestine intelligence service – and was a Haganah 'plant' in the Palestine Police. Later he was a key figure in the Haganah arms procurement efforts

The major problems were connected with shipping and provisions; money was scarce, so the Jewish soldiers created a special fund by saving their rations of whiskey and gin and selling them in return for canned meat. Other troops, hearing the story of Ha'apala chipped in, among them South Africans and Australians. Fuel too, was hard to come by; a veteran Haganah worker, Yehuda Arazi, who left Palestine with a price on his head, dressed in a Polish aviator's uniform, arrived to take over in Italy. Like Wingate much earlier, his only credentials were a scribbled note from Golomb; but it was enough; Arazi enforced a fuel levy on each Palestinian unit in Italy, and when the Palestinians began to leave for home, he assembled a pseudo-military unit of his own with the jeeps and trucks they left behind for him. He set up a mock camp, used false papers to get army fuel, and finally organized a twenty-vehicle garage, including a pump from which the boats could be fuelled. Also, he supervised the Mossad's remarkable radio network, and the secret workshops in which the transmitters were assembled. Within a matter of months, the Mossad had radio stations in Bari, Naples, Milan, Athens, Marseilles and Paris, all in constant contact with the boats, with the Mossad's own European Command, and with Palestine.

The nerve-centre of the Mossad operations of 1945 was in the back of the Jewish Soldiers' Club in Milan, where Arazi, Enzo Sereni's widow Ada and others, worked day and night in the organization of the Aliyah. The flow of refugees to northern Italy now included Jews from Germany and Austria, and involved tens, and later hundreds of thousands. Another network, under the command of Shmarya Zameret, was established in France. It was based mainly in Marseilles, and relied for the most part on the use of small ports strung along the Mediterranean coast. In France,

Operational head-quarters of the Mossad

153

850 refugees boarded the Haganah ship s.s. 'Unafraid' somewhere in Italy, only to be forcibly removed by the British in Haifa, and transferred to a detention camp in Cyprus

as in Italy, the newly liberated local populations, and sometimes even the authorities, were openly sympathetic, and often actively helpful. But it was inevitable that British Intelligence began to take increasing interest in the Mossad's activities, particularly in the location of the secret transmitters. Arazi and his co-workers managed to dodge detection, the elusive transmitters were shifted from one place to another, and a special house was purchased for the Mossad drivers who were responsible for transporting the refugees to the ports. Security became maximal; the refugees were not told until the last minute when their journey would start. Shipboard precautions tightened; tarpaulin was stretched across the bellies of the little boats in rows so that the refugees would

154

be able to stay in the holds, on collective hammocks; water tanks and makeshift toilets were laid on, but comfort was ruthlessly sacrificed so that more and more refugees could be taken aboard for each trip, and fear of detection dictated additional discomfort.

The first of the 'big' ships which Arazi bought was the *Pietro*; 150 tons and capable of nine knots per hour. One of the Mossad workers recalled the boarding of the *Pietro*, symbolic of all the other embarkations: 'The refugees walked to the ship, in the dark, in single file. We staked out a path for them with strips of white cloth tied to trees. On their backs, they carried all their earthly possessions. Many were sick, thirsty, pregnant – and frightened, but they walked in absolute silence. In front of them, and behind

The s.s. 'Pietro'

them, walked the young men of the Palmach, armed with submachine guns. The sea was calm; not a sound broke the stillness of the night. That was how 170 ma'apilim walked to the ship. A few Italian fishermen stood by to help them into the little tender which took them to the big boat. Each refugee was shown his own patch of tarpaulin, his blankets and the knapsack which served as a pillow. The captain was a huge Italian, but the crew were boys from Palestine. In the distance, at the British naval base of Taranto, the beacon of a lighthouse slowly revolved, its beams lighting up the water...' The Mossad commander was a member of Palyam (the naval branch of the Palmach) who knew Palestine's coastline by heart, and possessed a natural air of authority. He spoke in very bad French to the captain. Arazi made a quick last-minute check, addressed the refugees briefly, gave each one of the Palmach escorts a pistol and left. The *Pietro* raised anchor and sailed. Within eight days, she was in Palestine; that night, she prepared for a second voyage. She, too, took back to Europe Mossad workers for France, the Balkans, Belgium, Austria and Germany.

Thousands of refugees reach Palestine from Europe

The summer of 1945 passed, the autumn came with its winds and rain. Other bigger and better ships had to be bought – ships that could cram a thousand and more refugees into their airless holds – the *Enzo Sereni*, the *Palmach*, the *Bracha Fold*; the *Pietro*, once the pride of the Haganah fleet, became just an 'escort'. On the face of it, the bricha had little to do with the struggle for independence or with the growth and development of the Yishuv's ability to defend itself. But, of course, it was in fact crucial: it provided intense organizational and naval experience, under the most problematic of circumstances, for tens of young men who would later assume command positions in the War of Independence; also, it was not an isolated activity, it went hand-in-hand with preparations for, and the actual start of, the armed struggle which was to climax the ma'avak. As the British attack on 'illegal' immigration escalated, the Haganah came to rely increasingly on various underground auxiliary services, of which the most important and the most efficient were those that had to do with the manufacture and acquisition of arms and ammunition.

Problems of arms procurement

Although obtaining weapons had been a Haganah preoccupation since its establishment, and a matter of deep concern as long ago as the days of Hashomer, the years of World War II, and those which immediately followed it, witnessed the peak of this most secret of all the underground activities in Palestine. *Rekhesh*, the arms procurement branch of the Haganah, was responsible for everything and anything that had to do with getting hold of

156

weapons, whether it was the purchase or 'lifting' of tens of thousands of bullets, the securing of a single rifle, the theft of a tank, or the removal of arms from a moving train. It operated in Palestine and overseas, and like Ha'apala was run by an astonishingly small (under fifty) number of highly motivated, and eventually expert, Haganah members. The people of Rekhesh, in many ways, were a breed apart, even within the Haganah. It was on the arms of the Haganah that the security of the Jews depended, and on these arms that the Jewish state would arise, if arise it did. The responsibility was awesome, the secrecy total and, of course, the work dangerous in the extreme. Rekhesh was, in fact, nor more or less than an underground within an underground.

Acquisition of arms in Europe and elsewhere was only part of the problem faced by the Haganah. The problem of evading the constant British searches was no less difficult. *above*: The top of this palm tree in Kibbutz Gesher conceals a 'slik', a secret cache of weapons
left: Hiding a supply of hand grenades

157

Atlantic Ocean

North Sea

Moscow

London

Ravensbrück
Sachsenhausen

Belsen

Treblinka

Berlin

Chelmno

Warsaw

Lodz

Sobibor
Majdanek

Kiev

Drancy

Rhine

Buchenwald
Theresienstadt

Auschwitz

Belzec

Paris

Prague

Lvov

Danube

Dachau

Vienna

Don

Mauthausen

Budapest

Milan
Genoa

Bucharest

La Spezia

Belgrade

Danube

Black Sea

Marseilles

Portovenere

Sofia

Rome

Manfredonia

Istanbul

Gaeta

Naples Bari

Mediterranean

Sea

Haifa

Jaffa Jerusale

Red Se

EXTERMINATION AND
CONCENTRATION CAMPS

0   200   400
Km.

The operations were many and varied. Among the most typical in 1945 were those that involved the filching of ammunition crates from British bases. Each of these operations required great care: the crates were kept in the centre of British camps, under tarpaulin, closely guarded. There were always millions of bullets, but the Haganah orders were explicit: only a certain specified number of crates were to be taken so that the action could pass unnoticed. Each crate contained some 2,000 .303 calibre bullets and had to be carried out of the camp at night by Rekheshmen, usually across sand dunes and on to waiting trucks, and then to special caches in which the loot was hidden. These caches were called 'sliks' from the Hebrew word meaning 'to get rid of', and Rekhesh showed remarkable talent in the range and style of 'sliks' which it created.

For a long time, the Haganah relied primarily on explosives, which were cheap and could be easily concealed in knapsacks carried by its sappers. But even explosives were hard to come by in Palestine; a special ingredient was needed, 'chile potash' – a fertiliser which the Imperial Chemical Industries produced, and which it made available, traditionally, to the Arabs of Hebron and Nablus for firing the cannons which boom out to mark the start and the end of the Moslem holiday of Ramadan. In its dusty little offices in Haifa, Rekhesh printed special identity cards for its operators, and had special bills of lading and rubber stamps made which included the signature of the British Police Inspector for the Haifa area. Armed with these convincing documents, dressed as Arabs, and driving in trucks that bore license plates with Nablus numbers, the Rekheshmen received a substantial ration of the urgently-needed potash, unloaded it at a nearby kibbutz, gingerly transferred it into sugar sacks, burnt the original sacks, and deposited the entire load in a special 'slik' until the Rekhesh truck came to take it to the arms factory.

Many of the Haganah's hidden armouries were filled with weapons contributed by the Jewish soldiers in the British Army (including members of the Jewish Brigade) who fathered the bold idea of obtaining arms from British military railway transports. Guarding the railway and escorting trains was one of the main, if unglamorous, jobs of the Jewish units; it was logical, therefore, that the possibility of adding to the Haganah's meagre store of arms in this perilous but useful way occurred to the guards, and train robberies became a valuable source of firearms and bullets. As soon as word was received that arms were to be loaded on to a train, the Rekhesh people began the long process of detection: they learnt from which British units the military escort for a given train would be drawn. Through its connections with the railway

Rekhesh and train robberies

159

The 'Davidka', the affectionate nickname given to the mortar invented by David Leibowitz, was one of the most successful armaments in the limited arsenal at the disposal of the Haganah in the War of Independence. The photograph shows a Davidka on a war memorial in Jerusalem

workers, many of whom were Jews, the Haganah was occasionally able to get trains shunted off on to side tracks so that the crates of arms could be unsealed and their contents removed. Haganah's two key contact men on the railways were two brothers, Moshe and Eliav Paicovitch. Timetables and signals were studied and Haganah men were assigned to work on the railways to find out exactly how many weapons the train under study would include, just where the weapons would be located, and what sort of weapons they were. A Palmach unit was trained to jump on to the moving trains, to remove the seals from the crates, and to push each crate off the train at a pre-assigned place – all in a matter of minutes: The Haganah obtained much of its signals equipment in this way, and even part of its medical equipment. Some weapons, of course, were obtained through dealers; Arab smugglers brought rifles and bullets from the Western Desert; there were Englishmen who helped, sometimes for money, but sometimes also out of combined sympathy and guilt. The dissident organizations also acquired arms from British sources, though in much smaller quantities.

Rekhesh activities in Palestine were to assume greater and more dramatic proportions just prior to the British evacuation, late in 1947, as we shall see; in 1945 and 1946, the heart of Rekhesh was in Europe. Here, the operations were many-sided and intricate; they involved obtaining import licenses, packing, dealing with customs, trading companies, guards on ships and officialdom in a hundred guises. As far back as 1922, arms had been sent to Palestine from Vienna inside millstones, and later in suitcases and even in steamrollers. A major debacle had taken place in the 1930's, when 500 barrels of cement – containing bullets – were dispatched from Belgium. In Haifa, one of these fell from the crane, was smashed and its real contents exposed. By World War II, the Haganah had found more sophisticated means of concealment: meat grinding machines and washing machines were sent, in the dozens, from Italy, and often the sentimental Italian packers included a bottle of Chianti in the transport.

Attempts to salvage sunken vessels

The war had left in its wake an abundance of war material; not all of it could either be shipped or used in its present form, but the Haganah was rarely at a loss; Rekhesh workshops in Italy worked around the clock modifying, dismantling, cannibalizing and packing weapons. One example of their attitude that nothing must go to waste were the wrecked arms-bearing ships which lay at the bottom of Italian harbours after the war. Italian workers refused to raise or dismantle the ships, but Rekhesh decided that it was worth making the effort. Much of the equipment on the

160

sodden ships turned out to have been soundly waterproofed, and the dry TNT in hundreds of shells found its way to Palestine.

In Palestine itself, the emphasis was on the manufacture of arms, an activity launched after the Arab riots of 1929 and which now became pivotal. The home weapons industry, *Ta'as*, was run from a number of small workshops and factories, rather grandly known as Institutes, all of which were undercover, and the main one of which was in a tannery on the Tel Aviv sea shore. The first locally-produced arms were very primitive: tins filled with explosives and detonated by lit cigarettes. David Leibowitz, a Russian Jew who later invented the 'Davidka', the short range heavy spigot mortar used with much success in the early months of the War of Independence, tells the story of the first Ta'as attempts to create a rifle grenade in the early thirties.

Local arms production begins

'I was obsessed by the paucity of our arms and it seemed to me that we had to produce a grenade of our own, on the model of a Mills bomb. A carpenter in Mikveh Israel with whom I was friendly, and whom I trusted made me a wooden model. We cast it in metal, and I took it to a Haganah commander in Tel Aviv for approval... He sent for a man called Israel Yashpeh who was making grenades in his own apartment. Together with him, I set about making rifle grenades copied from a Russian rifle grenade of which we found a description in a book. It was constructed from electrical conduits and water pipes... we managed to make one that was successful. In order to test it, we went out on the sand dunes, pretending to be hunters'.

The next weapons were a hand grenade, and an improved 50 mm rifle grenade copied from an American one. The Ta'as work entered a routine; instead of working at night in back rooms of apartments, the industry moved to what was known as The Room. It was now 1935; The Room contained a small but complete arms factory. One corner was for making fuses, in another corner the grenades were filled with high explosives and put together. The rest of The Room was a store for the finished product. To The Room was added the first Institute, called Institute A; the weapons were hidden, when necessary, in the vats of the tannery and the guard outside was constantly 'occupied' with the casting of bricks by hand. Institute A was equipped with all kinds of fancy warning devices, including lights and bells, and was, in fact, never found by the British. The transport of parts between The Room, Institute A and other workshops was accomplished either by the Haganah's teenage couriers, on bicycles, or on the backs of donkeys.

Ta'as and its first products

Until the middle of World War II, the Haganah's only automatic weapons were the Italian Bredas, the US Brownings, the German

The Thompson sub-machine
gun (Tommy gun) — one of
the motley collection of weapons
acquired by Rekhesh
right: Ta'as girls assembling
hand grenades

Schwartzlose and a few US Tommy guns taken from the Western
Desert, burnt and often bloodstained, but these required very elab-
orate arms industries to manufacture. It was suggested that the
British Sten gun, improvised in England in the desperate days after
Dunkirk and easily made, would be perfect for the Palmach.
Rekhesh, working in Egypt, eventually got hold of one of the first
four Stens brought into that country and sent it to Tel Aviv. The
Institute made two prototypes, one an exact copy of the original,
and one with a collapsible butt. After testing them, Ta'as decided
to mass-produce them – but the main problem was to get hold
of high-grade steel for the barrels. In World War II Palestine,
there was no such steel to be found. Rekhesh undertook to comb
all of the secret stores in the country – all the rusty old rifles, so
carefully stored since the days of Hashomer were now brought to
the Institute, among them Napoleonic, Austro-Hungarian and Vic-
torian rifles, including Enfields and Winchesters from the 1870's.

In the armourers' corner of the Institute, the old barrels were

One of the early Ta'as products: a three-inch mortar

carefully removed, cut, rebored and fitted to the Ta'as-made Stens. The guns were then taken to the desert Kibbutz Ruhama, north-west of Beersheba, where they were tested and their sights calibrated. Not only steel but also aluminium was scarce in Palestine. Salvation came in the form of a badly damaged RAF plane which had made a forced landing near Caesarea. It was entirely dismantled by Ta'as crews and the aluminium used in the manufacture of grenades. Nearby, in the sand dunes, Ta'as created what came to be known as the RAF Institute which re-cast the aluminium by the incongruous and feeble light of a kerosene-powered generator.

Slowly, Ta'as expanded its scope; other 'institutes' sprang up. In addition to various types of grenades and Sten guns, the Haganah started to manufacture shells for two-and three-inch mortars, and finally the mortars themselves. The security was so tight that until the great arms searches of 1946 the British had no idea at all of the extent or efficiency of Ta'as. During one of the major

New weapons are manufactured

163

British troops carry out a search for illegal possession of weapons at Kibbutz Yagur, 1946. This particular search was only too successful

searches, at Yagur, they discovered dozens of two-inch mortars and their shells. Despite the strange markings (*Ozek*, the acronym of the Hebrew words 'One more step forward'), the British were unable to believe that these weapons had been locally produced. They sent samples to England for re-examination; the subsequent report indicated that the product must have been made in the United States and only assembled in Palestine.

In 1945, Ta'as set up its first bullet-making machinery in the Eilon Institute which was seven metres underground, built under a laundry, and had soundproofed workshops. It was located in a small kibbutz, and protected from intrusions by unwanted guests by a large sign posted outside which warned that foot-and-mouth disease had afflicted the kibbutz's cattle. A dipping trough was added for further proof that the kibbutz was, indeed, quarantined. The precautions extended to the establishment of a special shoe repair shop in the kibbutz so that the minute pieces of brass and other debris embedded in the sandals of the Ta'as workers of the Institute, would draw no attention. When underground conditions began to leave their mark on the pallid workers, Ta'as arranged for them to receive ultra-violet treatment and vitamins so that they would look like everyone else.

The workers of Ta'as, too, were a startlingly small group; drawn from all walks of life in Palestine; some were members of kibbutzim, others garage mechanics; there were young mothers, building contractors and one or two professional scientists among them. There was something shared in their personalities; they were

164

A spot document check carried out by British police in an attempt to identify 'illegal' immigrants, Tel Aviv, 1946

taciturn, reserved, had an air of constant worry. They worked under harsh physical conditions, subject always to the fear of sudden alarms, of raids and the need to gather up their blueprints and tools, and make for the nearest 'slik'. They spoke a language of their own, a perpetual code, and they lightened the burden of their difficult, anonymous lives by inventing their own 'in' jokes. They lived, and worked, in an atmosphere of such hermetic secrecy and caution that, in all of the years of its existence, only one or two Ta'as workshops were discovered, and only a handful of Ta'as workers were injured or killed, despite the daily risk. One of these, who was killed in an accident only a few days before the establishment of the State trying out a Ta'as-invented bomb that could be hurled from the window of a plane, once described the colleagues with whom he had worked for so long. 'I belong,' he wrote, 'to an odd fanatical band of a hundred lunatics – but the day will surely come when these illicit arms, these arms which we have made with our own hands, will determine the destiny of this land.'

Ta'as, Rekhesh, the Mossad, and in fact, the totality of the Haganah, largely depended for their security on their own watchdog – *Shai*, the underground intelligence service, founded in the autumn of 1940 by Avigur, Arazi and David Shaltiel. Shai (acronym of the Hebrew for 'Information Service') dealt not only with espionage and counter-espionage, but also with the screening of Haganah members, the checking of their credentials, the maintenance of a network of contacts with Arab agents and, above all, with the securing of information about the British CID. It boasted

Shai and security

165

a small tightly-knit corps of fulltime operators, but its work rested mainly on the assistance rendered to it by the hundreds, if not thousands of volunteers who functioned as its ears and eyes, and without whom its success would have been impossible. Shai's so-called British Department not only collected information about projected British actions against the Yishuv, but also leaked erroneous, carefully timed information *into* the Headquarters of the Palestine Administration; one such red herring being the man-power potential of the Haganah, always immensely and purposefully exaggerated. Shai differed from all other intelligence services in one important respect: whereas, under normal circumstances, an intelligence service is supported and aided by other security organizations, such as the police, the contrary was true of Shai. Among its more delicate responsibilities was its work with and against informers: it is interesting, in this context, to look at some of the figures of Jewish and Arab arms confiscated by the British in the years between the summer of 1936 and the winter of 1947; 1,376 bombs and grenades and nearly 5,000 revolvers were confiscated from the Arabs, while only 650 bombs and grenades and some 360 revolvers were taken from Jews – the relative position of informers on both sides is demonstrable.

Shai's 'British Department'

Shai also threw a protective screen around Ta'as and Rekhesh; it ensured that preliminary negotiations for arms deals were not traps set by the British; it saw to it that not even officers of the Haganah High Command knew the exact location of Ta'as workshops or were allowed to visit them; it trained and planted volunteer operators in the customs and postal services of Palestine to facilitate the import of weapons and ammunition; it set up voluminous files on Arab leaders, the heads of Arab armed bands and even the headmen of Arab villages. Additionally, Shai worked closely with a special cadre of Haganah lawyers, among them Yaakov S. Shapira, Mordechai Eliash and Aaron Choter-Ishay.

Kol Yisrael

A particular task entrusted to Shai, which gleefully accepted it, had to do with the Haganah's mobile secret transmitter, *Kol Yisrael* (the Voice of Israel) which played so dramatic a role in the ma'avak, broadcasting daily and provocatively in Hebrew, English and Arabic.

The underground station enraged the British – not only because it could and did jam the wireless networks through which the Palestine Administration communicated with the British ships hunting Ha'apala vessels – but mainly because they were never able to find the transmitter. No directional devices whatsoever helped: at one point, the CID imported costly equipment from England and even brought specially-trained Scotland Yard personnel to

Palestine to track it down, but in vain. Shai always managed to warn the station in time – and the truck in which it was installed moved on.

The Kol Yisrael broadcasts themselves were taken seriously by the Palestine Administration; they were translated at once and a dispatch rider sent daily with the text to the High Commissioner and the Inspector-General of Police in Jerusalem. The programmes began in the same way: a few whistled bars of 'Hatikvah'; but the background noises were frequently different. Sometimes listeners clearly heard the bucolic clucking and mooing which would make it appear that the transmitter was near a farm; at other times, the noises indicated urban surroundings, but always they were thoroughly misleading.

If only one Shai operation is to be selected out of the many, perhaps the most far-reaching, spectacular and yet characteristic, was the securing in May 1946 by the Haganah's intelligence service – through the good offices of a friendly Englishman – of the CID's 'Black List', a painstakingly compiled top-secret collection of the names and addresses of thousands of Haganah and other Jewish underground members throughout Palestine. The CID, which had spent years putting these files together, clearly intended to use them just as soon as the authorities gave the green light for massive action against the Jewish resistance movement. It was obviously imperative to get the files (which amounted to hundreds of pages) out of their hiding place, copied, and returned – as rapidly as possible. Shai accomplished the mission in full; with only a few days for the necessary preparations, it found all the cameras, photographic paper and chemicals required for photographing the list; located space in a kibbutz which could safely be set aside for teams of typists; stole into and out of the government office in which the files were kept; rushed them to the photographers and then to the waiting office staff which typed them (reading the negative prints through mirrors as positives) and finally even supplied Kol Yisrael at once with extracts for broadcasting. The British files not only included personal information about underground members but also substantial detail about the suspected whereabouts of arms caches. Although the British duly went ahead with their proposed swoop on Haganah personnel and institutions in June, 1946 as we shall see, the list upon which they so heavily counted was rendered totally useless. From its inception until its transformation in 1948 into the intelligence service of Israel, Shai justified the reluctant compliment paid it by General Barker, Commanding Officer of the British Army in Palestine, who bitterly described it as 'a perfect intelligence system'.

Acquisition of CID's 'Black List'

167

At the end of that critical summer of 1945, however, the overriding concern of the Yishuv was immigration, and the decreasingly successful attempt of the Haganah ships to break the British blockade of Palestine's shores. The plight of the refugees, the worsening conditions in the crowded DP camps, the contagion of post-war anti-Semitism (particularly vicious in Poland from which thousands of Jews were fleeing) and the obduracy of the British government began to attract world attention. Six million Jews had died in Nazi-occupied Europe as the result of man-made laws which the world had not opposed, neither in time nor with sufficient conviction. Now, the newly aroused conscience of the West questioned the moral validity of a new set of man-made laws which denied the survivors the chance to rebuild their lives in the land of their choice, Palestine. But the British refused to yield to any appeals, including an urgent request made by President Truman who asked that, in a one-time gesture of mercy, the British permit

US President Harry S Truman brought the full pressure of his office to bear on the British Prime-Minister's policies, especially regarding the refusal to allow refugees to land, but to little avail

Barely sea-worthy vessels set sail for Palestine loaded beyond the danger point with refugees

100,000 DPs from Germany and Austria to enter Palestine. Mr Attlee regretfully replied that it was impossible to accede to the Presidential request. But if the US government was so worried about the Jewish refugees perhaps it should join the British in trying to find a solution to the Palestine problem. In retrospect, it is clear that had Attlee let the 100,000 DPs come to Palestine, the turn of future events in Palestine, and, in fact, in the Middle East would have been different. But instead, following the classic pattern, another fact-finding body was established, the eighteenth to be sent to Palestine; the Anglo-American Commission of Inquiry duly went the rounds of Europe, it took testimony from DPs, from representatives of the British and American armies of occupation, from the leaders of British and American Jewry, and in February, 1946, it arrived in Palestine.

In the meantime, the crisis sharpened. The entrance certificates allowed by the White Paper were used up; official Jewish immigration into Palestine ground to an end. The British announced a new policy which in view of the situation, and the mood prevailing in Palestine, could be only construed as a deliberate provocation: 1,500 certificates would be given each month, provided the Arabs agreed. The Arabs, of course, refused their consent. After a while, the British government unhappily placed the 1,500 certificates at the disposal of the Jewish Agency, without Arab approval, but the number was patently ludicrous and the determination of the Jews to maintain the Ha'apala stiffened. A sub-war began; much of it fought on the high seas. The Royal Navy, its cruisers and destroyers, the RAF and batteries of coast guard stations, military

An immigrant ship is joined by an unwanted escort – a British destroyer – as soon as it enters Palestinian territorial waters

Legal immigration to Palestine ends

169

police launches, and radar installations were put into action. Also, the British began to detain the refugees whom they caught, on the pretext that Nazi agents might be among them. By the end of the year, there were hundreds of ma'apilim detained at Atlit, about eight miles south of Haifa, including a group of immigrants who had entered the country on foot from Syria and whom, the Haganah learned, the British planned to return there forthwith. Detention in Palestine was one thing, deportation from it quite another; the word alone bore horrifying associations. The Haganah High Command resolved to free the detainees; in many respects, the Atlit break can be seen as the actual start of the armed conflict, even perhaps as an initial stage of the War of Independence. At all events, it served notice on the Palestine Administration that the Jews were in deadly earnest.

The break from Atlit

The Atlit detention camp was located near an army base, with no easy access to it from any Jewish settlements. But the Haganah infiltrated several men into the camp, in the guise of teachers, and these established contact with the Jewish notrim who worked there. The plans for the break were completed; the Haganah Order of the Day specified that no harm befall the refugees and that all fire be held unless they were endangered. At dawn, on 10 October a Palmach task force of some 250 overwhelmed the Arab sentries; a small unit broke into the camp and prepared the refugees for escape while other units set up road blocks outside. The break succeeded, but it was accompanied by a series of mishaps; the refugees refused to leave their belongings behind; in the end, exhausted, they dropped their suitcases by the wayside, thus providing the British with a well-marked trail; radio communications between the various Haganah units broke down, and runners had to take over. The RAF, hovering overhead, reported on the refugees' movements. The Haganah, using a tactic it would use often in the months ahead, summoned hundreds of Jews from nearby kibbutzim and from Haifa to Beit Oren where the refugees assembled; in the ensuing confusion, it was impossible for the British to distinguish between 'illegal' immigrants and solid citizens, and eventually the British army and police units left. None of the refugees had been hurt, and all had escaped. The break proved, if proof was still necessary, that the Haganah was capable of initiating and carrying out complicated actions and that the Yishuv would back it to the hilt; also it warned that all British installations related to immigration – trains carrying troops and weapons, naval and aviation fuelling stations and even the harbours where British warships anchored – would, from now, become targets of the underground. A month later, the Palmach simultaneously at-

170

British troops evacuate their casualties from a blown-up police station at Sarona. A village founded near Jaffa by German Templars, Sarona, now known as the Kirya, is in the heart of Tel Aviv and houses government offices

Haganah troops blow up a British check-point on the outskirts of Haifa, 1948

tacked some 200 points on the British railway system from Rosh Hanikrah in the north to Gaza in the south; that same night, symbolically the anniversary of the Balfour Declaration, three British coast-guard cutters were blown up by Palmach frogmen using homemade 'limpet' mines, and a number of police stations on the coast were severely damaged.

'The Night of the Railways' was the first underground operation in which all the resistance movements in Palestine combined forces, including the right-wing Irgun Zvai Leumi (IZL) and *Lochmei Herut Israel* (LHI) – called by the British the 'Stern Gang'.

The 'Night of the Railways'

171

In these circumstances, which were to be repeated several times in the future, the command rested with the Haganah; but despite this provision, many members of the Haganah and particularly of the Palmach objected to the partnership on the grounds that a proliferation of underground movements was undesirable and that only one authority should exist. As individuals, it was the duty of all Jews to participate in the ma'avak, but a multiplicity of military forces would be fatal to the concept of one nation, one authority, one army. The dissident groups justified their continued separatism by claiming that they were prepared to battle the Mandatory Government in the only effective way, i.e. by refusing to recognize it at all, and found it hard, occasionally impossible, to abide by the tenets of Haganah discipline. Nonetheless, for a while, within the framework of a national resistance movement, the IZL and LHI, refusing to disband, agreed to coordinate their operations with the Haganah.

All through that winter and spring, Haganah boats arrived in face of greater and greater British efforts to keep them from berthing. In November, 211 refugees, who boarded s.s. *Berl Katznelson* in Greece – despite the endeavours of British agents to stop their embarkation – landed on the coast; a British warship approached, let down motorboats with armed sailors, and fired on the refugees, some twenty of whom were caught. It was the first major British counter-warning; the Royal Navy would no longer hesitate to use force against the ma'apilim; the unequal battle was on.

The front extended to the Jewish settlements; the British turned to the 'supporting population', in the first instance to the kibbutzim in the vicinity of landing beaches. Assisted by tanks, planes and artillery, the British Army assiduously combed the settlements, conducting arms searches, hoping that the Jews would either give in or fight back. In either case, the British could then claim that insurrection had broken out in Palestine. But the Jews chose a third, unexpected response: passive resistance. They refused to identify themselves, refused to help the searching parties, refused to disperse, and stood by while the British tore through the kibbutzim, unable to locate refugees or find caches of arms.

The technique of non-identification was demonstrated most memorably by the reception of the *Shabtai Lozinsky*, a Haganah ship which was disguised as a freighter making for Port Said. Nearing the shores of Palestine at night, she turned her bows northward; if she beached near Nizanim, a kibbutz in the south, perhaps she would be able to approach the shore unnoticed. But a storm broke out and the *Shabtai Lozinsky* waited all night for the sea to calm. She waited in vain; at dawn, the waves were still high and strong;

a British warship had appeared on the horizon and overhead an RAF plane hovered watchfully. The only chance was to run the ship aground; but even then it was impossible for the immigrants to land. A call for help went out to the settlements in the area; within an hour, thousands of Jews were making their way to Nizanim; so were units of the British Army. The commander issued a desperate directive: swim alongside the ship, he told his men, and as the immigrants jump from deck, catch them and take them to shore. One by one, the Palmachniks took the ma'apilim to safety. The destroyer, unable to come closer, let down motorboats, but the sea still raged and the motorboats capsized. On the sand, outnumbered, cold, wet and dead tired, the Palmachniks finally left to the British 125 of the immigrants – those who were too old, too sick or too scared to jump from the ship – who were captured by the British Army; but the other 723 mingled with the Jews on shore. Frantically, the British tried to sift newcomer from immigrant, to sort out the refugees and to arrest the members of the Haganah. But the crowd on the beach knew what it had to do: all the British questions received the same reply: 'Who am I? I am a Jew from the Land of Israel!' The Palestinians had

The Haganah ship, s.s. 'Shabtai Lozinsky' off-loads its cargo of 'illegals' through the surf near Nizanim at the site of the modern harbour of Ashdod

173

identity cards, and their clothes were different, but in an instant, shirts and trousers, skirts and blouses were exchanged and a new order rang out: Burn the cards! Two piles of identity cards flamed on the sand, while the Jews – Palmachniks, DPs, ordinary Palestinians – linked arms and danced around them. In the end, the British hauled everyone off to detention, but it took wasteful months to straighten out the purposeful confusion.

The Emergency
Regulations

That winter, the s.s. *Hannah Szenes* left Italy with a cargo of ma'apilim. She managed to elude the British naval dragnet, but at Nahariya, approaching the shore, she capsized on a sandbar, in high wintry seas. Someone from the Mossad suggested turning to the British for help, but the Palmach commander pointed out that a human chain could be formed and the refugees could be passed along it. At dawn, the British posses arrived: the ship, battered and empty, listed to one side in the water, only a blue and white flag near her, and a damp scrap of paper which informed the British that 'they' had reached land remained. The British acknowledged the message by subtracting the number of the ma'apilim on the *Hannah Szenes* from that month's quota of 1,500 certificates of entry. Also, all patience lost, they issued Emergency Regulations; now each Jew was viewed essentially as a political offender; each British soldier, detective and constable handled virtually unlimited powers. Palestine, once again, was under what amounted to martial law.

It was in this atmosphere of hostility and suspicion that the Anglo-American Commission Report was published in May 1946; it included a short-term proposal that 100,000 immigrants be admitted and that the land sale regulations of 1940 be annulled, and the long-term suggestion that the Mandate over Palestine, awarded to Britain by the long-defunct League of Nations, be extended under a UN trusteeship, aimed at developing self-governing institutions in Palestine. The British indicated that these recommendations would not be implemented, save for the 100,000 certificates which might be granted *if* the Jews disbanded what Mr Attlee called their 'private armies'. At a Labour Party Conference held soon after, Ernest Bevin made clear what the British decision really was: destruction of the Haganah. It was a decision given impetus by two episodes, one of which had to do with land settlement, the other with immigration.

In the spring of 1946, a British patrol stopped a bus travelling in the north of Palestine. Neither arms nor documents were found on any of the passengers but something about the bearing of a group of young men in the back of the bus aroused British suspicions; they looked like, and indeed were, Palmachniks. The

opposite: A selection of Israeli stamps on different themes concerning defence, and heroes of Hashomer, Haganah and the Israel Defence Forces

174

1

2

3

4

5

7

8

9

6

10

11

12

13

14

15

16

17

18

Emergency Regulations were invoked and the young men imprisoned. The Palmach attempted to rescue them, the unit was intercepted, but its members nonetheless managed to get away. In the subsequent search for them the British arrived at a small northern settlement on Mount Canaan, Biriah, arrested all its male settlers, razed the settlement, and ensconced themselves on the site as a miniature army of occupation. The Yishuv leadership determined not to abandon the ruined settlement; a new settlement would be established in the immediate vicinity, even though, according to the White Paper, the zone was prohibited to Jewish settlement, regardless of Jewish ownership of the land itself. The day chosen for the operation was Tel Hai Day; thousands of Jews from Galilee, members of youth movements and school children from all over the country marched to Biriah, carrying building materials, seedlings and farm tools. They marched all night, in soft, steady rain; when the sun rose, the British watched the Jews put up the new Biriah, raise tents, plant saplings and erect a fence. It was like the days before World War II – only then, the Tower and Stockade had been put up during the day so they would be standing should the Arabs attack by night. Now, it was the British who had to be evaded, and the work had to be done by dusk. The marchers carried placards and banners; at nine o'clock that morning, there was a brief ceremony, and the 'Hatikvah' was sung. The British District Commissioner in Safed warned that the army, which had taken Biriah before, would take it again, and in the afternoon, the British tanks appeared to roll over the tents and the trees.

Biriah destroyed –
and rebuilt
But some of the settlers refused to budge, and the army dug in, watching them. The next day, hundreds more Jews appeared at Biriah to set it up for the third time. On the fourth day the British Army sent in its reinforcements, so did the Yishuv. Despite the Sabbath, work went on. On Sunday, the British issued an official statement: twenty Jews could stay at Biriah. It was a moral victory, a fitting commemoration for the defenders of Tel Hai so long ago, but it served to confirm the British in their decision that the Haganah must be abolished.

The other British defeat, from which the British concluded that swift and drastic action must be taken against the Haganah at once, took place at La Spezia, a port on the Italian Riviera where two Ha'apala ships were caught, under British pressure. The 1,200 refugees refused to leave the ships; if forced to do so, they declared, they would sink the vessels – and themselves. Like Biriah, the scene was reminiscent of past times; as in Biriah, the British at first refused to give way. Royal Marines took up positions on the decks; the refugees dismantled part of the ships' machinery and

176

The s.s. 'Max Nordau' carrying nearly 800 refugees was the last straw as far as the British were concerned. Following its detention, British reprisal measures were intensified

proclaimed a hunger-strike. Their condition was pitiable and the British attempt to hunt down the Haganah ships in Europe, not just in Palestine, received much unfavourable publicity, considerably augmented by a protracted hunger strike undertaken concurrently in Palestine by fifteen leaders of the Yishuv. In the end, the Haganah ships, under heavy British escort, sailed to Palestine, the ritual of the subtraction from the month's quota of certificates having been punctiliously observed.

The prelude to Britain's retaliation bears the date of 14 May 1946. A Haganah ship, the *Max Nordau* (named after a noted Zionist leader and philosopher) was caught nearing the shores of Palestine; it was the largest transport the Haganah had organized thus far, with 1,760 men, women and children, all of whom had visas to Mexico, which had served them as exit permits. Also, it was the first embarkation from a port in a Russian zone of influence, and was to be followed by other sailings from Rumanian, Yugoslav and Bulgarian harbours, with Czechoslovakia, Poland and Hungary serving as transit for the refugees. The *Max Nordau*'s passengers, among them nearly three hundred orphans, were hauled off for detention in Atlit; her crew was arrested and the vessel, confiscated by the British, joined the *Enzo Sereni*, the *Tel Hai* and the *Wingate* in the special dock reserved in Haifa for such ships. Not long afterwards, the Palmach responded massively by blowing up – at one and the same time – eleven bridges which connected Palestine to the neighbouring countries. Ten of these bridges were either destroyed or badly damaged, and fourteen

s.s. 'Max Nordau'

177

TO THE BRITISH SOLDIERS
WHO WILL DIE
IN THE
Fight for The Freedom of Israel
STERN GROUP
"If I Forget thee O Jerusalem"
American Friends of Fighters for Freedom of Israel, 149 2nd Ave., N.Y.C.

Dov Gruner, a hero of the IZL, was wounded and captured after a successful break into Acre Jail. He was subsequently hanged by the British together with several comrades-in-arms. His execution set off worldwide repercussions — witness the poster of the American branch of LHI — and several British soldiers were executed in retaliation

Deportations to Cyprus

members of the Palmach killed in the fighting that ensued. The 'Night of the Bridges' in which hundreds of British police and soldiers were involved, underlined the crystallizing British belief that as a British military base Palestine would be less than ideal. General Barker personally visited Chaim Weizmann, President of the Zionist Organization, and warned him that such incidents would not be tolerated by the British, although at the same time he praised the courage and effectiveness of the Haganah forces.

Twelve days later, on 29 June, 100,000 soldiers and 1,500 police surrounded dozens of Jewish settlements, descended upon all the national Jewish institutions, including the Jewish Agency, putting them under virtual siege, imposed a curfew on all major cities with Jewish populations, and incarcerated 3,000 Jews in camps at Atlit, Rafa and Latrun. Twenty-seven settlements were searched for arms by a British task force of some three divisions, hundreds of settlers were dragged into barbed wire screening pens, and the kibbutzim were literally torn apart. Most Haganah leaders, forewarned by their familiarity with the British master-list, went into effective hiding and relatively few arms were found, other than the Haganah central depot discovered at Kibbutz Yagur. The heads of each settlement were asked to identify their members by name, those not identifiable as residents of the kibbutz would be held on the assumption that they were Palmachniks. But this time, too, the settlers refused to cooperate; they identified themselves only as 'Jews of Palestine'. 'The Black Sabbath', as that Saturday in June came to be known, represented an irreversible action; it heralded conscious preparations throughout the Yishuv for the ordeals of imprisonment and banishment and resulted in the creation of a siege mentality, in a collective grasp of what was entailed in a last-ditch stand, and in a total willingness on the part of the Yishuv to pay whatever dreadful price might be demanded for free immigration.

The Haganah reorganised itself once more, created new arsenals, invented new codes and drove deeper underground. Names and identity cards were changed, Rekhesh, Ta'as and Shai drivers received newly forged licenses and, using only the most marginal means, Haganah commanders made subtle alterations in their appearance: Yitshaq Sadeh grew a beard, some donned glasses, others abandoned khaki shorts and shirts and took to wearing business suits. Phase Two of the ma'avak had commenced.

By August, 1946, Palestine was a fully-fledged police state; ship after ship arrived (by now, manned almost entirely by Haganah crews); the detention camps filled up; the British, enraged, but still adamant, took another inexorable step: they deported the 'illegal'

178

Survivors of the Nazi Holocaust managed to reach Palestine – only to be deported by the British to special displaced persons camps in Cyprus

immigrants from Palestine to special camps on Cyprus, and began to intervene even more actively abroad, particularly by persuading various South American countries not to grant visas to refugees. The bricha became more complicated; new routes had to be found, at night, through forests and valleys. But Europe's frontiers could not be wholly sealed; all along the secret roads, men of goodwill reached out their hands and helped, and even Cyprus was nearer to Palestine than a DP camp in Germany or Italy.

Floggings and the death penalty

But continued immigration and settlement in the face of increasingly cruel and often irrational British counter-measures were not the only burdens which the Haganah, perforce, assumed in the tragic months of 1946 and the beginning of 1947. The dissident organizations, representing the will of only a small minority within the Yishuv, denied the authority of the national leadership and on their own initiative struck back at the British brutally; when the British took to flogging terrorists, the Irgun Zvai Leumi also resorted to abduction and the whip; when the British imposed the death penalty on the IZL and LHI, the dissident organizations retaliated by executing Britons and blew up a wing of the King David Hotel, containing the British administrative offices. The Haganah, harried, exhausted and preoccupied, refused to condone cold-blooded assassination – whatever the provocation and regardless of the circumstances. It was repelled by the idea of terror, both because of profound opposition to reprisals against individuals, and because

179

Most immigrants fought bitterly against forcible removal from the ships, as this picture of British airborne troops overcoming a DP on the Haifa quayside shows

terror would surely provide the British with an excuse to embark upon extensive punitive measures against the entire Yishuv. But the British lost all control: the government reacted to the operations of the dissident organizations, not as to the actions of a few hundred daring hotheads, of whom most of the Yishuv largely and loudly disapproved, but rather with wild denunciations of the entire Jewish population. Continued curfews, deportations without charge or trial, mass arrests and a series of other harsh punitive decrees were directed against the Yishuv in general, and the Haganah in particular. British troops, frightened in any case, were now forbidden to associate with Jews; the British Civil Service locked itself up in virtual fortresses, turned its offices and installations into compounds under heavy guard, barricaded itself behind barbed wire while the military, pressing London for permission to launch an all-out war against the Jews, behaved, and, in fact, began to envisage itself, as an occupation force garrisoned in an enemy land. Tanks rolled endlessly through Palestine's streets; no Jew was free of humiliating searches or the danger of arrest; and *habeas corpus* ceased to exist. The shadow that had fallen over Palestine could only lengthen – and lengthen it did.

Just as the Ha'apala scorned the White Paper's restrictions on Jewish immigration, thus the creation of settlements in prohibited areas made mockery of the White Paper in another vital respect. Eleven settlements sprang up overnight in the Negev and the coastal plain, making it clear that no strictures affecting Jewish settlement on the land could be truly effective, and that the Jews were not prepared to be confined to pales of settlement. The backing which the Yishuv gave to its elected leadership robbed the Palestine Administration of the power to govern, and turned it, in the eyes of the Yishuv, into an increasingly nominal, though lamentable, entity; and the Haganah's military operations underlined the significance of the Jewish underground as a factor in the Middle East.

In 1947 there were only two possible directions for the Mandatory government to take: either Palestine would remain an armed camp in perpetuity, a vast, expensive and restless British force arrayed for years against a ludicrously small, embittered, hate-ridden and stubborn foe – with no end in sight for either party – or, ending their thirty-year rule of Palestine, the British would get out, rid themselves of the whole frustrating untenable business, and make others take over the responsibility. The die was cast: in February, 1947, Mr Bevin announced in the House of Commons that the British government would refer the Palestine problem to the United Nations. It seemed unlikely that the British, however

The most famous immigrant ship of them all — the Haganah ship s.s. 'Exodus 1947'. The British treatment of the refugees reached its lowest point in this incident when – in defiance of world opinion – more than 4,500 refugees were forcibly returned, caged in wire pens on the deck, and again forcibly removed from the boat at their point of embarkation at Hamburg, by British troops

thwarted, would really withdraw, but the United Nations had no alternative other than to create a Special Committee on Palestine (to be known as UNSCOP) and despatch it, as so many other committees before it had been despatched, to Europe and to Palestine. But UNSCOP was unique: it was the first international body ever to investigate the Palestine problem and it was responsible to the nations of the world, not merely to the British or the US governments. Its term of reference stipulated that by 1 September 1947, it was to report back to the General Assembly of the United Nations, having gone into all 'questions and issues relevant to the problem'.

The eleven-man committee and a large secretariat arrived in Palestine in June: travelling in a convoy of twenty-six cars, in a country filled, as one of its members, Jorge Garcia Granados of Guatemala wrote, 'with armed men, hushed and waiting...', it interviewed all of Palestine's spokesmen, except the local Arabs who refused to acknowledge it, talked to representatives of the Yishuv and of the Palestine Administration, and later met also with the leaders of the Arab states. As the Anglo-American Commission of Inquiry had done, UNSCOP, too, went to Germany and Austria, interrogated DPs and took volumes of notes. But first, the British, in their strangely self-destructive mood, chose to demonstrate the impossibility of their position in Palestine by an act which only a year before would have been unthinkable. The

UNSCOP visits Palestine

181

above: Judge Emil Sandstrom of Sweden, Chairman of the United Nations Special Committee on Palestine (UNSCOP) *below*: Dr Chaim Weizmann addressing a meeting of UNSCOP

story of *Exodus 1947* is well-known; books and films have covered, in great detail, the consequences of the British decision to return to Germany the more than 4,500 ma'apilim who arrived in Palestine that July on a small wooden Haganah ship. The members of UNSCOP saw those refugees for themselves, heard dazed eyewitnesses tell the incredible tale of the boarding of the *Exodus* by British troops – dressed for combat in helmets and masks, carrying clubs, pistols and grenades – and, realizing the depth and determination of the Jewish underground, asked to meet with officers of the Haganah. The interview, held under conditions of maximum security, was revelatory; from it, the three members of UNSCOP present understood, for the first time, that the Haganah was a truly sovereign body. Garcia Granados, reporting the interview, quotes one of the anonymous officers as furnishing a working definition of the Haganah, a definition which was to prove important in UNSCOP's deliberations:

'We are not a band of conspirators, nor a private army, nor a political faction,' said the officer, 'We have no political aims other than those of the Jewish people... we are a free national volunteer army in whose ranks may be found practically every Jewish young man and woman capable of bearing arms. Our forces cover every Jewish rural and urban settlement... practically every household. Our members are drawn from all parties and social groups.'

The Chairman of UNSCOP, Judge Emil Sandstrom of Sweden, asked the Haganah spokesman whether his organization believed that any scheme relating to the partition of Palestine would be accepted by the Jewish community, and, if so, whether – in the event of the inevitable Arab resistance to a Jewish State – the Haganah would be able to cope with large-scale Arab attacks. The same question had been asked of the British Officer Commanding in Palestine in 1946 by members of the Anglo-American Commission. Then General D'Arcy had replied: 'If you were to withdraw British troops, the Haganah would take over tomorrow; it can hold Palestine against the entire Arab world.' Now, UNSCOP received an equally unequivocal and affirmative reply from the Haganah itself. In Geneva, that August, the Committee settled down to work out its proposals to the United Nations. Eight of the members agreed that there was only one possible solution; essentially the same solution recommended so much earlier by the Peel Commission: the partition of Palestine into two states, and an international enclave consisting of Jerusalem and its surroundings, linked by an economic union. A minority recommendation, upheld by the representatives of countries with large Moslem populations (India, Iran and Yugoslavia), suggested a federal Arab-

Jewish State. At midnight 31 August, in the former Palace of the League of Nations, the members of UNSCOP signed their names at last – just five minutes before the deadline – to their report, and waited for the General Assembly to convene.

The reaction of the Arabs, the British and the Jews, was predictable: the Zionist Organization, noting that carving of Palestine into two states entailed heavy sacrifice of territory, accepted the partition plan with tempered joy, and called for immediate termination of the British Mandate. The Arabs announced that they were unalterably opposed to both the majority *and* the minority recommendations; all Palestine must become an Arab State, or war would surely break out in the Middle East. The British, relieved that the Mandate would be ended, announced, ambiguously however, that they could only assist in the implementation of a plan to which the approval of *both* the Jews and the Arabs could be secured: they would not, in other words, cooperate in any meaningful or realistic manner. The United States, for its part, announced that, with the exception of a few minor adjustments, it would wholeheartedly support the partition plan, and so did the Soviet Union. British ambivalence notwithstanding, the great powers of the world, the two colossi of 1947, gave their official blessing to UNSCOP's majority recommendation.

The UNSCOP partition plan

The debates and discussion at the United Nations headquarters in New York lasted for more than two months; on 10 November, UNSCOP, accepting various suggestions, amendments and objections, issued its final report: it called upon Britain to withdraw from Palestine by 1 May 1948, and shortened the transition period preceding the actual creation of the twin states to two months, specifying that both must be established, at the very latest, by 1 July 1948. Also, it requested that a UN Commission, responsible directly to the Security Council, be appointed to supervise the birth of the two states and maintain order during the first two months.

UNSCOP recommends termination of the British Mandate

On 29 November 1947, the General Assembly, by a two-thirds majority, accepted the UNSCOP majority report: thirty-three countries voted in favour of it, six against it, and ten, including Great Britain, abstained. The United Nations had created its first ward; the world had sanctioned the establishment of a Jewish State; the dream that had inspired the Founding Fathers of the Zionist Movement and the first settlers, the pioneers of the Second Aliyah, the Jewish Legion and the Jewish Brigade, the Haganah, and the ma'apilim themselves – that dream of independence, of freedom, and of refuge – was now about to come true. But the rise of the Jewish State and its very survival would still, so it seemed on that tense November evening, depend on blood and fire.

The UN ratifies the Jewish State

6 The War of Independence

*Partition — Arab-Jewish strength — Etzion falls — Jerusalem under
siege — Independence is declared — Invasion — The Turn of the
Tide — Victory*

The UN Resolution to partition Palestine into a Jewish and an
Arab State and an international zone around Jerusalem was passed,
at Lake Success in New York, at one o'clock in the morning,
Jerusalem time, on the night between 29 and 30 November 1947.
It heralded the start of a war which was to rage between Jews and
Arabs from that day until 10 March 1949, nearly sixteen months
later; a war which cost the Yishuv 6,000 lives, assured the exis-
tence and set the boundaries, for years to come, of the State of
Israel; and forever changed the face and the destiny of the Jewish
People and of the Middle East.

In many respects Israel's War of Independence was unique,
unique in the balance of the opposing forces, in the war aims of
each side – the Jews bent on securing their still non-existent state,
the Arabs not merely on limiting the state-to-be or on changing
its government-to-be but on obliterating it -- and in the circumstances under which it was fought. It was a war with a singular
chronology: it began and ended at different times, in different places; and it was geared, initially, not only to the respective abilities
and conflicting aspirations of the combatants but to the attitude
and the timetable of the British Administration in Palestine and
the close to 100,000 British soldiers who were garrisoned there.

It was a war which consisted, for the Jews, of thirty-nine separate
operations, fought from the borders of Lebanon in the north to
the heart of the Sinai desert in the south-west and on the Red Sea
in the south; it saw the birth of the State of Israel, the metamor-
phosis of the Jewish resistance movement into the Israel Defence
Forces, and the total mobilization of the Yishuv, consisting of
650,000 people – ill-armed and only partially trained – to meet
the coordinated assault not just of Palestine's 1,000,000 Arabs but
of five regular Arab armies. And finally, it was a war which reaf-
firmed for all time the determination of the Yishuv to survive.

UN partition and war

The extent of the war

*opposite: A soldier of the
Palmach keeps a solitary watch
from an Israeli settlement over-
looking the Valley of Jezreel in
the Galilee*

185

Haganah strength   The foremost Jewish formation was, of course, the Haganah: within its ranks it included, all told, some 45,000 men, women and youngsters, of whom less than two thousand (the Jewish Settlement Police) were legally entitled to bear arms. The Palmach consisted then of four battalions, together comprising some 2,100 young men and women, on active service and about 1,000 more in the reserves. One battalion was based on the settlements of the Valley of Jezreel, one in the Galilee and the Jordan Valley, another in the Negev, and one was a Headquarters battalion which incorporated the Palmach's miniscule naval service, airforce, and its reconnaissance units. The rest of the Haganah fighting potential was divided into two: the Hish (field army), which numbered about 9,500, whose members ranged in age between eighteen and twenty-five, and sorely lacked fulltime training; and the *Him* or Home Guard, a militia made up of 30,000 men and women over the age of twenty-five, some of whom were members of kibbutzim and cooperative villages, others city-dwellers, all of whom, in the event of emergency, were to man defensive positions. There was also the *Gadna* (acronym of the Hebrew words for Youth Battalions) – 9,500 boys and girls from fifteen to eighteen years of age, who had had some paramilitary training, and who could be used as signallers and

British Army veterans   couriers. The backbone of the fledgling army were the 32,000
and DP 'graduates'   veterans of the Palestinian units in the British Army and of the Jewish Brigade Group who were now incorporated within various Haganah units and whose combat experience was to be invaluable, particularly in the artillery, the administration and the logistics required by the Jewish war effort.

There were also those Jews, mobilized by the Haganah in the DP camps of Germany, and in the detention camps of Cyprus; for the most part, it had been impossible to train them with live ammunition or with real weapons; and hundreds of them had learnt the arts of war with the aid of wooden rifles and dummy bullets. Nonetheless, with the establishment of the State, and their final entry to the land so long denied them, these, and many hundreds of other new immigrants, went straight from the boats which brought them to Palestine into combat units. But until 15 May 1948 – the end of the Mandate – they were not a factor.

Another source of manpower to be tapped mainly after the British had gone and the 'official' invasion had started, were the volunteers from overseas, chiefly young Jews from the Western world, fired by the excitement and challenge of Israel's rise, and moved by the peril which faced her in the days of her infancy. In all, there were only a few thousand of these, but they were to play a significant role in the formation of Israel's armoured corps,

186

airforce, medical corps and artillery. When the first shots of the war rang out, however, they too, were still far from Palestine.

Additionally, there were other small fighting organizations: the Irgun Zvai Leumi (largest of the dissident underground organizations) could call upon from two to three thousand members, many of whom, however, had received only spasmodic military training; the LHI, which was made up of a few hundred volunteers and whose people were trained mainly in sabotage activities.

The inventory of the Haganah armouries was not reassuring; a pre-war count did little to lift the heart of the High Command: 10,073 rifles (nearly 9,000 scattered throughout the country, and only the remaining 1,350 in a central depot); 1,900 machine guns, 440 light machine guns, 186 other guns. The entire Haganah artillery consisted of 672 two-inch mortars and 96 three-inch mortars: not one cannon, not one tank and a critical dearth of military vehicles. True, the machinery (weighing thousands of tons) for the up-to-date production of arms had already been obtained abroad, but it was impossible to bring it in until the British left. The Rekhesh had substantially stepped up its attempts to procure arms, but the existing supplies were patently inadequate for the uses to which they would be put. The 'airforce', separated from the Palmach and recognized as an independent unit, in November 1947, possessed nine light aircraft (only one with two engines) and, there were, that winter, a total of forty Jewish pilots in the country, twenty of whom were RAF 'graduates'.

Two members of IZL. The shoulder badge shows a rifle superimposed over a map of Palestine and the words *Rak Kach* — 'Only thus'

What of the Arabs? The advantages were clearly manifold: apart from the fact that their initiative gave them tactical superiority for many weeks, they were blessed by unhampered overland access to Palestine and to an Arab hinterland which was mobilized to assist the invading armies in all respects. Most of the densely-populated Arab areas were adjacent to each other, providing the Arabs with depth and the possibility of moving freely from one front to another, while few, if any, of the Jewish areas of Palestine were contiguous. Also, generally speaking, the Arabs controlled most of the hilly or mountainous part of Palestine, and it was easy for them to attack the low-lying Jewish settlements and towns. But there were other non-topographical differences: an absolute superiority of arms, and an overwhelming superiority of manpower conscripted, volunteer or potential. Finally, there was the tangible encouragement and support of the British.

The Arabs' strength

The tally, however, cannot be completed without some reference to the handicaps with which the Arabs started the war; they were unable, at any stage of the conflict, to unite among themselves or to create a unified command. The 'volunteers' and the invading

Arab irregular forces attacking from one of the walls of the Old City of Jerusalem

King Abdullah, ruler of the Hashemite Kingdom of Jordan

armies supposedly enthusiastic about the 'Holy War' and the promise of its glittering booty, had little in common with the Palestinian Arabs – and found it unnecessary to conceal their disdain for them. The Arab commanders tended to be unreliable and had no echelon of experienced junior officers under them. The various Commands were made up of often brilliant and brave individuals who were incapable of, and unused to, team work. Noteworthy as 'hit and run' snipers, the Arabs did poorly whenever well-planned operations, requiring group effort, were called for; and the very structure of Arab society, in Palestine itself, and in the neighbouring Arab states, highlighted all these disadvantages.

In this context, the question of motivation cannot be overlooked; the Jews were faced by a simple equation: prevail or perish; when all else is said and done, it was this which made the Yishuv win the war. But the Arabs were spurred on by emotions which had nothing to do with survival, and which, in the end, were to prove ineffectual, inadequate to the challenge.

In Palestine itself, on the eve of war, there were more than 1,000,000 Arabs; only 6,000 of these were trained veterans of World War II, but almost all Arab villagers had handled arms from childhood on – and knew something, however elementary, about guerilla warfare. Also, there were hundreds of Arabs who had served in the ranks of the Palestine Police, in all-Arab units, and close to 2,000 soldiers of the Transjordan Frontier Force (an entire battalion of which was disbanded by the British at the start of 1948, thus releasing its members for service with the Arab armed bands).

188

Arabs burning and looting Jewish shops in Jerusalem's commercial centre

Sir Alan Cunningham was Britain's last High Commissioner of Palestine. David Ben Gurion (*below*) led the Yishuv in its struggles in the War of Independence

The Arab Legion of Transjordan, a crack British-officered Bedouin force, numbered about 7,400, and the Arab Liberation Army – financed by the Arab states through the good offices of the Arab League – was already in operation in Palestine by 30 November. With the departure of the British, Transjordan, Syria, Lebanon, Iraq and Egypt became active and formal participants in the war, representing a combined Arab population of some 40,000,000.

For most of the Yishuv 30 November was a day given over to celebration, to mass rejoicing, and to prayer – despite the news that seven Jews had been killed in an Arab ambush of a bus on the road to Lydda. Next day, the Arabs of Palestine proclaimed a three-day strike; David Ben-Gurion went to see the High Commissioner, Sir Alan Cunningham, at Government House in Jerusalem. Sir Alan received the Chairman of the Jewish Agency coldly, without a word of congratulation. 'I suppose you are happy about the Resolution,' was all he said. Ben-Gurion tried to discuss the future; he requested photostat copies of the land registry deeds, detailed information about the available supplies of food and fuel in the country, and asked for permission to establish an armed militia which would keep law and order during the transition period and escort Jewish transport on the main roads – the vast majority of which ran through Arab inhabited Palestine. The High Commissioner promised to think over these requests and to reply to them. Within a day, another news item jarred the Yishuv; the Jewish commercial centre in Jerusalem was set afire by an Arab mob; eye-witnesses reported that the British police had stood

189

by, taking action against the Haganah when it tried to help. A pattern, not unfamiliar, began to emerge, and the mood of the Jews shifted and darkened.

The next weeks were tense. The Arab League met in Cairo and resolved to send troops, in the guise of volunteers, to all the Arab states neighbouring Palestine; the process of major Arab infiltration had already started and the British were neither hindering nor stopping it. On 7 December, the High Commissioner asked Mr Ben-Gurion to see him again; the British, His Excellency announced, had decided to evacuate Palestine as soon as possible. Of course, it would be a complex operation and it would take time; the British army had large stocks in the country which would have to stay there and these would have to be put in order before the British went. Mr Ben-Gurion asked for whose benefit these stores would be maintained, but the High Commissioner did not reply.

Mr Ben-Gurion returned to Tel Aviv and convened a series of emergency meetings, some with the leaders of the Yishuv, others with the Haganah High Command. It was at one of these meetings that a fundamental principle was laid down which was to guide the Yishuv throughout the spring, and, eventually, to ensure Israel's victory. The map, unrolled, revealed that the area allotted to the Jewish State by the United Nations, was, like Gaul, divided into three: in the north, from Metullah to Tirat Zvi, the Jews were in the minority, scattered and surrounded on all sides; in the centre, from Acre to Beer Tuvia, there was a Jewish majority, and the sea to the west, but even here the roads were dominated by the Arabs; Jerusalem could be easily cut off, and Jaffa posed a permanent threat to Tel Aviv. The Negev, demographically, resembled the north, except that it was far less densely settled by Jews.

'Not one settlement to be abandoned'

A high-ranking Haganah officer suggested that perhaps, since it was impossible for the Yishuv to fortify or man so many non-contiguous areas from north to south, certain settlements should be abandoned; after all, where *would* the necessary soldiers and the arms come from? How *could* money be raised in sufficient quantity, or soon enough? Would it not be sounder to make a stand only where really sizeable Jewish populations existed? But the proposals for evacuation of the smaller and more remote Jewish outposts, near Gaza, Acre, Jerusalem and the north were turned down. In the sea of uncertainty that now lapped over the Yishuv, one binding decision stood out, rock-like; the Jews would hold on to everything; not one of Palestine's 300-odd Jewish settlements would be abandoned, regardless of its size, of Arab harassment, of the looming invasion.

Chaim Weizmann's aphorism was proved true. 'No people has

190

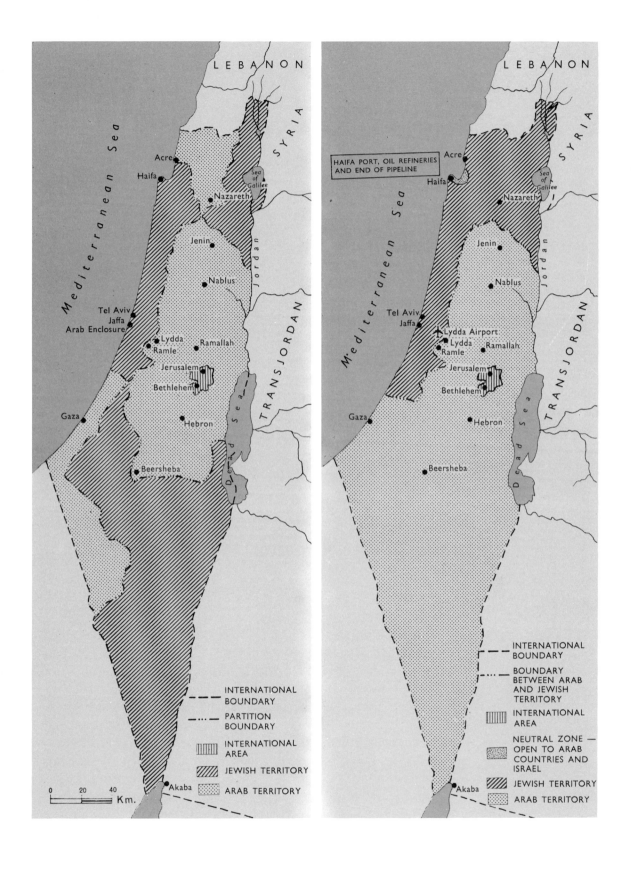

LEBANON

SYRIA

Mediterranean Sea

Acre

Haifa

Sea of Galilee

Nazareth

Jenin

Nablus

Jordan

Tel Aviv
Jaffa
Arab Enclosure

Lydda
Ramle

Ramallah

Jerusalem

Bethlehem

Gaza

Hebron

Dead Sea

TRANSJORDAN

Beersheba

Akaba

– – –	INTERNATIONAL BOUNDARY
– · –	PARTITION BOUNDARY
‖‖‖	INTERNATIONAL AREA
⫽⫽⫽	JEWISH TERRITORY
∴∴∴	ARAB TERRITORY

0   20   40
Km.

LEBANON

SYRIA

Mediterranean Sea

HAIFA PORT, OIL REFINERIES AND END OF PIPELINE

Acre

Haifa

Sea of Galilee

Nazareth

Jenin

Nablus

Jordan

Tel Aviv
Jaffa

Lydda Airport
Lydda
Ramle

Ramallah

Jerusalem

Bethlehem

Gaza

Hebron

Dead Sea

TRANSJORDAN

Beersheba

Akaba

– – –	INTERNATIONAL BOUNDARY
– · · –	BOUNDARY BETWEEN ARAB AND JEWISH TERRITORY
‖‖‖	INTERNATIONAL AREA
∷∷∷	NEUTRAL ZONE — OPEN TO ARAB COUNTRIES AND ISRAEL
⫽⫽⫽	JEWISH TERRITORY
∴∴∴	ARAB TERRITORY

The noose around Jerusalem tightened and the city was encircled and cut off. The raising of the siege was one of the most daring and dramatic incidents of the war. Here a food convoy reaches the besieged city

ever received a state handed to them on a silver platter'. The concept of localized defence was set aside; in its place came a strategy based on national defence, not the defence of a given settlement but rather of the Yishuv in its entirety. New weapons would be needed, of course; the time had passed for only rifles, machine guns and grenades; tanks, fighter planes and even warships would determine the outcome.

There were those who still doubted that the situation would become acute enough to warrant such horrendously expensive means, who were sure that the UN would take action soon against Arab depredations, who believed that the British, on the very eve of their departure, would suffer a change of heart. But the consensus within the Haganah High Command was that, somehow or other, the Yishuv would have to prepare itself for the zero hour; delegations were sent off at once to raise money abroad, to order arms, planes and heavy military transport in the hope that these could be brought into the country in time.

The Jerusalem road The situation worsened daily; the Arabs escalated from sniping at Jewish cars and trucks to blocking Jewish traffic, in particular on the lovely, winding road that meandered, largely through Arab-held territory, from Tel Aviv to Jerusalem; the Jerusalem road, whose defence by the boys and girls of the Palmach, formed a chapter of its own in the story of the war. Losing the road to Jerusalem meant risking the loss of Jerusalem itself; the narrow corridor from Jerusalem to the coastal plain had to be kept open, whatever the cost, or Jerusalem, already encircled, would be strangled to death. And so it happened that the defence of the road – in many ways, the hardest, the most dangerous and the most dis-

192

Arab irregular forces burn a truck ambushed on its way to Jerusalem

couraging assignment of the entire war – was handed to a relatively small task force of Palmach youngsters.

Sha'ar Hagai

The most dangerous part of the road was the beautiful valley known as Shaar-Hagai in Hebrew (Bab-el-Wad in Arabic) whose steep forested sides sheltered the nests of Arab snipers. At Shaar-Hagai, men and vehicles alike were easy prey; and many men and vehicles met their end there.

January, 1948. Not only was the Jerusalem–Tel Aviv road a death trap, but Arab attacks had increased all over the country – in the Negev, in the Galilee, in the outlying quarters of Jerusalem and even on transportation within Jerusalem itself. At Gush Etzion, a bloc of four settlements perched in the Hebron Hills, on the side of the road connecting Jerusalem, Bethlehem and Hebron, the endurance of the Jews, and their ability to withstand aggression, were put to a severe and crucial test. The four settlements were under siege until on the very eve of Israel's independence, they fell to the enemy. The story of the Etzion bloc – frustrating, gallant, tragic, and wasteful in terms of human life – typifies, better than anything else, the early spring of 1948 in a riven land.

The attack on the Etzion Bloc

In December a Haganah convoy, making its way through the hills to the Etzion bloc, was attacked and ten of the boys in the convoy were killed; in the middle of January, the Arabs, a thousand strong, mounted an assault on the bloc itself, under the command of one of the most gifted and best-known of the Arab military leaders, Abdel Kader el Husseini, who was related to the Mufti of Jerusalem. The Arabs, making sanguine and detailed plans for carting away their spoils, were sure that the settlements would crumple at once. But the convoys that had journeyed to

the Etzion bloc all winter had brought more than arms and food with them; they had brought squads of Palmachniks and now these Palmachniks opened fire upon the attackers. By night, the Arabs had fled, but the settlements were left critically short of arms.

In Jerusalem, the Haganah assembled a platoon of volunteers, half Palmachniks, half university students who were members of Hish, and assigned them the task of reinforcing the bloc. It was 15 January; stumbling through the hills, one of the boys sprained an ankle and was ordered to base, with two of his comrades as escorts. The remaining thirty-five went on, but they never reached the Etzion bloc. Years later, Arabs from the vicinity and British police records supplied part of the missing information. Trapped by hundreds of Arabs, the thirty-five boys had fought back in vain. The British reported afterwards that one of the murdered boys still held a stone in his hands, the only ammunition left to him. But valour was not enough; on 17 January, the British brought thirty-five mutilated bodies to Etzion to be buried in a common grave.

January, February, March... the situation at Etzion was acute; sporadic contact with the settlements was maintained by the Haganah's plucky Piper Cubs, nicknamed the 'Primuses' (for the primitive sputtering kerosene cooking stoves on which many Palestinians cooked), while from the bloc itself, the Palmachniks and settlers did their best to disrupt Arab communications along the Hebron road by putting up road blocks and laying mines. But the siege had to be broken, or the settlements were doomed. On 27 March, a convoy of thirty-three trucks, four armoured cars and twelve armour-plated buses set out for Etzion. The transport carried 140 Hish members and an escort of one hundred Palmachniks. By noon, the trucks were unloaded and the convoy began to wend its way back to Jerusalem. The vehicles were desperately needed for duty on the Jerusalem–Tel Aviv road. Near Bethlehem, the Arabs had set up a mammoth road block and attacked in force. A 'Primus' overhead reported that the road was impassable and the convoy was ordered back to the Etzion bloc. But it was too late; only a few of the trucks could turn around. The battle went on all day and all night. From Jerusalem, Haganah HQ told the fighters to hold on; by morning the British would come to the rescue. Late next morning a British unit duly appeared; it had come to take the defenders of Etzion back to Jerusalem, but first it disarmed them. In full view of the gleeful Arabs, the British insisted that all the Jewish weapons be collected and turned in. The battle had lasted for thirty hours; an estimated 3,000 Arabs

above: Danny Mass, commander of the ill-fated thirty-five volunteers killed in a vain attempt to reach Etzion
below: A Piper-Cub on patrol duty

opposite: Shaar-Hagai, the road to Jerusalem, lined with the shattered skeletons of lorries and armoured cars burnt out in courageous attempts to reach the beleaguered city. These skeletons still remain today as war memorials

Canadian-born Dov Joseph
(later Israel's Minister of
Justice) was civilian Governor
of Jerusalem during the siege

had participated in it; fourteen Jews had been killed, many more wounded. The casualties were grievous, but for the Haganah troops the sight of the armoured cars – some of them brand-new and still shining – which had to be left behind on the road, was almost unbearable.

The Etzion bloc was now connected to the rest of Jewish Palestine only by air. On 4 May, the fighting was renewed: Transjordan's Arab Legion, which was still part of the British forces in Palestine, began the seventh and final onslaught on the settlements; a few days later, hundreds of Arabs advanced on Kfar Etzion, which was cut off from the other three settlements of the bloc. Sixteen times the Arab Legion, and hundreds of Arab villagers following in its wake, broke through Kfar Etzion's defences, and sixteen times the attack was repulsed. But the end had come: devoid of even the most primitive means for continuing to resist, faced by the Legion's tanks, the bloc was overrun. A message was sent to Jerusalem: 'Establish contact with the Red Cross.' There were only fifteen Jews alive in Kfar Etzion and they were shot on surrendering; late that afternoon, the Red Cross arranged for the settlers of Masuot, Revadim and Ein Tsurim to be driven into Arab captivity.

In the mean time, the war for Palestine's other highways moved into a critical stage. In March, many of the men and much of the Jewish armoured transport had gone; the roads to the north and south were blocked, and Jerusalem was cut off from the coastal plain. The UN Implementation Committee, charged with overseeing the creation of the two States, came to Palestine, observed, and returned to voice its doubts as to the viability of the Jewish State-in-the-making. The United States was also on the verge of changing its mind; if the slaughter of Jews was to be the price of a Jewish State, perhaps the State should wait. Maybe the solution was trusteeship, rather than independence. Since 29 November, 1947, 1,200 Jews had been killed in Palestine, and the toll was rising daily. But the Yishuv was determined to bring the State into being.

Operation 'Nachshon'

Clearly, Jerusalem, as always, mattered most to the Jews. If Jerusalem fell, a mortal blow would be delivered to the State, and the will of the Yishuv to stand firm before the Arab attack might dwindle. The road to Jerusalem must be freed and the Arab noose choking the city loosened. The immediate answer to Jerusalem's plight was *Operation Nachshon* (named for the first Jew, who, according to legend, crossed the Red Sea in the exodus of the Children of Israel from Egypt); it took place between 3 and 15 April, and involved a force of 1,500 fighters, consisting of Palmach

196

and Hish units three times the number used in any previous Haganah operation. Their arms came from all over the country; every kibbutz and outpost was called upon to contribute weapons from its own sparse stores. The night before the operation began, a four-engine Dakota plane, touching down on a secret air strip in the south, brought the first consignment of arms purchased by the Haganah in Czechoslovakia, and these were rushed, still packed, to the Nachshon HQ. Operation Nachshon (commanded by Shimon Avidan), in which the Jews took the initiative for the first time, forced open the Jerusalem road for long enough to permit three giant convoys – bearing arms, ammunition and food – to enter the city and it was on these convoys that Jerusalem was to live until the 'Burma Road' was opened a month and a half later.

Jerusalem's population in 1947 included 100,000 Jews (one-sixth of the Yishuv) of whom 2,000 – pious, scholarly and other-worldly – lived in the crowded Jewish Quarter in the southern section of the Old City; and about 65,000 Arabs. Although the entire Jewish population of Jerusalem was sealed-off from the coastal plain by November, and although from then on, there were incessant Arab attacks on all the Jewish sections, it was the small group of Jews in the Old City who were in the greatest danger – and it was upon them that the eyes of the entire Yishuv were riveted during the first winter of the war.

The Arabs, in full view of the British, had barred the Old City to all Jewish traffic; now and then, a truck was allowed into the quarter with food and medical supplies, and a few Haganah soldiers and a limited quantity of arms, mostly revolvers, were smuggled into the quarter in December and January. The Arabs, and the British, obviously hoped that the Jews, half-starved and now isolated from the rest of the city, would leave. 'From a military point of view,' wrote Dov Joseph, the Canadian-born member of the Jewish Agency who was to be the governor of Jerusalem during its agony, 'the Old City represented a dead loss of energy and men. From a supply point of view, it presented an insoluble problem.' But it was inconceivable that the Old City be abandoned.

In new Jerusalem the Jews set up an Emergency Committee in December 1947; they rationed food and saved water, cut the use of fuel to an absolute minimum, established a Home Guard, and kept their morale high by listening to the frequent broadcasts of the Haganah's secret radio station 'The Voice of the Defender'. A similar attempt was made to organize life within the Jewish Quarter: a tiny civil defence unit was set up, and a handful of Haganah members did its best to distribute food equitably, to see that schools were kept open, and the population of the quarter

Yeshiva (theological college) students receiving training with sten guns

Situation in the Old City of Jerusalem

197

were given training, at least, in first aid. Tenderly and with remarkable patience, the boys and girls of the Haganah coped with an unfamiliar community; all that mattered to the Jews of the Old City was that they be allowed to work, and pray, and live in permanent proximity to the Wailing Wall and to the Temple Mount – even though direct access to these Holy Places had long been denied them by the Arabs. All that mattered to the defenders was that the quarter continue to resist.

On 20 April, the Eve of Passover, the last food convoy after Operation Nachshon, made up of some 300 trucks, brought provisions to Jerusalem. One other convoy, twelve trucks strong, loaded with military supplies, got through on 17 May, but it was to be the last. The siege was now complete.

On 13 May, the British began to withdraw from the Old City; within a matter of minutes the Haganah had readied itself to meet the onslaught of some 20,000 well-armed Arabs who had waited, for weeks, for the British to leave so that the Old City could be made theirs. On May 14, Sir Alan Cunningham drove out of Jerusalem, boarded a plane at a nearby airstrip, and flew to Haifa. The Union Jack was hauled down at Government House: a few people in Jerusalem, and in Haifa, waved goodbye to the departing British entourage, but there was no fanfare, and there were no speeches. The British departure, on which so many hopes and fears were pinned, went by, virtually unnoticed by the population of Palestine – except as a starting signal for the open confrontation between the opposing forces.

The British withdraw from the Old City

The battle for Jerusalem now raged within, and without the walls. From 14 May until 11 June 1948, 300 people were killed in Jerusalem's streets and houses, 1,400 wounded, and over 10,000 shells lobbed into the Jewish sections of the city by the Arab Legion. Jewish Jerusalem, its various quarters linked up in a series of desperate hand-to-hand battles which lasted for over sixty hours and which had begun as soon as Sir Alan had left, faced its uncertain future grimly. Exhausted, nervewracked, but not disheartened, Jerusalemites, munching their daily ration of 1,000 calories, washing themselves in half cupfuls of water, and subjected to the constant pounding and hammering of the Legion's artillery, worried less about their own fate than that of the Jewish Quarter in the Old City.

The battle for the city

On 18-20 May repeated attempts to break into the Jewish Quarter through the Jaffa Gate were made by a unit of the Etzioni Brigade, but it was forced to retreat, and suffered heavy casualties.

On 19 May, a tiny force of the Palmach took Mount Zion and broke through to the Jewish Quarter. The force held its position

opposite: Members of the Haganah keeping watch on Arab positions on the walls of the Old City of Jerusalem

Golda Meir, today Prime Minister of Israel, paid a clandestine visit in 1948 to Emir Abdullah of Transjordan to try to avert war at the eleventh hour

right: Jerusalem undergoes its nightly bombardment

Hostile British attitude

for several desperate hours, but was forced to withdraw when promised reinforcements of the Etzioni Brigade failed to arrive.

But the Jewish Quarter was in its death throes. By 27 May, there was nothing to eat; nothing to shoot with; 100 Haganah members were dead and many wounded. The Arab attacks were unremitting and the Arab Legion pressed for a surrender, promising to protect the civilians from the mob. On 28 May, the quarter gave in; 290 Jews between the ages of fourteen and seventy were taken prisoner by the Legion; 1,200 old men, women and children were passed through the lines to the New City. Within a short time, the Jewish Quarter was a mass of debris, its synagogues razed, its homes looted. Thus it was to wait, violated and disfigured, for nineteen years before the Jews returned to it again.

The first phase of the War of Independence can be dated from 29 November, 1947 until the British commenced their withdrawal during April, 1948. It was marked by the hostile presence of the British, whose withdrawal from Palestine was phased in accordance not only with the organizational requirements of the British Army, but with those of the Arabs. Allied in anti-Jewish intent and mood, the Palestine Administration and the Arabs divided up the task of proving that the Jewish State, even if it were to be established, would not be viable. The Arabs did the fighting; the British planned their evacuation in such a manner that it would be easy for the Arabs to take over from them. First, they withdrew from all the contiguous Arab territories, the so-called Arab Triangle (Jenin-Tulkarm-Nablus) and Hebron, and at the same time, in the middle of December, 1947, from Tel Aviv and the coastal plain. Latrun,

200

a key outpost on the Jerusalem road, was also turned over to the Arabs. Then, they left the Jerusalem corridor and the Arab part of the Negev. The Arab Liberation Army was now free to operate in the Triangle and it made its headquarters, under Kaukji's command, in the very centre of Palestine. Arab extremists from Egypt took over, again openly, from the British in Gaza. Although the British stayed for a while in the Galilee, their presence in no way deterred the formation there of new Arab units. The same held true, as we have seen, for Jerusalem and for Jaffa. In addition to the Jerusalem road, the Arabs had, of course, also blocked the only road in the Negev which connected the south with the Jewish population in the centre.

A last-ditch attempt was made to persuade the seemingly moderate Emir Abdullah to keep out of the war. Mrs. Golda Meir, today prime minister of Israel, crossed the border at night and met the Emir secretly. He openly admitted that it was too late; he was committed to go to war against the infant state, and moreover, the authority to coordinate all the Arab armies was in his hands.

The second stage of the fighting began with British withdrawal and terminated with the Arab invasion of 15 May. This stage witnessed intensive local offensives aimed at achieving Jewish territorial contiguity, and to prepare for the invasion.

Now the contours of the final outcome were beginning to shape up; in the north, *Operation Yiftach* (commanded by Yigal Allon) substantially and dramatically changed the Jewish position. It had three objectives: the taking of key strongholds, the liberation of the northern roads, and the preparation of the Galilee for defence before the invading Arab armies entered it from Palestine's northern borders. But even before Operation Yiftach began in the Upper Galilee, and *Operation Ben Ami* (commanded by Moshe Carmel) began in the Western Galilee, a number of important towns were captured by the Jews: Tiberias and Tsemach on the shore of the Sea of Galilee, the harbour city of Haifa on the Mediterranean, and Beisan in the heart of the Beisan Valley. Later, two other large towns were taken: Jaffa, near Tel Aviv, and Acre, in western Galilee.

The focal point of Operation Yiftach was the campaign for yet another of these towns, Safed. Northernmost and highest of Palestine's towns, Safed had been a celebrated centre of Jewish mysticism in the sixteenth century, and, now, in the twentieth century, its small Jewish community still devoted itself to scholarship and to the interpretation of the Jewish Law. The Arabs of Safed, on the other hand, were known to be zealous fighters, perennial trouble-

Arab forces bringing down the body of their commander, Abdel Kader el Husseini, killed during the battle for the Castel, one of the key hills on the approaches to Jerusalem

Operation 'Yiftach'

201

Street fighting in Haifa. The Arab part of the city was captured after a brief fight and thousands of its Arab inhabitants fled by land and sea to Lebanon

makers and ardent nationalists, and trouble had begun in the town in the middle of December 1947. A Jew had been killed in one of Safed's three Arab sections and a few days later, the Arabs had attacked the solitary Jewish quarter *en masse*; they had been driven off but the attack heralded the start of a five-month siege of the quarter. Most of the Jews of Safed had lived there all their lives; many still remembered the lesson of World War I when much of the Galilee had been cut off from the rest of Palestine, and the Jewish community left prey to endless and cruel Arab raids. Then, 10,000 Jews had lived in the town; now, there were less than 2,000 and arrayed against them were not only Safed's 12,000 Arabs but an Arab force numbering 3,000 men collected from all over Galilee and serving under one of the most notorious Arab commanders, Adib el Shishakli; also there were some 700 Syrian 'volunteers'.

On 14 April, the British withdrew from Safed. Before they left, they ceremoniously turned over to the Arabs not only the police station in Safed itself, but also the vast and traditionally impregnable police fort (one of those built by Teggart during the 1936–39 riots) which, from the top of Mount Canaan, dominated the entire area; as well as the ancient Citadel in the heart of the town. Only then did the British bother to notify the Jews of their departure.

Relief arrives in Safed

Huddling in their picturesque, vulnerable quarter, bullets flying around them, the Jews waited fearfully for the Arabs to close in for the kill. All of the northern roads were in Arab hands: there was no way for help to reach them; no way to defend themselves against the final attack. But that night, a platoon of Palmachniks, the spearhead of Operation Yiftach, marching through the moun-

202

tains, miraculously entered the quarter from the rear, bringing with them not only food and arms, but hope. Jewish Safed, no longer alone, set about fortifying itself; all through the Passover holiday, under ruthless bombardment, old men, women, and children, lacking even cement and nails, improvised barricades made of broken rocks. As they worked, they sang the strange new songs which the Palmachniks taught them, and wondered, in their hearts, if a few Piats and home-made spigot mortars, a few fresh-faced youngsters in tattered clothes and knitted caps, could possibly prevail over the Arab might. There was talk of evacuating the children to Haifa, but the Palmach commander refused to let them go. Long after the war had ended, he explained his reason: 'It was very hard to say "no", very hard to see the small children running around the narrow crooked alleys of the old city which was taking such terrible punishment. I knew I was assuming a tremendous responsibility but I had to take the chance. If the children had left, morale would have dropped and we needed every bit of confidence we could call upon. Besides, we couldn't spare the troops to escort hundreds of children and their mothers through the perilous mountains into safety.'

On 1 May, the Arabs opened a large-scale attack on Ramot Naphtali in the northern hills, near Lebanon; if the settlement fell, the Arabs could take the valley below, stop the Palmach from bringing reinforcements to Safed, and end the fragile dream of Jewish victory in the Galilee. Ramot Naphtali had been founded in 1945 by two organizations of Jewish ex-servicemen, one named after Orde Wingate. It had been subjected to heavy shelling all spring, and the women and children had already been taken out. By May, the village was no longer a farming community but a tightly-knit outpost upon which the fate of much of the Galilee depended. The 'Primuses' dropped arms and provisions to Ramot, evacuated the wounded and did their pathetic best to 'bomb' the enemy emplacements which encircled it. After a few days, Ramot was without radio communication, and its ammunition was almost gone. On 10 May, unable to reach the settlement herself, Orde Wingate's young widow, Lorna, leaning from a Piper Cub, dropped a Bible onto Ramot. With it, she threw a note: 'This Bible accompanied Wingate on all his campaigns and inspired him. Let it represent a covenant between us – in victory or defeat, now and forever.'

Time and again, the Arabs were pushed back from Ramot. They might have persisted and taken it, after all, but the Palmach mounted its assault on Safed; the Arabs brought up their guns from Ramot, but the Palmach was ready for them. The battle for

Orde Wingate had been one of those who had laid the foundations of the Israel Army's tactics. In the country's hour of peril, his widow, Lorna Wingate, lent moral support

Release of Safed

203

Colonel Moshe Carmel, commander of Operation 'Ben Ami' in western Galilee and OC Northern Command

the town – one of the most ferocious of the war – began; it lasted only one night and all Safed trembled with the sound of gunfire and shells. But by dawn the ancient Citadel in the centre of the town was in the hands of the Palmach and the town was quiet – at last – for the first time since the winter. Only a small group of Syrians remained on the roof of the municipal police station, and then it, too, was taken. About this time an Arab unit joined the Haganah, the Arab-el-Heib Bedouin tribe from a village east of Rosh Pinah; barefooted but helmeted, its name temporarily changed to Pal-Heib, it entered action with the Palmach in the Galilee, a veteran Palmachnik on a white horse at its head.

In Lebanon, across the border, the Mufti and his entourage had been busy planning the announcement of an Arab government to be temporarily headquartered in Safed; the conquest of the town's Jewish Quarter was to be a harbinger, the sign and symbol of the Arab conquest of Palestine. The story of the Jewish offensive and of Safed's defeat spread like wildfire from one Arab village to another and within a week, all Arab Galilee was alive with rumours of a vast Jewish host moving northwards. As they had done in Tiberias and Haifa, thousands of Arabs fled in panic.

With the fall of Safed, and on the eve of the Arab invasion, the Yiftach force took the range of hills stretching along the Lebanese border, thus blocking one of the major entrances into Palestine. From now on, the emphasis was on the northern frontiers: the Palmach carried out a series of raids across enemy lines, including demolition of the bridges connecting Syria and Lebanon with the Galilee, and the destruction of a large enemy base, northeast of the upper reaches of the Jordan River.

The conquest of Galilee

At the same time, Operation Ben Ami (one of the few Jewish amphibious operations) restored to the Yishuv the Western Galilee which was to have been outside the borders of the Jewish State – and which, save for sporadic contact from the sea – had been cut-off from the Yishuv for months. Operation Ben Ami started with a force which stormed and took 'Napoleon Hill' east of Acre. Another force landed, in small boats, at a Jewish village just south of Nahariya and marched inland to the main road from Acre to Beirut. This sea-borne force cleared the Arab village of Samaria, together with an armed convoy which came up from Haifa Bay after detouring Acre. The convoy then drove on past Nahariya and succeeded in relieving the beleaguered kibbutzim on the Lebanese border.

The two most fertile parts of the Galilee were now in Jewish hands; only the hilly centre still remained Arab; but the day was not far off when all of Galilee would be Jewish.

204

In the south, matters had also improved, slowly but discernibly. Only about 1,000 Jews lived in the Negev in some twenty-seven settlements, dotted sparsely across a huge territory inhabited by over 100,000 indigenous Arabs as well as some 200,000 refugees. Not only were the roads almost entirely closed to the Jews, but the pipe-lines upon which the settlements depended for their existence stretched over miles of land and were the target of endless Arab attacks. The Arabs, not unreasonably, took for granted that if their direct onslaughts on the Jewish settlements failed to drive the Jews out of the Negev, hunger and thirst would certainly do so. Not only had nature and the enemy seemed to join forces against the Jews in the south; but the Haganah itself was unable to provide the Palmach's Negev Brigade with more than the bare minimum of essential equipment. Even transport was lacking; most of the Palmach patrols had to reconnoitre on foot, inadequately armed, across miles of sand and scrub.

The Negev settlements

Out of these hardships sprang a new breed of Haganah fighters, the commando units of the Negev; the toughest, most admired, most feared and least conventional of all the Jewish forces in the war. Restless, bearded, hardened by wind and sun, they were forever on the move, scouring the reaches of the Negev, pitting themselves, their stamina and their reputations first against the Palestinian Arab bands, later against the fanatical Moslem Brotherhood whose members were already infiltrating into the south of Palestine from Egypt, and who were soon to fight under the command of regular Egyptian officers.

By the early spring of 1948, although the coastal road to the north was still blocked by the Arabs, a small parallel unpaved road (actually a dirt track) had been opened and it was thanks to this second road that Jewish convoys could get through to the south at all. But even this road was perilous; it passed close to three large and inimical Arab villages of which the most aggressive, and the one most often used as a stronghold for snipers, was Breir. Something had to be done to make the road less of a death trap; the Haganah arrived at a conclusion which was entirely at one with its general philosophy, and with its tradition. A new Jewish settlement would be put up next to Breir, Breir would be neutralized and the road, at last, made safer. Examined today, in the context of what was going on in Palestine then, the decision to establish a new settlement anywhere seems breathtakingly bold, but to the Haganah High Command it was merely a matter of commonsense.

Operation Abraham, named for a boy who had been killed in an attack on one of the Negev-bound convoys, resulted in the

Bror Hayil

14th May, 1948. The Jewish State comes into being and the Declaration of Independence is signed in Tel Aviv

creation of Bror Hayil. The official report is typically laconic: 'On the night between 18 and 19 April, infantry units mined the entry paths to the new settlement being established near Breir. The action ended at 01.30 on 19 April. At 02.00, a convoy with troops was sent to the site. At 03.00 the main Palmach convoy set out. The entire force was ready by 04.30, and work started at once. At dawn, the operation ended and the camp was formally turned over to a Palmach unit. Bror Hayil is now in control of the situation.'

Breir was silenced; another Jewish outpost had been founded in the Negev; and on 12 May, in a coordinated action from north and south, the dirt track was finally taken by Jewish troops and Breir itself fell – three days before the Arab invasion. The road northwards was open; the siege of the Negev temporarily broken.

At midnight on Friday, 14 May, to the salute of seventeen guns, the British High Commissioner sailed from Haifa; the Mandate ended. That afternoon, just before 4 PM, the leaders of the Yishuv (with the exception of most of those from Jerusalem who had no way of reaching the coastal plain), and a few selected guests, met in the small, shabby art museum of Tel Aviv. Inside, in front of a huge photograph of Theodor Herzl, David Ben-Gurion, his voice steady, read out the Proclamation of Independence of the State of Israel including the sentence 'We call upon the sons of the Arab people dwelling in Israel to keep the peace and to play their part in building the State'. It ended with the words: 'Our call goes to the Jewish people all over the world to rally to our side in the task of immigration and development and to stand by us in the great struggle for the fulfilment of the dream of generations for the redemption of Israel. With trust in the Rock of Israel, we set our hands to this Declaration, at this Session of the Provisional State Council, on the soil of the Homeland, in the city of Tel Aviv, on this Sabbath eve, the fifth of Iyar, 5708, the fourteenth of May, 1948.'

Then, at last his voice breaking, Mr Ben-Gurion read out the Jewish State's first Ordinance: 'All the laws enacted under the Palestine White Paper, 1939, of the British Government, and all deriving from it, are hereby declared null and void.'

That night, the armies of five Arab states invaded Palestine. This marked the third stage of the war – the checking of the invasion by a combination of passive and active defence tactics, which lasted until the first cease-fire on 11 June.

It is relevant at this point to ask why the invasion? Surely, it was already apparent to the Arab world that, in the six weeks which had passed since Operation Nachshon, the military position of the Jews, though still serious, was immensely improved; the area assigned to the State by the UN was largely in Jewish hands; surely the Arab world knew that the military strength of the Palestinian Arab bands, and the various volunteer troops associated with them, had been shattered. About a hundred Arab villages had been taken by the Jews; the Western and Eastern Galilee were partly under Jewish control; the siege of the Negev had been partially lifted and even parts of the Jerusalem road were no longer in Arab hands. But each Arab country had made its own calculations. Transjordan's King Abdullah wanted all of Palestine, in particular Jerusalem. Iraq, in addition to the blood relationship between her ruling dynasty and that of Transjordan, wanted an outlet to the Mediterranean, even via Transjordan if need be, and was, therefore, anxious to demonstrate solidarity with Abdullah; Syria lusted for the Galilee, and also hoped to gain access to the Mediterranean via the Western Galilee. Lebanon's powerful Moslem community had long looked wistfully at the Central Galilee; and Egypt, though she had no territorial ambitions as such, was obsessed by the idea of being acknowledged as the supreme Arab power. Over and above these individual reasons, there was the shared lure of a quick victory, that entrancing vision conjured up so adroitly by the British.

The largest, most organized and best-equipped of the invading armies was that of Egypt; massed in the south, at El Arish, Abu Ageila (at the junction of the main roads to the Sinai Peninsula) and at Rafa, it was in possession of fairly accurate information about the Haganah's manpower and armouries, but knew astonishingly little about the extent of preparedness or the spirit in the kibbutzim and other Jewish settlements in Palestine – a deficiency which was to prove crucial.

On paper, the Jewish forces in the Negev seemed to justify the Egyptian self-confidence; there was the Negev Brigade of the Palmach (commanded by Nahum Sarig), made up of two battalions; further north the Givati Brigade (commanded by Shimon Avidan), and the twenty-seven settlements, consisting of a few dozen young people organized in more or less military units; and five larger settlements. A few Jewish settlements lay on the actual invasion routes of the enemy (the Rafa-Gaza-Ashkelon road, and the Auja el Hafir-Beersheba-Hebron road) but these were underpopulated by any standard and hardly likely to deter the Egyptians from their thrust towards Tel Aviv. The task of these forces was to attempt to halt the relentless Egyptian advance.

above: Shimon Avidan, a senior Palmach officer, founded the 'German Squad', led Operation 'Nachshon', and commanded the famous Givati Brigade.
below: Nahum Sarig, commander of the Palmach's Negev Brigade

The Egyptian invasion began simultaneously at two points: the main route was along the coast from Rafa, through Khan Yunis to Gaza, while lesser units were assigned the job of eradicating some of the smaller kibbutzim, including Nirim, Kfar Darom, and

A force of Palmach armoured cars sets out on patrol in the Negev

Beerot Yitshaq. This turned out to be rather more difficult then the Egyptians expected; at all three outposts, the invading troops had to withdraw, with heavy casualties; particularly at Nirim which was made up of Palmach veterans who forced the Egyptians, disorganized, badly hurt and terrified, back to Rafa. Even the ensuing Egyptian artillery bombardment failed to soften up Nirim. The Egyptians, carefully keeping their distance, settled down to a systematic shelling of the stubborn settlement, and decided to concentrate their efforts to reach Tel Aviv on another point; Yad Mordechai, on the road between Gaza and Ashkelon.

Yad Mordechai   The attack on Yad Mordechai, named for Mordechai Anilewitz, first commander of the Warsaw uprising of World War II, began on 19 May when the Egyptians actually penetrated the kibbutz perimeter. That day, they were repulsed, but their attack was resumed on the morrow. Four times, on 20 May, the Egyptians attempted to storm the settlement, each time they were beaten back. Bloodied and fatigued, the settlers begged the regional command for help, for ammunition, for reinforcements. Their dugouts and emplacements were ruined; there was not even enough cover left in the settlement for the wounded; but the heartbreaking appeals from Yad Mordechai were in vain. There was no way to reach it in time – Israel was under attack from the south, the

208

north and the east, and the ravaged settlement had to manage as best it could. On 23 May, the attack continued; two Egyptian task forces, made up of light tanks and armoured cars, broke through and it was decided to evacuate Yad Mordechai. 'We are no longer in a position to defend ourselves,' signalled the settlement, 'our losses are too heavy.' But that night, tearing through the Egyptian lines in ten dilapidated armoured cars, the Negev Commandos arrived; they helped to take the wounded out and volunteered to try to hold the Egyptians; it was a gallant but hopeless effort. Before sunrise, the surviving settlers of Yad Mordechai, having defied two infantry battalions, an armoured battalion and an artillery regiment, broke through the enemy lines and reached the settlement of Gvar Am. The attack on Yad Mordechai had cost the Egyptians 300 casualties, and five expensive days. It was those five days which were to make possible the creation of a Jewish line of defence further northwards and the reinforcement of the Negev. Yad Mordechai, which fell on 24 May, was the first Jewish settlement to be overrun in the course of the Egyptian invasion; but on 5 November, in *Operation Yoav*, it was to be retaken – and resettled.

Now, the way north was clear for the Egyptians. Moving rapidly, the invasion force reached the Arab town of Majdal (Ashkelon), overran the Jewish settlement of Nizanim (which, cut off and pulverized from the ground and air, surrendered) and finally arrived at Yavne north of the large Arab village of Isdud (Ashdod) 20 miles south of Tel Aviv! At the same time, another Egyptian column, not much smaller, racing from Auja el Hafir, on the Sinai border, through Bir Asluj, reached first Beersheba, then Hebron, then Bethlehem and finally the southern outskirts of Jerusalem itself. There, at the settlement of Ramat Rachel (founded in 1926 by the Labour Battalion), the headlong northward rush of the Egyptians was halted by Hish's Etzioni Brigade (commanded by David Shaltiel, later succeeded by Moshe Dayan), and reinforced by a task force of Palmach's Harel Brigade (commanded by Yitshaq Rabin, later succeeded by Yosef Tabenkin).

In the southern coastal plain, the main Egyptian invasion force was still tied down in heavy battles against the Negev and Givati brigades.

War was not new to Ramat Rachel; it had been entirely destroyed in the Arab riots of 1929 and the settlers were determined to survive the War of Independence. In the course of ten days, Ramat Rachel changed hands six times, but it was finally held by the Jews, and the Egyptian attempt to break into Jerusalem from the south was halted, and finally completely defeated.

The Palmach Harel Brigade was commanded by Yitshaq Rabin (*above*), later to become Chief of Staff of the IDF in the Six-Day War

below: Yosef Tabenkin, son of Yitshaq Tabenkin, labour leader and one of the Palmach's founding fathers, took over command of the Harel Brigade from Yitshaq Rabin

The first truce

above: Shlomo Shamir, commander of the Palmach's Seventh Brigade
below: Michael Ben-Gal, commander of the Kiryati Brigade

opposite: The shattered water tower of Kibbutz Yad Mordechai still remains as a monument to the settlement's heroic defence, its fall and its recapture

The main Egyptian force now established a line of fortification which reached from Ashkelon on the Mediterranean up to Hebron, Bethlehem and the southern approaches to Jerusalem. Although the capture of Tel Aviv was 'postponed', the Negev was wholly isolated from the rest of the country.

The Kiryati Brigade, (commanded by Michael Ben-Gal), was entrusted with the defence of Tel Aviv, and its periphery as far as Ramle. Kiryati was also held in readiness to defend Yavne, a necessity which, fortunately, never occured.

Throughout April and May, the Jews continued trying to open the Jerusalem road: the focal point of their endeavours was the Arab-held police fortress at Latrun which blocked access to Shaar-Hagai. The newly created 7th Brigade, (commanded by Shlomo Shamir), assisted by a Givati task force, was assigned the job; but the assault was difficult, its human price prohibitive, and a series of frontal attacks tragically failed. The road to Jerusalem remained closed.

One day late in May, after the 7th Brigade had captured a series of Arab villages in the central plain, Yosef Tabenkin had a brainwave: was it perhaps possible to cut behind the 7th Brigade positions and find an alternative to the Latrun road? An immediate decision was made: a patrol composed of only a handful of men set out entrusted with the mission of finding just such a route. They were convinced that a way could be found. In the course of one long night threading their way on foot between boulders and brambles, dodging Legion patrols, stumbling along goats' trails and across gulleys, the three boys reached the other end of the Jerusalem road. When the group told Palmach HQ in Tel Aviv that they had come from Jerusalem, no one believed them, but they had, in fact, found an emergency route to the Holy City.

On 1 June, a unit of the Harel Brigade made its way along the secret road, a track six miles long across the Judean hills, which was instantly dubbed the 'Burma Road'. One stretch of the Burma Road was impassable even for jeeps, and here, at the so-called Jeep Junction, men and mules, for weeks, carried supplies for Jerusalem on their backs. 240 men, mostly new immigrants, twice nightly, for an hour and a half each way, heaved loads, often weighing more than sixty pounds each, on their backs. Out of the darkness, clambering over the rocks, they came, in single file. Every now and then, they dropped their loads and rested, but no one had to tell them to carry on; they were bringing food to the fighters, and to the children, of Jerusalem, and each night until the rocks were cleared and the entire road readied for transport, the human assembly line kept going and supplies continued to get through.

210

Colonel David Marcus, a volunteer from the USA, who was drawn to Israel to help in its defence in its hour of peril. He was shot accidentally by one of his own sentries just before the first truce and raised to the rank of major-general posthumously

Hish's Alexandroni Brigade, (under the command of Dan Even later succeeded by Ben Zion Ziv), was deployed in the Hefer and Sharon valleys facing strong Arab forces in the hill regions and in the plains. It managed to clear a belt along the central coastal plain, pushing the enemy forces back, albeit with only limited success.

It was at this stage of the war that one of those rare and forceful personalities, drawn now and then from the world outside to the cause of Jewish self-defence in Palestine, appeared on the scene. US Colonel David ('Mickey') Marcus, a West Point graduate and a Jew, had felt impelled, much like Wingate years before, to place the sum total of his military know-how and his considerable organizational abilities at the disposal of the embattled Haganah High Command. A brave and dedicated leader, he was accidentally killed, by a sentry on the Jerusalem road, a few hours before the first truce. Before his death he had made a real contribution to Israel's military thinking and organizational concepts.

At 6 AM on 11 June, the UN enforced a ceasefire, known as the first truce. The Jews had met the threat from the south with what a contemporary commentator termed 'a mixture of improvisation, courage, able fieldmanship and luck' – and they were entitled to be optimistic about the future and proud of their tenacity. But Jerusalem was still in dire peril. The Jordanians hammered at the city from east and north, and the Egyptians, contained at Ramat Rachel, lurked in the south. The Jerusalem Command not only comprised the city, but extended eastwards as far as the Dead Sea. An additional force in Jerusalem was the Harel Brigade which fought in Jerusalem itself on the hills of both sides of the road from the plain to the besieged capital. The fate of Jerusalem depended on the ability of her tired, hungry population to stick out the siege, and this, in turn, depended on getting the minimum of food, arms and ammunition to it.

The first truce lasted for twenty-eight days and it changed the tide of the war. The truce conditions included the proviso that new immigrants of army age should not be allowed to enter Israel, except when acceptable to Count Folke Bernadotte, head of the Swiss Red Cross who was appointed UN Mediator in Palestine; it was also, of course, forbidden for either side to increase its stock of war material.

Searches for arms   The attempt to find arms had begun in the dark days at the start of the war; in Eastern Europe, the men of Rekhesh, working against time had knocked on Polish, Czech, French and Rumanian doors. The US had declared an embargo; the British would certainly not help, but a response had come from the Czech Government, and the Rekheshmen gathered tensely and expectantly in Prague, and to a lesser extent, in Paris.

The prices were high; hundreds of thousands of dollars for a single far-from-new aircraft; but money was the least of the problems. It was agreed that arms and planes be bought in the name of another country, but how were they to be brought in to Israel? The Yugoslavs had agreed to let the Haganah use their ports and airfields where Rekhesh ships awaited the precious cargoes. Perhaps the most famous of the fleet was the s.s. *Borea*; flying a Panamanian flag, bringing cannons, shells, machine guns and some 4,000,000 bullets packed in 1,000 crates buried under 450 tons of onions, starch and canned tomato juice, she had reached Tel Aviv on 13 May. A British coast cutter approached her; there were the customary exchange of signals and the usual check. Then, just before she docked, the British decided to inspect the *Borea* again A British officer informed the captain that the vessel would have to sail to Haifa for an overall inspection on suspicion of smuggling. There were twenty-four hours to go before Israel's independence: cables flew back and forth between the *Borea* and the anxious Rekhesh party on shore; finally, chained to a British warship, the *Borea* made for Haifa. At midnight, the British officer looked at his watch. 'The Mandate has ended,' he said to the *Borea's* captain, 'Go on your way. Shalom.' The *Borea*, which arrived back in Tel Aviv to see the first Egyptian bomb fall, not very effectively, on the city, became the first ship to unload in a free Jewish port.

During the truce, total secrecy had to be maintained; the UN, not the British navy, was on the alert and fighter aircraft were desperately needed; a number of planes had been bought in Czechoslovakia, and a group of American volunteers arranged for Rekhesh to get other planes, including a few old Constellations, from US Air Force surplus. The rights of two defunct airlines were bought and the Panamanian flag used again. By 11 June, the Israel airlift, named *Operation Balak* had made thirty flights, and had delivered over one hundred tons of cargo. It began officially on 20 May 1948, from a Czech airfield known in the Haganah code as 'Etzion' and ended on 12 August of that year.

Towards the end of May two important State documents were published; one was a Defence Order authorizing conscription in times of emergency and stating that Israel's standing army would be composed of 'land forces, a navy and an airforce'. It declared that 'compulsory enlistment' would be instituted, that each citizen serving in the Israel Defence Forces would be required to take an oath of allegiance to the State, and forbade the establishment or maintenance of any armed force other than the Israel Defence

Conscription

213

Forces. Also, a Control of Manpower Ordinance was issued, authorizing the mobilization of all Israelis between seventeen and fifty-five. On 31 May, an Order of the Day was published.

It read, in part: 'On the establishment of the State of Israel, the Haganah has emerged from the underground and has become a regular army... Without the Haganah's experience, planning, skill in operation and command, its devotion and valour, the Yishuv could not have held its ground in the dreadful trial of arms it had to face during these six months and we would not have attained the State of Israel.' It was signed by David Ben-Gurion, Israel's first Prime Minister and Minister of Defence.

The soldiers of the IDF were called upon to take an oath of allegiance, and did so on 28 June, seven months after the start of war. Now, Yaakov Dori, Haganah Chief of Staff, Yigael Yadin, its young archaeology student-turned-Chief of Operations, and thousands of others, were sworn in to the *Zva Haganah Leyisrael*, or the IDF. The first commanders were Yosef Avidar, ordnance; Moshe Zadok, manpower; Eliahu Ben Horin, training; Issar Beeri, intelligence; Aaron Remez, airforce; Gershon Zack, navy; Shmuel Admon, artillery; Emmanuel Shacham, engineers; and Yıtshaq Almog, signals. In many respects, the swearing-in was a formality; it made 'legal' what had been 'illegal'; it legitimized a force that had existed for years. To the young army the Haganah bequeathed not only its men and accumulated experience, its table of organization and its weapons, but also the victories of the past few weeks.

In June, some 50,000 men were engaged in combat on both sides: by the time the first truce ended, on 9 July, 1948, there were some 100,000 combatants, and most of the additional manpower was Israel's. The war had entered its fourth stage, that of the major offensives on the northern and central fronts. On 11 June, both the Jews and the Arabs held well-defined positions; the Syrians had a bridgehead on the Jordan River in Galilee, at the settlement of Mishmar Hayarden which they had totally destroyed, and where some of their best troops were concentrated. From Mishmar Hayarden they hoped to control the Upper Galilee by advancing on Rosh Pinah. The Arab Liberation Army, under Kaukji, was still in the central Galilee, its supply line originating in Lebanon, its area of control including Nazareth. But the IDF was entrenched both in eastern and western Galilee and the Arab Liberation Army was, in effect, trapped, though it seems to have been unaware of this fact. In the narrow waist of the country, in Samaria, (the Arab 'Triangle'), the Iraqis were still firmly lodged in a position to threaten both the Hefer and Esdraelon Valleys.

As for the Arab Legion, it not only dominated the Old City and

214

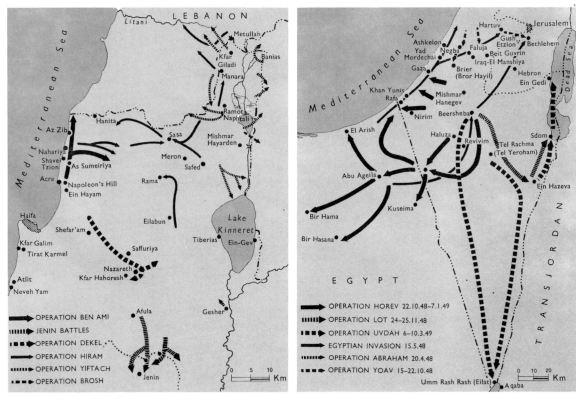

Map 1 (top left):

LEBANON

Litani

Mediterranean Sea

Metullah
Kfar Giladi
Banias
Manara
Ramot Naphtali
Az Zib
Hanita
Sasa
Mishmar Hayarden
Nahariya
Shavei Tzion
As Sumeiriya
Meron
Acre
Napoleon's Hill
Ein Hayam
Rama
Safed
Haifa
Eilabun
Shefar'am
Kfar Galim
Tirat Karmel
Saffuriya
Tiberias
Ein-Gev
Lake Kinneret
Nazareth
Atlit
Kfar Hahoresh
Neveh Yam
Afula
Gesher

Jenin

→ OPERATION BEN AMI
┅ JENIN BATTLES
╍ OPERATION DEKEL
→ OPERATION HIRAM
┅ OPERATION YIFTACH
╍ OPERATION BROSH

0 5 10 Km

Map 2 (top right):

Mediterranean Sea

Hartuv
Jerusalem
Ashkelon
Yad Mordechai
Negba
Faluja
Gush Etzion
Bethlehem
Iraq-El Manshiya
Gaza
Brier (Bror Hayil)
Hebron
Ein Gedi
Khan Yunis
Rafa
Mishmar Hanegev
Nirim
Beersheba
El Arish
Haluza
Revivim
Sdom
Tel Rachma (Tel Yeroham)
Abu Ageila
Ein Hazeva
Bir Hama
Kuseima
Bir Hasana

Dead Sea

TRANSJORDAN

E G Y P T

→ OPERATION HOREV 22.10.48–7.1.49
┅ OPERATION LOT 24–25.11.48
╍ OPERATION UVDAH 6–10.3.49
→ EGYPTIAN INVASION 15.5.48
┅ OPERATION ABRAHAM 20.4.48
╍ OPERATION YOAV 15–22.10.48

Umm Rash Rash (Eilat) Aqaba

0 10 20 Km

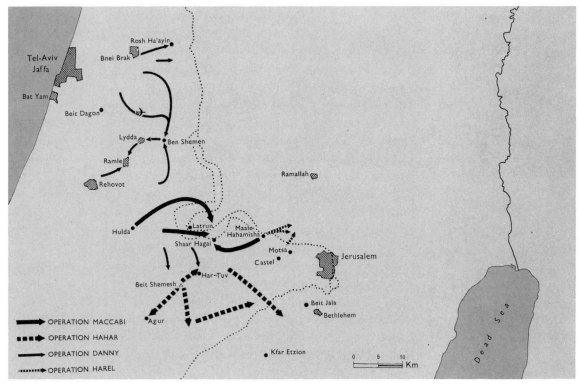

Map 3 (bottom):

Tel-Aviv Jaffa

Rosh Ha'ayin
Bnei Brak
Bat Yam
Beit Dagon
Lydda
Ben Shemen
Ramle
Ramallah
Rehovot
Hulda
Latrun
Maale Hahamisha
Shaar Hagai
Motsa
Castel
Jerusalem
Beit Shemesh
Har-Tuv
Agur
Beit Jala
Bethlehem
Kfar Etzion

Dead Sea

→ OPERATION MACCABI
╍ OPERATION HAHAR
→ OPERATION DANNY
┅ OPERATION HAREL

0 5 10 Km

Moulah Cohen took over command of the Palmach's Yiftach Brigade from Yigal Allon

the environs of Jerusalem but much of the valley below, including the Arab towns of Lydda and Ramle, and it was unpleasantly close to Tel Aviv. The Egyptians occupied a large area of Palestine along the western coastline from Rafa via Gaza to Majdal Ashkelon and as far as Yavne, on the one hand; and in a thinner band, stretched from Auja el Hafir to Beersheba and as far as Ramat Rachel. They were also deployed from west to east, from Majdal Ashkelon to Hebron and had cut off the entire Negev.

As far as Israel was concerned, there were three critical fronts: the Negev, the centre with Jerusalem embedded at its heart, and upper Galilee. It was anguishing to have to decide which front should receive priority, but the army's weight was finally thrown in two directions: the north where it hoped to hurl the Syrians back across the border, and the centre where it hoped to take Lydda and Ramle and prevent the Arab Legion from joining up with the Egyptians in the coastal plain and to drive them away from Tel Aviv.

On 9 July, when the truce ended, Israel's Ten Day Offensive began; a series of sharp, short, decisive and victorious engagements. Clear-cut and business-like, the army, understanding that holders would be keepers, and that the borders of the State would have to be secured before the UN rushed to impose another truce, lunged into action. When the Ten Day Offensive was over – stopped, as the Israelis had predicted, by a UN ceasefire – 677 square miles of Arab controlled territory had been taken by the IDF; the threat to Tel Aviv, Haifa and the coastal plain obliterated; the corridor to Jerusalem widened, and the siege of Jerusalem finally lifted, a deep hole gouged out of the Arab territory in the centre of Palestine and all the main Arab bases in the Galilee overrun. Twenty percent of the effective Arab fighting force had been lost – and the War of Independence won – though not ended.

Operation 'Danny'

Operation Danny which started on 9 July involved the entire stretch of country from Tel Aviv to the southern reaches of Jerusalem, though it did not involve Jerusalem itself. It was directed primarily against the Arab Legion, although it operated also against the Iraqis, and, in certain sections, against the Egyptians. The battle aims in the first phase were roughly as follows: the enemy was to be hit hard wherever and whenever possible; territory was to be taken; the Israel line to be pushed towards the hilly, more easily defensible parts of the central sector; and Jewish control assured over the crucial crossroads and such vital installations as the Lydda airport and railway system. Above and beyond these goals, initiative was to be wrested from the enemy for good.

The force entrusted with Operation Danny (named after Danny

216

Mass, the commander of the last reinforcements sent to the Etzion bloc) consisted partly of infantry, partly of armour, partly of the Palmach, partly of the Hish. Given both limited artillery and air support, (headed by Yigal Allon and staff officers of the Palmach) it was the largest and most varied Jewish formation to function on any front under one command since the war had commenced. The new task force was made up of the 8th Armoured Brigade under Yitshaq Sadeh; Palmach's Yiftach Brigade under the youngest brigade commander in the IDF, Moulah Cohen; Palmach's Harel Brigade and the Kiryati Brigade from Tel Aviv.

Two forces, one starting near Tel Aviv, and hitting out towards the southeast, the other starting from Gezer and striking northeast, were to join forces, in a pincer movement, at Ben Shemen, an agricultural village for children east of Lydda which had been sealed off from the rest of the Yishuv for months. Having met up, the brigades were to mount an assault on Lydda, in the hope that Ramle, to the west, would surrender. A joint attack was duly launched on Lydda from the rear; it was typified by a daring raid carried out by a mechanized battalion of the 8th Brigade, and by bitter door-to-door fighting by the men of Yiftach. The lesson was not lost on Ramle; on 12 July, Ramle surrendered to the IDF. The immediate danger to Tel Aviv was removed; and a far more effective Jewish line of defence created in the centre of the country.

Within two days, the Palmach had reached the Latrun-Ramallah crossroads, and at the same time, an advance force of Harel, moving northwest, joined up with Yiftach, thus encircling Latrun. At any moment a UN truce might be announced. The Arab Legion rushed reinforcements from Latrun in an attempt to meet up with the Egyptians, and left only a garrison in Latrun itself. The Israelis desperately pushed on towards Latrun – but the Arab garrison there fought back. In the last hours of the draining effort, a small task force was brought into action; a mechanized infantry company, supported by two tanks and artillery; on 19 July, the last of the Ten Days, the Israelis tried to topple the Legion by attacking Latrun from the northwest – but one of the two lone tanks broke down and the attempt to pluck Latrun from the bed of nettles failed. Latrun remained in enemy hands – and stayed there until June, 1967.

But further north, the Harel Brigade had driven a wider wedge between the Egyptians and the Legion, and Har-Tuv, taken earlier in the war by the Arabs, became the first Jewish settlement to be liberated. Operation Danny had succeeded, in the main: it had been both costly of men and nerve-wracking; and it might have succeeded altogether had the second truce not been enforced. In part,

The Palmach's 8th Armoured Brigade captures Lydda Airport

Lydda and Ramle captured

217

Palmach forces of the Northern Command Force open an attack on Kaukji's Arab irregulars at Sasa in upper Galilee

it had been fought along classic lines; in part, it had been made up of guerilla raids, the tactics of 'little war'; by day, it had been one sort of campaign, by night, another. It had been punctuated by mistakes and miscalculations, but it had accomplished its chief goal: Lydda and Ramle were taken, and with them, symbolically, Modiin, a tiny village where the Maccabees had been born 2,000 years earlier, and which now became part of the Jewish State.

Operations 'Brosh' and 'Dekel'

The ten days' fighting also included two campaigns in the north; one, *Operation Brosh* (Cypress), under the command of Mordechai Makleff, was aimed at the Syrian bridgehead at Mishmar Hayarden in the Upper Galilee. The Syrians were so effectively dug-in that, despite repeated attacks, the insufficiently armed Israeli forces were unable to dislodge them. The Syrians managed to hold their ground until the onset of the second truce declared by the United Nations. The other, *Operation Dekel* (Palmtree) in the lower Galilee including Nazareth and the surrounding hills, was much more successful. The attack mounted by a combined force of armour and infantry resulted in the capture of the whole area; the Arab forces commanded by Kaukji were put to flight. The operation was commanded by Ben Dunkelman, later succeeded by Chaim Laskov. The overall commander of the front was Moshe Carmel.

The second truce

The second truce began on 19 July 1948, and no date was set for its termination. It was used to bring about certain far-reaching

218

changes in the structure of the Israel forces: four 'fronts' or commands were established and all troops in each front were now under the control of front commanders, rather than, as in the past, regional brigades in which not all the soldiers were under the brigadier's command. Moshe Carmel was appointed GOC, Northern Command; Dan Even was named head of the Eastern Command; Zvi Ayalon was given the Central Command and Yigal Allon made commander of the Southern Command. Uri Brenner became acting commander of the Palmach. Furthermore, it was decided that, in view of conscription, which would probably water-down the quality of the army, the IDF would be a strictly disciplined force, based on regulations as well as on convictions. Ranks were introduced, officer messes were opened and a military police corps, its uniforms resembling those of the British, was established. Israel was alive and strong, but her borders were neither well-defined nor tenable and the Negev was still under siege. Count Bernadotte, who saw himself as a statesman of stature rather than as a referee, made clear that his vision of the future included ceding the Negev to the Arabs – and probably restricting Jewish immigration into Israel. The Yishuv found itself contemplating not small concessions or minor adjustments for the sake of peace but the annulment of the State's purpose. If Jews were not to enter the Jewish State, when, if and in whatever number they chose, Israel would be reduced to a farcical entity, rendered trivial and meaningless. The same *reductio ad absurdum* would occur if it were to be deprived of territory; much of the Negev was arable, and it was unthinkable to have it snatched away to appease the states that had begun the war. Incongruously enough, in view of everything that happened in Palestine over the past fifty years, the world still seemed unable to grasp that the Yishuv would never abandon its demand for free Jewish immigration – and the Mediator apparently shared this lack of comprehension.

Count Folke Bernadotte, the Swedish United Nations mediator, was assassinated in Jerusalem during the second truce

Count Bernadotte busied himself with talks at the British Foreign Office and the US State Department; the British were not displeased by his views; if the Negev were to be excluded from the Jewish State after all, it might serve an ideal alternative to British bases in Egypt. Bernadotte also recommended that Lydda airport be internationalized and that Haifa harbour be permanently placed under UN supervision.

When Count Bernadotte's plan was published, it turned out to be worse than most Israelis had anticipated: the Mediator formally proposed that the Negev be annexed by Transjordan, that the UN supervise all Israel air and sea ports and that a 'special status' be created for Jerusalem, including the New City.

Infantry and armoured Palmach units go into action during the fight for Beersheba

Israel, horrified, reminded the UN that Bernadotte's suggestions could hardly be seriously considered, and rejected the plan in its entirety, stressing its indignation at the proposal to rip Jerusalem from the Jewish State and, essentially, turn it over to the Arabs. By September, Bernadotte himself understood that his plan for Jerusalem was unfeasible and suggested UN control for Jerusalem; but before anything developed along the new lines, Bernadotte was struck down by assassins on a quiet street in a residential area of Jerusalem and the situation became more chaotic than ever. Arab violations of the ceasefire were incessant, and the UN was unable, or unwilling, to take action. Jewish concern over the fate of the Negev increased; there seemed no solution other than to take up arms again. By October, the Egyptian Army in the south had been greatly reinforced, and the Egyptians had no reason to expect much trouble from the few Jewish settlements which, cut off from the State, continued to resist them. Contact between these settlements and the IDF was maintained throughout the summer by an airlift (*Operation Dust*) which often involved as many as eight flights a night, but the air was no replacement for land; besides, time pressed; if the *status quo* was not changed soon, the final agreement regarding the south might be disastrous.

Operation 'Ten Plagues'

The IDF prepared to mount *Operation Ten Plagues*, known also as Operation Yoav, (after a Palmach commander killed in the defence of kibbutz Negba) which was intended to drive the Egyptians out of the Negev, once and for all. The force mustered for Operation Ten Plagues included the Givati Brigade, the Yiftach Brigade, the Negev Brigade, the 8th Brigade, and, later, the 9th Brigade

220

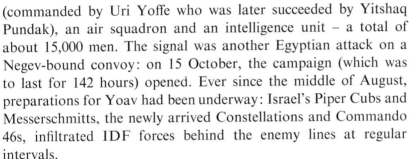

(commanded by Uri Yoffe who was later succeeded by Yitshaq Pundak), an air squadron and an intelligence unit – a total of about 15,000 men. The signal was another Egyptian attack on a Negev-bound convoy: on 15 October, the campaign (which was to last for 142 hours) opened. Ever since the middle of August, preparations for Yoav had been underway: Israel's Piper Cubs and Messerschmitts, the newly arrived Constellations and Commando 46s, infiltrated IDF forces behind the enemy lines at regular intervals.

Now, taking the enemy by surprise, the IDF moved, hammering two massive wedges into the long Egyptian line which ribboned from north of Gaza right up to the foothills of the Hebron range, and severed much of the Egyptian army from any contact with its already over-extended lines of supply. Then, the main effort shifted to the major Negev crossroads, which were in Egyptian hands; when the crossroads fell to the Israelis, the siege of the Negev lifted; the isolation of the south ended at last. Painfully aware of the UN tendency to intervene whenever the Arabs were in danger, the IDF hastened to exploit its initial success, and on 21 October, Beersheba was stormed from the west and taken. As had been predicted, a UN ceasefire was ordered forthwith. Time had run out and the Israelis could no longer move, nonetheless, they managed to connect the Sdom area with Beersheba before the ceasefire took effect on the entire southern front.

The fall of Bethlehem and Hebron to the IDF on the central front would have only been a matter of hours, but the IDF was ordered by the government to stop in its tracks. On 17 November,

left: Jeeps of the Palmach's 'Negev Beasts'
right: Dr Ralph Bunche succeeded Count Bernadotte as UN Mediator in Palestine

Capture of Beersheba

221

above: Zvi Ayalon, head of
the Central Command
below: Uri Yoffe, commander
of the Ninth Brigade in
Operation 'Ten Plagues'

Operation 'Hiram'

the United Nations itself, in the person of Bernadotte's successor, Dr Ralph Bunche (later to be awarded the Nobel Peace Prize for his efforts in Palestine) proposed that the Israelis, though withdrawing their combatants, be allowed to maintain a garrison in the Negev. Despite the ceasefire, mopping-up operations went on in the Hebron hills, and the Egyptians continued to evacuate the south – partly by sea, an operation which resulted in the sinking by the small Israeli Navy of two enemy warships, one of them the flagship of the Egyptian navy, the *Emir Farouk*.

Only the so-called Faluja pocket still resisted the Israelis in the south; in this U-shaped area, which, towards the end, was only some three miles wide, an entire Egyptian brigade was trapped with its equipment. It had no way of rejoining the other Egyptian units – by this time in full flight – but it continued valiantly to hold out. Even direct talks between the Israeli commander and the Sudanese brigadier at Faluja, Said Taha, were of no avail; the brigadier, whose intelligence officer was a young major named Gamal Abdel Nasser, refused to surrender. It took weeks before the stalemate was resolved, but in the course of the armistice talks held by the UN at Rhodes, it was finally agreed that the Faluja pocket be evacuated.

No sooner was the southern front quiet than the north began to simmer; Kaukji's troops, hastily re-equipped by the Lebanese, began again to harass the Jewish settlements in the Galilee. Kaukji took trouble to announce that neither he nor his force were represented at the UN and were, therefore, not obliged to abide by the ceasefire. In one raid, directed against the settlement of Manara in the Naphtali range, the Israelis rose to the challenge; the time had come to put an end to the last Arab provocation. The sixty-hour offensive mounted against the Arab Liberation Army at the end of October, 1948, was named for Hiram, King of Tyre, to whom King Solomon had given 'twenty cities in the land of Galilee'. Led by Moshe Carmel, it was a four-pronged attack, supported from the air and by artillery, on the Liberation Army's remaining positions; in the eastern Galilee; near Safed and below the Acre-Safed road. The Syrians helped from Mishmar Hayarden, but the Israelis were in full pursuit, and neither the Syrians, the Lebanese, nor the Arab Liberation Army could withstand the onslaught. *Operation Hiram* lasted two and a half days; it cleared the Galilee, drove Kaukji out of Israel, broke up the Arab Liberation Army forever and even, briefly, took the Israelis across the border as far as the Litani River into Lebanon.

Israel returned to concentrating on peace: by the middle of December, almost all fighting in the Negev had ended but the

222

Egyptians still refused to consider peace talks. The feeling grew in Israel that the enemy must be forced to the conference table; that if Egypt led the way to negotiations with the Jews the other Arab states would follow in her wake; and that peace, genuine and lasting, was worth even another round of the war – if no other way could be found to bring the Egyptians to their knees. Operation Horev (which lasted from 22 December to 7 January), resulted in the Egyptian-Israel armistice talks which began in Rhodes as soon as Horev ended.

Operation Horev began with a diversionary attack on the Gaza Strip, but its real and secret objective was the crossroads at Auja el Hafir, from which the IDF could cut through the Sinai desert, finally endangering the entire Egyptian force. The subterfuge worked; the Egyptians rushed reinforcements to the Gaza Strip, while the major Israeli columns raced southwest – to the accompaniment of wind, sand and rain storms. The advance was not made, as might have been expected, along the only road from Beersheba southward to Bir Asluj, but along the remains of what had once been a Roman road – perhaps one along which Titus' armies marched on their way to Palestine in 70 AD. The Egyptians were taken unaware by the sudden appearance – seemingly out of the blue – of the IDF, and though they fought hard to hold Auja, on 27 December, the junction fell to the Israelis. The Egyptian soldiers (and officers) surrendered in thousands, opting for imprison-

Operation 'Horev'. Israel troops dig in during the closing period of the war in Sinai

The Israelis' dash southwards

223

Egyptian soldiers surrender to advancing Israeli troops. Such scenes became familiar again in 1956 and once more, in 1967

ment rather than death in the wilderness. It was the first but not the last time that Israel's army, although faced by such numbers, was to witness the dreadful spectacle of its erstwhile enemies perishing of thirst in the sand – a spectacle which, though no one then knew it, was to be repeated twice again in the following two decades.

The first stage of Horev accomplished, the Israeli thrust continued; the IDF swooped deeper into Sinai. On 28 December, Israeli forward troops crossed into Egypt from Auja el Hafir, took the strong position of Umm Katef, occupied Abu Ageila, the major crossroad of northern Sinai, the larger force turned northwards to El Arish, the main Egyptian base in Sinai, from the rear. A smaller force advanced southwest towards the Suez Canal, took the airfields of Bir Hama and advanced to within 50 miles from the Canal which was still in the hands of British forces. The third force moved southwards, took Kuseima, Kuntilla and Bir Hama in the heart of Sinai. All Egyptian airfields fell into Israeli hands and several airplanes were captured intact. The Egyptians, stunned and demoralized, broke lines and ran. It was, without question, the greatest victory of the war, and it was followed by a great political blunder. The Southern Command had received approval to drive a wedge into the Egyptian lines south of Rafa and the entire Egyptian army was cut off. At this point the Royal Airforce attempted to intervene and in the ensuing fight British Spitfires were shot down. The world held its breath. The resultant storm in the House of Commons had the effect of convincing the British to recognize the new State! A more important result was that the Egyptians realized at last that the continuation of the war was futile and agreed to enter into direct negotiations under the auspices of the UN with Israel at Rhodes on one condition: that Israel's wedge south of Rafa must withdraw. A second political blunder was made – the victorious Israeli troops had to beat a retreat on 9 January 1949. Israel had lost an important bargaining position and committed a third political blunder by accepting an armistice agreement with no guarantees instead of insisting on a peace treaty which certainly could have been achieved. The Israeli government gave in to British and American demands, and by 31 December 1948, the Israelis were virtually gone from the desert.

Operation Horev had a significant postscript: on 12 March 1949, while Tel Hai Day was being celebrated in Israel's schools, a small parade of Israeli soldiers took place in the courtyard of the police station at Eilat (Umm Rash Rash) on the tip of the Red Sea – 155 miles south of Beersheba. It marked the final phase of the War of Independence and of *Operation Uvdah* (Fact), a campaign which began on 6 March (while the Israel-Transjordan talks were being held on Rhodes) and ended five days later with the conquest of the southern Negev and the securing of the western shores of the Dead Sea, Massada, Ein Gedi and the Judean wilderness. The poet Yitshaq Lamdan's phrase 'Massada shall not fall again!' received renewed significance.

The time had come for Israel to implement her claim to her newly acquired territory.

Once again, veteran Palmach scouts were called into action; for hours they ransacked their memories, maps and notes, recalling paths, hills and valleys, reconstructing the dimensions of boulders, the length of wadis, the kind of plants that grew here or there. A tiny 'task force' piled into two jeeps and bounced over dry river beds and mountains to check the lay of the land for itself; it

above: A young platoon commander in Operation 'Horev' was killed moments after this photograph was taken
below: A group of officers confer during Operation Horev. First left, Nahum Sarig, centre, Haim Bar-Lev

225

returned home to finalize the battle plan. The Golani Brigade commanded by Nahum Golan, would move southward through the Arava wilderness, the Negev Brigade, along an interior desert route, taking with it a team of engineers and technicians to spread nets on the sand so that the IDF anti-tank guns, jeeps and half-tracks (which carried the infantry) would be able to proceed across the dunes, and so that a landing strip, the 'Field of Abraham' (about thirty miles north of Eilat) could be readied for transport planes to disgorge men and equipment. The point of contact would be Eilat.

Israel's GHQ issued stern instructions forbidding direct attack on the Jordanians; they were to be persuaded to fire first. The starting signal went up: the Negev Brigade moved southward, as did Golani, which advanced along the Arava, close to the border, clearing one Jordanian strongpoint after the other. It was only after a Negev Brigade column had been spotted a few days later by a reconnaissance plane that the Jordanian forces were ordered to withdraw, and Eilat fell to the Israelis, as planned, in a classic pincer movement. The Commander of the Southern Front cabled Prime Minister David Ben-Gurion and the Chief of Staff: 'Happy inform you operation accomplished according to plan including liberation of Gulf of Eilat stop Israel's flag hoisted over Umm Rash Rash police station stop Southern Army rejoices (signed) Yigal Allon.' On 10 March, the Negev Brigade reached Eilat: by 3 PM that day the little police station was occupied; and before dusk the Golani spearhead arrived. An armistice agreement between Israel and Transjordan was signed again rather than a peace treaty. Allon commenting to a group of his senior officers summed up the campaign in the words, 'we have won the war, but lost the peace'. Uvdah faced the world with a *fait accompli*; it was the epilogue of the War of Independence. 'We have come to the end of the map' the Palmach task force reported when it reached the Red Sea; it had come also to the end of a war which – though it did not bring peace to Israel after all – guaranteed its existence, and made it a fact.

above: Nahum Golan, commander of Palmach's Golani Brigade
below: Yigal Allon was commander of the Southern Front during the latter part of the War of Independence

opposite: A dramatic race through the southern desert resulted in the hoisting of a hand-inked Israeli flag at the police station of Umm Rash Rash on the shores of the Gulf of Aqaba – today the thriving town of Eilat

7 Terrorism and Retaliation

Haganah to Israel Defence Forces — The Fedayeen — Sinai Campaign — Occupation and Withdrawal — Suez — End of the Second Round

The War of Independence ended; the dust settled on Israel's roads; from passing jeeps and buses, throughout the country, tired young men and women yelled to each other jubilantly that it was over at last. Shabby uniforms were peeled off and once-precious rifles returned to the stores. But no one, least of all the thousands of veterans rushing to be demobilized, was unaware of the fact that peace, in any full or final meaning of the word, was far off. At best, despite the victory, the situation of the young State was still most precarious; her borders were inordinately long (some 600 miles) and her neighbours unreconciled to her existence. The proximity of her military bases, ports and airfields to enemy territory was alarming; and the armistice agreements, painfully negotiated under the auspices of the United Nations with Egypt (February 1949), Lebanon (March 1949), Jordan (April 1949) and Syria (July 1949) were replete with unsolved problems and unlikely to attain permanency or to form, as Israelis hoped they would, transitions to a changed, sounder relationship between Israel and the Arab states.

The agreements were seen as a transitional stage between war and peace in which both sides would undertake peace negotiations and undertake to prevent regular or irregular military actions against each other. Nevertheless, the Arab leaders now found new, if less dangerous, ways of continuing the war. Denying recognition to the Jewish State, they sealed off the frontiers they shared with it. In the main, the Arabs refused entry permits to anyone holding a visa for Israel; and most travellers to the Middle East armed themselves with two, and some even three, passports. In addition, the Arabs imposed an economic blockade on Israel, and on those who sought to deal with her economically. The blockade proved most effective in the Suez Canal and Gulf of Aqaba. There, at the tip of the Sinai Peninsula, at Sharm es Sheikh, massive Egyptian

opposite: The Sinai Campaign (October 29–November 5, 1956) broke the ring of Arab encirclement, destroyed huge concentrations of Egyptian armaments and eliminated terrorist bases in the Gaza Strip and Sinai and raised the blockade of the Straits of Tiran. Here, an Israeli jeep enters a canyon in the Sinai Peninsula

229

General David Shaltiel, one-time commander of Haganah forces in Jerusalem (in glasses), and Colonel Abdullah El-Tel (in Bedouin headgear) negotiate in Jerusalem the Israel–Jordan Armistice Agreement, which was signed in Rhodes on April 3, 1949

guns commanding the Straits of Tiran guaranteed that for seven years not a single ship could call at Israel's new port of Eilat, on which so many hopes were pinned. The Arab boycott was virtually worldwide; it included 'black lists' of companies which dared to trade with Israel, bans against aircraft bound to or from Israel flying over Arab territory, the barring of the Suez Canal to Israel shipping – despite the 1888 Constantinople Convention which specified that passage through the Canal must be allowed freely and at all times, in war and peace, to all nations.

Terrorist raids into Israel

But the attempt to isolate the country, to starve it out, and to wither its economic potential was reinforced also by actual physical violence – even as the ink dried on the armistice agreements. The infiltration of armed gangs from the Arab states into Israel began as early as 1949; at first, the crossings, though certainly undesirable, seemed innocent enough. Groups of Arab marauders, infiltrated sporadically to steal cattle, to plunder fields, to filch from the Jewish border settlements. Before long, it became clear that this harassment was exceedingly well-organized, that it was, in fact, backed by the Arab states themselves and that essentially it constituted the first stage of a small and unrecognized war. As the toll rose, and murder joined theft and arson, the Israelis turned to the United Nations for help; but the UN proclaimed itself unable to halt the infiltration, or to stop it from escalating. Besides, said the UN officials, there was no real proof that the raiding was not spontaneous, a lamentable result of post-war displacement, an unfortunate phenomenon but one that would eventually disappear.

There seemed, in the first turbulent years of the 1950's, little that Israel could do against the repeated violations of the armistice agreements. Besides, the population was preoccupied with problems

230

of growth and development stemming, almost entirely, from the mass immigration that now overwhelmed it; problems which inevitably expressed themselves in the changing character and aims of the Israel Defence Forces. In July, 1950, the Knesset (Israel's Parliament) unanimously passed the unique 'Law of Return'; legislation which gave the right of immigration to all Jews, and automatically conferred Israel citizenship on all Jewish immigrants. In May, 1948, there had been some 650,000 Jews in Palestine; by the end of 1964, over 1,200,000 refugees had been absorbed. Hundreds of thousands of Jews from the camps of Cyprus, and from those of Germany, Austria and Italy, from the Arab lands of the Middle East, and from North Africa, made their way to the Jewish State. They came from over seventy countries, and almost without exception, they were destitute. Food, clothing, housing, had to be urgently provided; the immigrants had to be settled, given jobs, their children schooled and taught Hebrew. The task which confronted Israel in those years was gigantic; but it was also crucial. The Law of Return expressed the guiding principles of the Zionist movement, it was literally the *raison d'être* of the State; and accordingly, Israelis buckled down individually and collectively to face the challenge. Tent cities, sheltering the immigrants, blossomed briefly and unattractively all over Israel, metamorphosing into not more attractive but rather more solid clusters of tin and asbestos huts; makeshift clinics and schools were set up; as many immigrants as possible settled on the land. It was a period of incessant activity, of no order of priority, of errors, and of austerity. The population's standard of living dropped; what had sufficed for one family in 1948 had to be shared with at least two other families in 1951; world Jewry gave generously but even the most magnanimous donor abroad was spared the short rations, the often-intolerable crowding, the confrontation with new citizens who knew little or nothing about the motivation or past history of the early settlers.

Roumanian immigrants aboard an Israeli vessel were among the hundreds of thousands of refugees who streamed into Israel in the years following Independence

In the years that followed the War of Independence, development towns and tens of new moshavim and kibbutzim sprang up throughout the country, their populations drawn from both new immigrants and old-timers. This mass settlement recalled the efforts and drive of the pre-State pioneers; as had been true before 1948, the redemption of the Land and its settlement was more than a mere matter of statistics, though these were impressive: indeed they were a national duty and privilege. They established the Jews as a majority throughout the new State; they developed its enormous agricultural, industrial and commercial potential and they utilized all of its available natural resources.

Considering the unorthodox composition and values of the un-

Mass absorption

231

above: Yigael Yadin, Chief of Operations in the War of Independence, was Chief of Staff of the Israel Defence Forces from 1949 to 1952. Today he is Professor of Archaeology at the Hebrew University of Jerusalem.
below: Mordechai Makleff was Chief of Staff of the IDF from 1952 to 1953. He had been a Brigade commander during the War of Independence

The Israel Defence Forces organize

derground movements which had so recently coalesced into an army, it was perhaps only natural that the Israel Defence Forces be chosen to serve as an important instrument for the rehabilitation and acclimatization of the newcomers. Granted, it was not the standard job of an army to teach immigrants to read and write or to master a new language, to man playgrounds for children, to run soup kitchens or to act as a living bridge between different cultures; but then, this was not destined to be an ordinary army; its concerns were unlike those of most military establishments; it saw itself as an integral link in the continuity of Jewish history in general, and of the Yishuv in particular; and it both was and wished to remain – primarily – a citizens' army.

With the formal end of the War of Independence, some sort of permanent defence system had to be created; a demobilization policy planned and implemented; thought given to the army's structure. The Israel Defence Forces became based on four elements: a small regular army, national service or conscription, the reserves, and territorial defence based on the settlements. It was also decided that both men and women would be liable to national service, and that special forces would be mustered to deal with Israel's special requirements. The most problematic of these elements, without doubt, was the regular army. It was one thing to volunteer for an underground movement at a time of heightened crisis, to become a soldier when freedom was in the balance; and another matter to opt for a life-long military career. The answer lay in the *kind* of standing army that was to be created: a small, highly trained and motivated mobile force made up largely of officers and NCOs might attract young Israelis, the more so if specialization were stressed. The Training Command opened a variety of specialist schools; officers were encouraged and helped to acquire university educations, and sent abroad for additional high-level military training, mostly to England and France. The army built its own housing estates and set up central stores for army personnel and army families. Acceptance into the commissioned ranks was solely a matter of merit and spit and polish were kept to the minimum without sacrificing *esprit de corps*. Also, this was to be a young army; free from cant or from artificial limiting traditions. The Chief of Staff, Yigael Yadin, was all of thirty-three when he was appointed in 1949, and his colleagues were rarely older.

Women, though not allowed to participate in combat, and serving in separate units, were in no sense regarded as just auxiliaries. The women's corps (known as *Chen* or charm – the fortuitous acronym of the Hebrew for 'women's army') was very much part

232

of the Israel Defence Forces, and women served – and still serve –
both in the regular army, and in the reserves – upon which, in
the final analysis, Israel's defence has always depended. Boys and
girls were to do national service, from eighteen until twenty or
twenty-one, remaining in the reserves until their middle forties.
For obvious reasons, Israel's Arab citizens were exempted from
compulsory military service, but hundreds of Arabs, Christians
and Moslems willingly volunteered for various positions in the
defence establishment. However, the Druze community of 35,000
and another minority, the even more tiny Circassian community,
had a special request: it demanded that it be subject to conscription.
All young male Druze serve in the IDF, or more often in the ranks
of the Border Police, and do so with conspicuous valour. To ensure
that, even in war, the bulk of the population could go on living a
normal life until the very last minute, one of the world's speediest
mobilization systems was devised. The radio, newspapers, notices,
posters, letters and telegrams were all used; reservists presented
themselves for registration on certain days, in given places, according to prepared lists; duly registered, examined and classified, they
were posted to units and there given code words which, when
broadcast or published, served as the signal for the reservist,
equipment in hand, to present himself. In a country lacking defensive depth, characterized by grotesquely elongated frontiers
shared with states whose leaders endlessly and loudly reiterated
their determination to launch a second round of the war as soon
as feasible, the speed and efficiency of mobilization were far from
being merely an exercise in agility. In the autumn of 1950, the
Israel Defence Forces held its first major manoeuvres: it turned
out that within less than forty-eight hours all reservists had received
their signals, picked up their gear, and arrived at assigned frontline
positions.

But, as had been true since the first days of the Yishuv, much
of Israel's defence still lay in the hands of her border settlers. All
through the War of Independence, the settlements had served as
anvils, the Haganah as a hammer; and, to a large extent, it was
between these that the State of Israel had been forged. The Israel
Defence Forces searching for means to combine military service
with agricultural life, finally evolved the concept that led to the
formation of *Nahal* (acronym of the Hebrew words for 'Fighting
Pioneer Youth'). Nahal, whose like existed nowhere else, was to
make possible the settlement of isolated parts of the country, and
thus considerably to increase Israel's defensive power in those critical areas. Special forms of recruiting permitted groups of members of pioneering youth movements – the nuclei of future settle-

above: Moshe Dayan was Chief
of Staff of the IDF from 1953
to 1958 and commanded the
Suez Campaign. Since 1967
he has been Minister of
Defence.
below: Chaim Laskov was
Chief of Staff of the IDF
between 1958 and 1960. Today
he is Director of the Israel
Ports Authority

Nahal

233

An Israeli fighter pilot of the 1950's in the cockpit of his plane

ments – to remain together throughout their national service; together, to receive military and agricultural training within the framework of established kibbutzim; ultimately, and still together, to join frontier settlements as civilian farmers. Possibly no other aspect of the Israel Defence Forces so succinctly described its innovatory nature.

Hand in hand with the newly-defined structure, with new textbooks, and new regulations, the Israel Defence Forces also acquired new equipment. Meteors took the place of Messerschmitts and Spitfires; frigates took over from the armed fishing fleet that had done yeoman duty in 1948; tanks replaced the armour-plated trucks whose carcasses still line the Jerusalem road. But the major emphasis was not on equipment, nor even on structure, but on people, on personnel, on the making of Israel's army from the human point of view. Most of the young men who had served during the war with the IDF had entered civilian life at last, many of them for the first time since childhood. Who would, or could, replace them? The Israel Defence Forces set about schooling thousands of young immigrants; turned itself into Israel's largest and probably most successful educational institution; created an Education Corps which taught far more than citizenship or marksmanship, which prepared and gave lessons in geography, in history, in grammar to youngsters who had never been to proper schools, whose environment was culturally deprived in the extreme.

Escalation on the borders

It was, for the most part, on problems such as these that the Israel Defence Forces concentrated in the opening years of the State's first decade. The unease on the frontiers, the growing depredations from across the borders, these, perforce, were the domain of the Armistice Commissions, the subject of constant, fruitless discussion. But, by 1952, the number of border incidents totalled over 3,000; once again, Jews were murdered on the roads and in the suburbs of cities, in the fields and in their homes. In 1953, the Israel Defence Forces, unbearably stung, formed a tiny unit (it numbered only some 20 men at first) charged with responsibility for carrying out punitive raids, for hitting back across the borders, for trying to end the growing Arab terror. By January, 1954, this small unit, combined with paratroopers, had carried out tens of actions; it had attacked Arab Legion camps, Egyptian positions, Egyptian headquarters in the Gaza Strip (which, though supposedly demilitarized, served as a jumping off point for the incursions into Israel) and Syrian emplacements.

Groomed to become the hard-hitting fist of the IDF, the special force trained rigorously in night fighting, in judo, learnt the devious arts of reconnaissance and penetration into enemy bases;

234

learned to assault from the rear, frontally, and from the flank – anywhere and anyhow as long as it was on enemy ground. A new brand of Israeli warrior emerged; tough, resourceful, limitlessly courageous – like his predecessors – but professional. These were no longer farmer-soldiers, these were commandos, élite troops, men who knew that the terror must end and who understood that it was up to them to end it.

In 1955, the situation worsened; Egypt decided to make fuller use of the armed bands she had supported for months. The *fedayeen* came into existence; formations of armed raiders dedicated to the continuing harassment of Israel, and to her eventual destruction. They based themselves mainly in the Gaza Strip, but fedayeen camps sprung up also in Jordan, Syria and Lebanon; wherever there was a convenient springboard for driving deeper and deeper into Israel; for mining roads, ambushing traffic, blowing up wells and destroying homes. Within a year, the Jewish death toll stood at over 400, including children, close to a thousand Jews had been wounded, and the total number of fedayeen actions now neared 12,000.

A medical orderly tends an Israeli soldier wounded in one of the reprisal raids that preceded the Sinai Campaign

'We cannot' declared Israel's Chief of Staff Moshe Dayan, 'save each water pipe from explosion or each tree from being uprooted. We cannot prevent the murder of workers in orange groves or of families in their beds. But we *can* put a very high price on their blood, a price so high that it will no longer be worthwhile for the Arabs, the Arab armies, or the Arab states to pay it.' The Israel Defence Forces set the price; it blasted enemy installations at Khan Yunis, Kuntilla, Kalkilya, demolishing the Teggart police fortresses out of which the *fedayeen* functioned. The crisis was so assiduously fanned that only eight years after the War of Independence, the Yishuv, seeking only time and tranquillity enough to develop the new state, found itself at war again.

The immediate prelude to the Sinai Campaign was the so-called Czech arms deal of 1955. This agreement between a Soviet satellite and the government of Egypt provided Egypt with a vast supply of arms, including fighter aircraft, tanks, troop carriers, armoured vehicles, destroyers and submarines. It underlined Egypt's intention to 'reconquer Palestine' as the Egyptian president, Gamal Abdel Nasser, put it in January 1956; and increased, fourfold, the disproportion between the military strength of Israel (to whom arms were denied by most of her friends) and that of her greatest and most dangerous enemy. The implications were not to be avoided : Israel turned her attention to a renewed attempt to find arms somewhere, (meeting with a generous response from France) and to settling the borders faster than initially called for in develop-

Call to arms again

235

A Nahal girl soldier, somewhere in Galilee, continues the Palmach tradition of farmer-soldiers

ment blueprints. In 1946, thirteen new settlements had made clear to the British that the Negev would not be given up by the Jews; ten years later, in 1956, five new Nahal settlements rose in the south to make the same statement. As 1956 wore on, Israeli intelligence advised, and the Israel Defence Forces later confirmed, that the Sinai Peninsula was being turned into a massive Egyptian base and readied for attack: jet airstrips were created close to the Israel border; field supply stations strung out all along potential axes of advance; fuel, ammunition, medicine and food stocked in quantities wildly exceeding anything that could conceivably be needed by the Egyptian forces garrisoned in Sinai.

If any doubts at all remained as to Egypt's intentions, they were dispelled by the unification, in October, 1956, of the Egyptian, Syrian and Jordanian high commands, under an Egyptian Supreme Commander. In 1948, a joint command of this kind had also been set up, but then it had served as an unsuccessful device for coordinating the various Arab armies; in 1956, however, the unified command was a serious attempt to create a genuinely monolithic military structure. In the summer of 1956, Nasser seized and nationalized the Suez Canal, dramatic token of the fact that Egypt was unlikely to be restrained from attacking Israel by world public opinion, or even by UN action. It was Nasser's most flamboyant gesture of defiance.

Egyptian dreams of victory

October, 1956 was a long, tense, hot month: each day brought new and more ominous developments. For the first time, Syrian infantry moved into Jordanian territory, taking up positions near the Israel border along the Jordan River. Political commentators abroad speculated about Nasser's motives: the Egyptian military junta seemed designed to bring into existence an Arab Empire sweeping from the Atlantic in the west to the Persian Gulf in the east and to the sources of the Nile in the south. The destruction of the Jewish State under Egyptian leadership would sky-rocket Egypt's prestige, already on the ascendant. Egypt, Syria, Jordan and Palestine formed a natural bloc and Egypt, inevitably the dominant Arab power, would finally attain that position of political and military supremacy in the Arab world that the Egyptian leader so coveted. In the Arab elaboration of this enticing fantasy, the lessons of 1948 were forgotten, and only the temptation remained.

But in Israel, the facts and figures of grim reality took precedence over political commentaries or analyses. The equation was familiar and simple, and the Israelis, contemplating it, accepted its logic: it would have to be the few against the many again; an economy pared to the bone would have to mount a war effort against an economy rich in oil; a politically isolated democracy would have

236

to pit itself against a large totalitarian military alliance, ceaselessly pampered both by the east and the west. Commentary condensed itself into a few eloquent facts: Arab bombers were less than fifteen minutes flying time from Israel's major cities, and even less from her bases. A sudden air attack would leave Israel's fields blackened and useless, her towns paralysed, her army fragmented and unable to move. The State's perilous geostrategic situation demanded an obvious course of action: the initiative would have to be wrested from the enemy. The Sinai Campaign, a classic example of an anticipatory counter-attack, began secretly to take shape.

The campaign had three main objectives: the decisive defeat of the Egyptian army and the removal of the war threat it posed, the final destruction of the Egyptian army bases (including the fedayeen camps) in the Sinai Peninsula and in the Gaza Strip and the opening of the Suez Canal and of the Gulf of Akaba to Israel's shipping. On 24 October, in total secrecy, Israel began to mobilize her reserves. Seven days later, by 5 November, less than a hundred hours after the first Israeli transport planes crossed the Sinai frontier, the men and vehicles of the Israel Defence Forces had travelled hundreds of miles, by road, and over wholly trackless wastes; had attacked and defeated the enemy on his own ground; had captured an area two and a half times as big as the whole of Israel. The meticulous preparations (however hurried); the faithful execution of plans; the elasticity, courage and obstinacy of officers and men alike, all these were to bear their fruit and result in a second victory over the Egyptians.

It took four days to mobilize the reserves, to assemble, equip, deploy and limber up the troops who were soon to face three full Egyptian divisions plus two additional brigades – over 30,000 Egyptian soldiers in all, in territory as harsh and as formidable as any in the world. The routines, rehearsed so often and so tediously, paid off; despite snags and mistakes, the mobilization proceeded as scheduled; word of mouth, telephone, telegrams were all employed and when the four days were up, Israel had nine brigades ready for action. The element of secrecy was pivotal; only GHQ knew the truth, that a campaign for life or death was being mounted against the Egyptians. For public consumption, but more especially for the edification of Egypt's military leadership, rumours spread that Jordan was to be attacked, troops massed and a curfew was declared on the Jordan-Israel frontier. At IDF headquarters, the final touches were put on the battle plan; on a four-phase operation, the success of which was entirely predicated on surprise, shock, speed and risk. The plan was so designed that should the United Nations intervene (and they had a tendency to intervene

Assaf Simchoni was commander of the Southern Front during the Sinai Campaign. He was killed in an air accident during the last hours of the war

Israel prepares for war

overleaf: In desert warfare, mastery of the sand dunes is a major problem and challenge

237

Israeli paratroopers played a decisive role in the Sinai Campaign. At right, dug in at the crucial Mitla Pass, where they linked up with IDF overland forces

whenever the Arabs were in trouble) or should the Egyptians prove more militarily competent than expected, the campaign could be called off and its first phase presented to the world as only another reprisal raid.

On 29 October, the Sinai Campaign began under the command of General Assaf Simhoni, GOC Southern Command. After sunset, a parachute battalion was dropped near the fourteen mile-long Mitla Pass in the Sinai Peninsula, east of Suez; that pass of which it was said that whoever commanded it, commanded all access to the Suez Canal from central Sinai. The rest of the para-troop brigade assembled, deceptively, on the Jordanian border – in the diametrically opposite direction – and then set out for an overland advance and a link-up with the paratroopers at Mitla.

Operation 'Kadesh'
gets underway

The start of the campaign (known in Israel as *Operation Kadesh*, for the Biblical site where the Children of Israel probably organized for their attempt to penetrate the Promised Land) was depicted by operations chief, General Meir Amit. 'At 14.30 hours, I arrived at the airfield,' he wrote, 'the transport planes were arranged in a U, their noses pointing to its mouth... Groups of paratroopers stood by each plane, checking equipment, cleaning weapons. At 15.00, they began to emplane; at 15.10, the first formation taxied to the takeoff runway. Within seven to eight minutes. all the aircraft were aloft and those of us standing on the ground waved "Shalom".' As they crossed the frontier, the paratroopers could see their bri-gade column below them, also moving west, on wheels and cater-pillar tracks. A day and a night, and more, would pass before they

240

would meet again at their desert rendezvous, at the monument in Sinai named for a British officer, Colonel Palmer, who had twice been governor of the Peninsula. Thirty-nine minutes after the planes crossed the border, the first parachutes opened. Before the sun had sunk, the troops had started to dig in near the monument, and by sunrise on 30 October, they were ready to hold the area until the overland forces joined them. As was to be true of the entire campaign, it was highly unconventional from the beginning. The paratroop battalion was the only Israeli force in all of Sinai's vast expanse; a solitary battalion, limited as to support weapons; some hundred miles, as the crow flies, from the Israel border; with considerable enemy forces blocking the lines of approach to and from it; that battalion was now vulnerable in the extreme.

Egypt's 'Eastern Headquarters' was quick to react. A mechanized brigade was dispatched to Mitla, ordered to advance to the monument. On 30 October, the first Egyptian aircraft appeared over the paratroopers' position, and the first battle of the campaign was on. But the Israeli overland troops were by now on their way to Mitla, taking three major Egyptian bases en route, scattering the astonished terrified Egyptians into the desert; Kuntilla, Themed, Nakhl fell to the Israelis, alternately fighting and slogging their way through sand so thick that vehicles bogged down, either to be repaired at once by the mobile workshops accompanying the force, or left behind. The brigade made military history by the rapidity and tenaciousness of its advance. It was a considerable achievement for men who were civilians only a few days before.

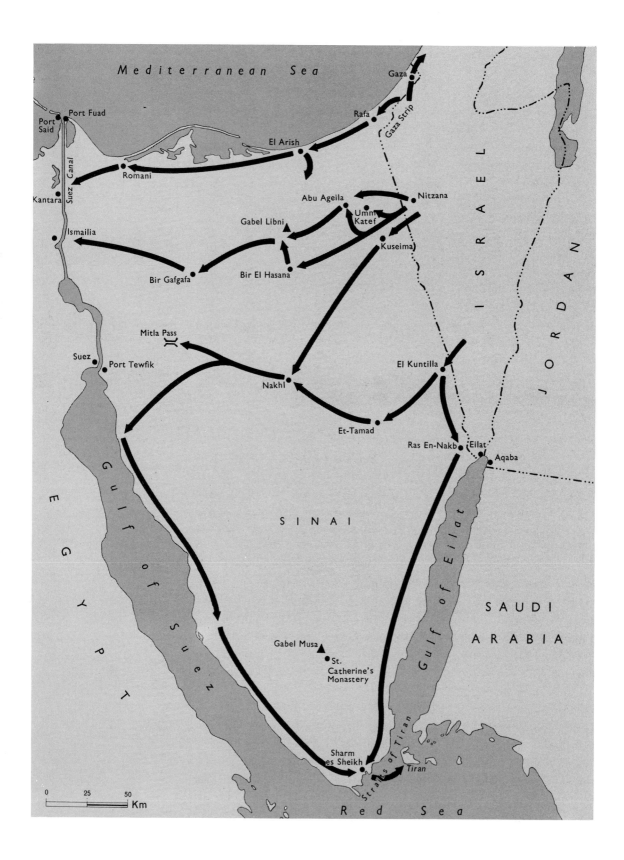

Mediterranean Sea

Gaza

Port Fuad
Port Said
Rafa
Gaza Strip
El Arish

Suez Canal
Romani

Kantara
Nitzana

Ismailia
Abu Ageila
Gabel Libni ▲
Umm Katef
ISRAEL

Kuseima
Bir Gafgafa
Bir El Hasana

JORDAN

Mitla Pass
Suez
Port Tewfik
Nakhl
El Kuntilla

Et-Tamad

Ras En-Nakb Eilat
Aqaba

EGYPT
Gulf of Suez
SINAI
Gulf of Eilat

SAUDI
ARABIA

Gabel Musa ▲
St. Catherine's Monastery

Sharm es Sheikh
Straits of Tiran
Tiran

0   25   50
Km

Red Sea

The appointment at the Mitla Pass was kept; the link-up was made; but the pass sheltered two concealed Egyptian battalions, entrenched in hidden positions in caves and on the cliffs, and the battle for the pass was to be costly. Bloodied and triumphant, the brigade reached the heights above the enemy, and won the pass. The way across the girth of Sinai was now open and the brigade advanced westwards.

In the meantime, another armoured force, led by Colonels Yosef Harpaz and Uri Ben-Ari, travelling the hot hard central axis, took the road junction at Kuseima, assaulted and captured the bristling Egyptian military complex at Abu Ageila in Sinai's heart, and headed for Ismailia, on the Canal. A third force, moving on the northern axis, and under the command of General Chaim Laskov readied itself to take the Gaza Strip, broke through, captured the Egyptian strongholds of Rafa and El Arish, mopped up and raced on its way to Kantara, to the Canal; while the Ninth Brigade (made up in its totality of no-longer-young reservists) led by veteran Colonel Avraham Yoffe, set out from the vicinity of Beersheba – along the southern axis – for an unprecedented 240-mile trek across the wilderness to the southern tip of Sinai, to Sharm es Sheikh. In many ways, the story of the infantrymen of the Ninth Brigade encapsules the story of the whole campaign; illustrates its

Among the commanders of the IDF armour were Colonel Uri Ben-Ari (with binoculars), *left*; Colonel Benjamin Gibli (*top*) and Colonel Haim Barlev (*bottom*), today Israel's Chief of Staff
opposite: Map of the Sinai Peninsula, showing the axes of the Israeli advance

243

*The race to Sharm
es Sheikh*

marathon quality, the stupendous gains which were made, and the effort that went into making them.

Southern Sinai, the Sinai Peninsula proper, is moon-country, desolate, mountainous, rent by ravines, and almost impassable. Its sands are deep, shifting and treacherous; it has neither shade nor water to offer; and it has been most accurately described as 24,000 square miles of rugged nothingness. But if the Gulf of Aqaba was to be opened up, if the Egyptian naval guns at the Straits of Tiran were to be put out of commission, if the Red Sea was to become available to Israel, this scorching, bleak, utterly inhospitable desert had to be crossed – and Yoffe and his men, a caravan of 200 oddly assorted vehicles, crossed it faster than any troops had ever traversed such terrain before. There was not a vehicle that did not bog down in the dunes, not a half-track that was not used for towing; not a man who did not have to push and pull guns and jeeps uphill and down. But 180 vehicles made it, and on 5 November, Yoffe cabled the Chief of Staff from Sharm es Sheikh, 'Praise the Lord, it is finished,' he announced. The Egyptian stronghold had put up minimal resistance at Sharm es Sheikh; after six hours of fighting they surrendered and the Straits of Tiran were open.

The march of the Ninth Brigade was the last battle of the Sinai Campaign. All the objectives had been met in a lightning, driving

assault. The campaign had not been fought for territory or gain, but the booty was massive; as they fled in the desert, the Egyptians abandoned hundreds of thousands of weapons; behind them, they left their tanks, their troop carriers, their artillery and their vehicles, and millions upon millions of rounds of ammunition. Nor had it been fought for captives, but some 30,000 Egyptians had been scattered in the desert by the onrushing IDF, hundreds doomed to lose their way, to perish of thirst and exhaustion. Nonetheless, some 5,000 prisoners were taken, largely as an act of mercy, eventually to be returned for the one Israeli in Egyptian hands.

Silenced Egyptian guns at Sharm es Sheikh on the southern tip of the Peninsula, November 5, 1956, no longer threaten the Straits of Tiran

The Egyptian defeat was absolute: a third of Nasser's army was broken, his airforce destroyed and Sinai was in Israeli hands. It might – and should have been – the end of hostilities.

Nasser's defeat

But Israel's war, though it ended in the campaign's only victory, was not the only war of the Sinai Campaign. France and England entered the fray: 'Operation Musketeer' was an attempt to seize the Canal from Nasser while Egypt was distracted by the Israelis and Russia by the rebellious Hungarians; a peerless opportunity – or so it appeared in Paris and London – to reassert the waning influence of the west in the Middle East. Had Operation Musketeer not taken place, Israel would probably have controlled the whole Canal; the Egyptian military junta would have been shaken;

Operation 'Musketeer'

so would Nasser, who now emerged in the eyes of the Egyptians, and much of the rest of the world, as a heroic figure staving off three attacking powers. But the French and the British intervened on the pretext of separating the combatants; on the second day of the campaign, they issued a joint ultimatum to Israel and to Egypt, insisting that the fighting stop. Israel agreed but Egypt rejected the ultimatum and the French and British launched their abortive attack on Port Said. In New York, the United Nations Assembly met in emergency session; the USSR threatened that a world war might break out; and the USA panicked. The Assembly demanded a ceasefire; demanded that the British and French evacuate the Canal Zone, and that Israel withdraw to the armistice lines of 1949. The pressure was intense; it came from both east and west; and the French and British backed down. In the climate thus created, little heed was paid to Israel's warning that the Middle East would only erupt and spill over into war again if the Israelis retreated either from Sinai or from the Gaza Strip.

Zvi Zur succeeded Chaim Laskov as Chief of Staff of the IDF in 1960. The men and equipment of the IDF were consolidated greatly during this relatively peaceful period.

opposite: By March 1957, Israel had withdrawn, not only from Sharm es Sheikh, but from the entire Sinai Peninsula and the Gaza Strip

The UN, adamant, adopted a proposal to set up a United Nations Emergency Force to patrol the borders between Israel and the Gaza Strip, as well as Sharm es Sheikh, to secure freedom of navigation through the Straits of Tiran. Alone in the face of the international clamour for withdrawal, bound by her straitened circumstances to consider the consequences of the cutting-off of US aid, and now informed, in no uncertain terms, by the great powers of the world that if she did not withdraw, she would bear responsibility for a third world war and the resultant calamity to man, Israel retreated; her troops left Sharm es Sheikh and the Gaza Strip in March 1957.

Once again, the dust settled on Israel's roads and, from passing jeeps and buses, tired young men yelled at each other that it was over, at last. No one was jubilant this time, but, at the very least, there was hope for peace. The menace of Arab attack, of the 'second round', was over; the myth of Arab unity had been dispelled – perhaps forever – for not a single Arab state had come to Egypt's rescue after all; the UN had undertaken active, objective supervision of the frontiers – though this, as demonstrated less than ten years later, proved singularly ineffective; and the IDF had won its laurels – even though it was deprived of the right to wear them.

247

8 The Third Round

El Fatah — U Thant and UNEF — Nasser blockades the Straits of Tiran — Mobilization — The Six Day War — The Wheel turns full circle

To the extent that Israel had known peace at all since 1948 – and at best it could only be defined as a minimal, highly tentative state of non-war with neighbours that remained adamantly dedicated to the idea of her annihilation – the period from 1957 to 1967 formed, if not exactly halcyon years, at least an era of relative serenity. The State grew and prospered, the cities swelled, and as the standard of living rose, life, for most Israelis, became notably easier. People began to travel abroad, and for the first time there was even a trickle of emigration from the Jewish State. But quasi-normalcy was hard to get used to: Israelis indulged in long bouts of self-criticism. Oldtimers talked nostalgically about the lost challenges of pioneering and warned about the ill-effect on the nation's youth of fulfilled national aspirations, while the youth itself seemed critical and restless.

Peace, real and lasting peace, appeared as elusive as ever, and although the borders were more relaxed following the Sinai Campaign, there was still constant, if sporadic, trouble with Arab terrorists. *An uneasy peace*

From 1963, Levi Eshkol was Prime Minister and Minister of Defence; prior to this, he had served the nation in many key capacities, particularly as Minister of Finance. One of his major concerns had always been the qualitative and quantitative strengthening of the IDF. Though for years he symbolized Israel's striving for peace, he never lost sight of the need for active defence and to this end he and the General Staff led by the Chief of Staff General Yitshaq Rabin devoted time, thought and energy.

The Israel-Egyptian border was the quietest; the 4,000-odd men of the United Nations Emergency Force patrolled Sharm es Sheikh and the Gaza Strip; and in 1962, Nasser committed the bulk of his army to a protracted war in the Yemen. It was unlikely, despite the incessant Egyptian declarations about continuing the Holy War

opposite: An Israeli keeps watch across the Suez Canal. The third round is over but is it the last?

249

Gamal Abdel Nasser, President of Egypt

with Israel, that any major Egyptian military action could or would be launched against the Jewish State. Not that the Egyptians were wholly pre-occupied by the fiasco in Yemen; Nasser actively encouraged and supported the various terrorist organizations (chief among them the *El Fatah* founded in 1965) that operated both from Jordan and from the Gaza Strip. But his relationship with the Jordanian Government, and in particular with King Hussein, was as discordant as ever, and the rivalry between the two for supremacy in the Arab world had not softened perceptibly over the years.

A more serious source of trouble was Syria, traditionally the most intransigent of Israel's enemies. From 1960 on, largely as a result of a new rapprochement between Cairo and Damascus, the Syrians had sent bands of infiltrators across the Israel frontiers; had sporadically bombarded the kibbutzim that lay so temptingly beneath the Syrian hills within effortless range of the Syrian artillery emplacements dug in above them; and had turned Israeli fishermen on the Sea of Galilee into sitting ducks for Syrian snipers. In many respects, the situation on the Israel-Syrian border resembled a small war, but in the main, it was controllable. The Syrians made attempts to divert the course of the Jordan and its flow to the Sea of Galilee, in order to negate the plan for irrigation of settlements in the arid areas of the Negev. When the Syrians blasted the Jewish settlements too hard or too long, the Israel Airforce would act, and the border would be quiet for several weeks or months. The terrorist incursions from Jordan were also kept in hand; every now and then, the Israel Defence Forces, goaded beyond endurance, mounted massive reprisal raids on terrorist bases in Jordan, and the Israel–Jordanian borders settled down for a while.

Egypt and Syria join forces   But in 1965, the situation worsened; that year there were some thirty Fatah raids on Israel from Syria and Jordan, and within the next months Syrian aggression against the Israel settlements escalated sharply. Throughout the early spring of 1967, there were almost daily terrorist attacks on the border settlements, and in April an air battle took place which resulted in the downing of six Syrian MIGs by the Israel Airforce. The Syrians promptly charged that Israel was planning a large-scale action against them, and by the beginning of May an ominous series of events began to unfold. Cairo and Damascus, bound in an official mutual defence pact, disclosed that General Mohammed Fawzi, the Egyptian Chief of Staff for the UAR, was in Syria to make final arrangements for the implementation of the pact; a state of emergency was declared in Egypt; and Nasser, claiming that he moved

250

A unit of the United Nations Emergency Force parades for the last time in the Gaza Strip before pulling out

in response to Syria's desperate plight, ostentatiously concentrated troops in Sinai with the full political backing and support of the Soviet Union, whose Ambassador to Israel had refused Levi Eshkol's invitation to see for himself that there was no truth in the allegations of troop concentrations opposite Syria. Arab agitation for war had been a characteristic of the Middle East for so long that many Israelis tended to disregard this outburst, and to pay little heed to Nasser's announcements.

But on 16 May, Nasser made the new and critical move, which was to lead him to disaster in less than a month: he demanded that the United Nations Emergency Force vacate Sharm es Sheikh and the Gaza Strip. Two days later, in a cable formally submitted to the United Nations, he repeated this request, stressing that the UN force had been stationed along the Israel-Egyptian border since 1956, only by virtue of Egypt's consent. Now that consent was abruptly revoked. History will certainly record that had the UN Secretary General asked Nasser for permission either to delay or phase-out the UNEF withdrawal, the Six-Day War would probably not have broken out. But U Thant, though mentioning 'serious misgivings', acquiesced at once. On 19 May, to the accompaniment of Egyptian jubilation and despite consternation almost everywhere else, the sky-blue and white flag of the United Nations came down in the Gaza Strip and at Sharm es Sheikh – and the Egyptians took over. Having unexpectedly met with no resistance from the United Nations, Nasser took an even more decisive step; on 22 May, he announced an Egyptian blockade of the Straits of Tiran; all entrances to the Gulf of Aqaba would be sealed to the Israelis by mines, land batteries, boat and air patrols; any Israeli ship attempting to pass through the Straits would be fired upon and sank if it refused to return to the port of Eilat.

U Thant gives way before Nasser's threats

251

King Hussein of the Hashemite
Kingdom of Jordan

Ever since the Sinai Campaign, the Straits of Tiran, Israel's only outlet to Asia and Africa, had been free and open; in April 1958, the UN Conference on the Law of the Sea (ratified by thirty countries, though not by Egypt), had unequivocally confirmed Israel's right of navigation through the precious narrow waterway leading to the Red Sea. Under other circumstances, it would have been unthinkable for such a flamboyant breach of an international convention to be countenanced, but Nasser, secure in Soviet support and intoxicated by his own propaganda, was not concerned with world opinion. The closure of the Straits, Nasser declared, 'might be an opportunity for Israel to test her forces and to find out that everything written about 1956 and the occupation of Sinai was utter nonsense. 'We must be ready,' he added, 'to enter all-out war with Israel.'

Much of the western world was aghast; in Washington, President Johnson termed the blockade illegal; so did the British and Canadian Foreign Offices. But France, declaring herself perturbed, was hostile to Israel, and Moscow shrilly blamed Prime Minister Eshkol for 'a dangerous worsening of tension.' Harold Wilson, prime minister of Great Britain, flew to Washington and Ottawa in a vain attempt to persuade his counterparts to dispatch an international naval task force to secure free navigation in the Gulf of Aqaba. The Kremlin, having poured aircraft, tanks, weapons and instructors into Egypt since 1955, continued to incite and back the Egyptian leader. Alarmed at last, U Thant flew to Cairo hoping to pacify Nasser but it was already too late; the Arab war hysteria was in full force; he coolly informed the UN Secretary General that no Israeli shipping would be allowed to pass through the Straits of Tiran.

The USSR pours oil on troubled waters

Israel prepares for war

Encircled and threatened, Israel began an urgent search for diplomatic intervention; her Foreign Minister Abba Eban, visited Paris, London and Washington, hoping to learn whether any of these nations intended to carry out the guarantees they had given to Israel when she withdrew from Sinai in 1956. But the answers everywhere were either negative or vacillating; and the tension deepened; the brief, memorable period of Israel's isolation had begun, and with it that test of her nerve and fibre which came to be known as the *konnenut* or preparedness; it was the agonizing prelude to the Six-Day War. The problem was no longer just the blockade of the Straits; Israel's very existence was at stake; her enemies massed in force around her borders.

On 30 May, King Hussein threw in his lot with that of President Nasser; despite Israel's assurances that if Jordan kept out of the looming war it would go unscathed, Hussein signed an anti-

Israel military pact. The 'Hashemite Harlot,' as Nasser had labelled him only a few days earlier, was forgiven; throughout the Arab world, mass demonstrations called for the destruction of the State of Israel, the extermination of her citizens, the final victory of Pan-Arabism over Zionism. On 4 June, a mutual defence pact was concluded between Egypt and Iraq. Their leadership temporarily reconciled, the Arabs were persuaded that the moment had finally arrived – after nearly twenty years – to deal a death blow to the Jewish State; and their enthusiasm for war knew no bounds.

The Egyptian contribution to the anticipated blow, in addition to military and political leadership, was to consist of the annihilation of the Israel Airforce, and the cutting off of Eilat and the southern Negev from the rest of Israel, thus complementing the earlier achievement of blocking the Straits. By the end of May, the Egyptians had close to 100,000 soldiers, over 900 tanks and a similar number of cannon in Sinai. The Syrians, for their part, were to attack Israel from the same directions they had chosen in 1948 – although this time they hoped for greater success. One Syrian force would lunge along the Mishmar Hayarden-Safed-Nazareth route, another across the Jordan Valley, south of the Sea of Galilee; both forces to meet victoriously in Haifa. Some six brigades, and 260 Syrian tanks were to be involved in this effort. The Jordanian assignment, relying on seven brigades, about 270 tanks, and 150 cannon, plus the assistance of at least one Iraqi brigade, was to throttle the Israeli part of Jerusalem, conquering large sections of it. Also, the Jordanians were expected to paralyse a number of Israel airfields, and two Egyptian commando units were transferred to Jordan for this purpose. In all, the Arab forces directly involved in June, 1967, comprised some 1,500 tanks, about 1,300 pieces of artillery, and over 500 planes. They represented a combined potential Arab strength, deriving also from Iraq, Kuwait, Saudi Arabia, and Algeria, of some 547,000 soldiers, 5,404 tanks and over 900 combat aircraft.

Levi Eshkol led Israel as Prime Minister from 1963 to his death in 1969, as well as its search for peace before and after the Six-Day War

Mobilization

Against the background of the feverishly accelerated attempt to stave off war; faced by the sight and sound, on radio and television screens, of frenzied mobs throughout the Arab world invoking her end; pitted against a war machine whose quantity was overwhelming, Israel, in those last days of May and the first days of June 1967, readied herself for the third time in nineteen years, to defend her right to exist. In all her towns and cities, in all the kibbutzim and villages, citizens grimly cleaned out basements and cellars for use as flimsy air raid shelters; parents and children filled sandbags and dug trenches; young men quietly answered the call to arms. By 1 June, all hopes of peace evaporating, the population took

253

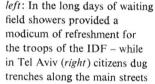

left: In the long days of waiting field showers provided a modicum of refreshment for the troops of the IDF – while in Tel Aviv (*right*) citizens dug trenches along the main streets

stock, sighed and accepted the three most relevant facts regarding its immediate future: that no power in the world outside would, or perhaps even could, move in time to succour the Jewish State; that war was inevitable; that if the Jews of Israel were to live, there was no alternative other than victory. Life no longer followed a routine; civilian transport was mobilized and the roads all but emptied of traffic; youngsters helped bring in the harvest and deliver mail; preparations were made to protect windows with tape, to respect black-out precautions at night and housewives started stockpiling food; the waiting game went on.

Tension rises   In the Negev, hot, dust-covered Israeli troops whiled away the long hours, counting the days and straining at a leash which daily grew more taut. Tel Aviv filled with foreign correspondents. On Saturday, 3 June, the newly appointed Defence Minister, General Moshe Dayan, held a press conference. Asked whether Israel had lost the military initiative, General Dayan answered calmly, if ambiguously:'If you mean to say we stand no chance in battle,' he said, 'then I cannot agree with you.' He also remarked that Israel does not ask for the help of foreign soldiers. That weekend, the tension seemed somehow to lessen; for the first time in weeks, soldiers came home on leave; some of the foreign correspondents, disappointed, decided that war had been averted after all; Israel, hemmed-in, had given way to Nasser and they might as well go home. But others, sensing the ever-increasing tension, stayed on, did their homework, and marvelled at the two and a half million

Jews of Israel, turned almost overnight into a single community.

Although the exact numbers were classified, of course, and Israel's deployment secret, most of the press corps were familiar with the rough figures, and with the awesome ratio of forces. All told, Israel had at her disposal some 800 tanks and 300-odd combat aircraft. Against the seven Egyptian divisions in the south, the IDF had three task forces commanded by Maj. General Yeshayahu Gavish, GOC Southern Command, respectively under Maj. General Yisrael Tal, Maj. General Avraham Yoffe, and a third under the command of Maj. General Ariel Sharon. Each of these formations, known in Hebrew as *Ugda*, was a self-contained, large force created for the emergency. In addition, Israel also had several independent units – infantry and armour – opposite the Gaza Strip, a unit in Eilat and combined units elsewhere in the Negev. It was not an immense war machine that waited in the desert during those draining spring days, but it was superbly trained, highly motivated, and schooled to move fast and hard. Many of the officers and men who fought in the Six-Day War had encountered the enemy before; in 1948, in 1956, in reprisal raids and retaliatory actions; many of them had lived through the riots of 1936-39 or had served in World War II. All knew that six million Jews had perished in the Holocaust and that extermination was not impossible. In the most literal sense of the words, many of the soldiers, airmen and sailors of the IDF were the direct heirs, the grandsons, in fact, of the Watchmen who had shouldered arms for the same defensive purpose

The line-up

255

in the same land, only slightly more than half a century ago; and they knew not only what had to be done but how to do it.

In the years since 1956, the IDF had changed and developed; the Airforce, the Paratroopers, the Armoured Corps and the Artillery, had been built up; the gap between the small standing army and the all-important reserves had narrowed appreciably; a territorial defence system had been built up and incorporated within the framework of field units; planes, tanks, artillery and electronic devices were improved, jacked-up, adapted. The ingenuity that had made Ta'as possible was still at work, and Israel's Ordnance Corps, hard-working magicians, got new power from old tanks by changing components, altering engines and improving cannons. But more than the technical achievements, more than the stress on accuracy and flexibility, the IDF had forged strong ties between the front and 'rear', taught soldiers to believe in what they fought for, and the 'rear' to know that the IDF could be relied upon. Throughout the konnenut, these were the feelings that prevailed, and the lassitude and dissatisfaction of the past few years were swept away by the gathering crisis and by the knowledge that it would be weathered.

The story of the Six-Day War has been told often before; few non-global wars have been described so extensively, so quickly and so colourfully; given such symbolic values and woven so fast into a legend. The sober, expert military evaluations still remain to be made and this is not the place to make them. But neither can the story be omitted, for above all else, it affirmed the calibre of David's sling and reminded sceptics everywhere about Goliath.

The celebrated pre-emptive counter attack began at about 7.30 AM on Monday 5 June and it lasted all day; non-stop, wave after wave of Israel's silver needle-nosed Mirages and her deadly arrow-shaped Mystères (flown by pilots who were to fly some eight to ten sorties before night fell), flying low in a wide curve over the Mediterranean, raked and blasted Egypt's airfields. Within only six hours, the Israel Airforce had destroyed some 280 Egyptian aircraft on the ground, smashed 20 more in combat, turned its attention to Syrian and Jordanian airfields and put 52 Syrian planes and 20 Jordanian aircraft out of action. All in all, the day's unprecedented kill amounted to over 400 enemy planes; Israel had won absolute command of the air from Sinai to the tip of Galilee. That night, the Chief of Air Staff, Maj. General Mordechai Hod, broadcasting to the nation, told the people of Israel what the IAF had done.

So swiftly had the Airforce done its skilled avenging work that later, on the same first day of the war, it found time also to

top: General Mordechai Hod, Commander of Israel's Airforce in the Six-Day War and *below*: General Ezer Weizman, now Israel's Minister of Transport, who were together largely responsible for the remarkable calibre of the IAF which Weizman headed for eight years. *right*: two of the 400 enemy planes destroyed by Israel's pilots in the first hours of the war

opposite: For the second time in a decade, thousands of defeated Egyptians were taken prisoner in the desert and the Gaza Strip. The sign held by one of the prisoners, reads 'Allah'.

give powerful, invaluable support to Israel's land forces. Someone eventually asked General Hod to analyse the reasons for Israel's victory. He gave a series of replies, but one in particular seemed conclusive: years of planning, he said, had gone into the air strike; years of practice, methodical intelligence work, tight operational control; imagination, discipline and concentration. That day, the same furious surge forward was repeated on the ground in Sinai; Israel's armour ploughed its way across the desert all day and all night, clashing in combat with the Egyptians. More tanks were involved in those battles in the desert than had ever fought against each other anywhere before, more even than at the bloody battle of El Alamein. Pushing on, in one of history's fastest mechanized advances, against sometimes ferocious resistance, inimical terrain and minefields, backed and aided by the IAF, the Israel Defence Forces, using the same three axes along which it had raced in 1956, cut off the Gaza Strip, took Khan Yunis, El Arish and Gaza itself; advanced on Abu Ageila; on Kuseima and Kuntilla further south, and pressed on – from all three routes – to the Suez Canal. The mailed fist had struck – and all that went before it was demolished.

On the central front, under the command of Maj. Gen. Uzi Narkiss, action also began. Goaded by the Egyptian Chief of Staff

Counter-attack in Jerusalem

of the United Arab Command, the Jordanians, unheeding Israel's secret messages that if they refrained from action they would remain untouched. started to shell Jewish Jerusalem and the settlements along the border. The Jordanian army entered the UN building in Jerusalem (the Government House of Mandatory days), even though UN personnel were still in it. The Israelis now moved. With breath-taking rapidity, the counter-attack started; Government House was taken and the battle for Mount Scopus launched. The fighting on the Jerusalem front was cruel and costly, and the city itself suffered civilian casualties, but the word that reached Jerusalemites in their improvised shelters that night was of impending victory.

If not the longest day in history, 5 June 1967 was long enough. Algeria, Iraq, Kuwait, the Sudan and Yemen all declared war on Israel – and a conference of Arab oil-producing states decided to embargo oil supplies to any country giving aid to Israel. In New York, the United Nations met in emergency session to hear Egypt's Ambassador claim that his country's armed forces were defending themselves against a 'treacherous' attack, and the Security Council discussed a demand for an immediate ceasefire.

But by 6 June, Israel's armour had carved even deeper into Sinai, the Governor of the Gaza Strip had formally surrendered to the IDF, and thousands of Egyptians were taken prisoner. Virtually all of the Egyptian army remaining in Sinai had been outflanked; its escape routes cut off by the Israeli forces nearing the Canal. On the central front, the Old City of Jerusalem was surrounded;

left: Maj. Gen. Uzi Narkiss, Commander of the Central Front which included Jerusalem *right*: An artillery duel in the Gaza Strip; in the foreground jeeps with recoiless guns

260

Kalkilya, Jenin, Hebron and Bethlehem had fallen to Israel – and Latrun, in Jordanian hands since 1948, was occupied by the IDF. In the north Syrian artillery kept up a steady heavy bombardment of the kibbutzim below the hills – but no troops had moved yet.

By Wednesday, 7 June, the Egyptians were in full retreat in Sinai and the Israeli forces making for the Canal had linked up. The Egyptian losses were staggering, about a third of the massive Egyptian army was hit – killed, wounded or in captivity. 600 Egyptian tanks were damaged or captured and almost all of Egypt's airforce gone. It was not only in the air and on the land that the Egyptians crumbled; not a single Israeli vessel was hit, not one Egyptian commando or saboteur landed behind the Israel lines. But on the night of 5 June, Israel's navy did more than defend Israel's shores; it attacked Port Said and Alexandria. After the Sinai Campaign, Egyptian apologists blamed the French and British armies for Israel's successes, but now Egypt had been defeated by Israel alone.

Demoralized and terrified the Egyptians scattered in the pitiless desert; they fled throughout Sinai, even evacuating Sharm es Sheikh. Israeli marines, paratroopers and troops landing from patrol boats steaming down from Eilat arrived there to find it empty. The Straits of Tiran were back under Israel control, a blue and white flag went up again – this time it was Israel's. The blockade that had begun the war was over; the sea lane was open again.

But the capture of Sharm es Sheikh, which should have been climactic was overshadowed by another victory. On Wednesday

overleaf: The fall of Jerusalem brought the Jews back to the Western ('Wailing') Wall – their most sacred site. General Shlomo Goren, Chief Chaplain of the IDF prays at the liberated Wall

The battle for Jerusalem was bloody, much of it hand-to-hand fighting. Mordechai ('Motta') Gur (centre) commanded the break-through of the paratroopers into the Old City on June 7, 1967

evening, Israel announced full control of the Old City of Jerusalem. Israelis, glued to their radios, could hardly believe it. At this historic moment, Prime Minister Levi Eshkol turned to the Arabs and offered them Israel's sincere hand in peace. Behind the historic announcement lay hours of tenacious, punishing fighting much of it hand to hand and street to street. Cautioned to avoid damaging the many holy places of the Old City, fighting an enemy for whose monarch Jerusalem had been a glittering diadem to be flaunted throughout the Arab world, fighting in a heavily built-up area, the Israeli troops were badly hurt. But they forced open the way to Mount Scopus and pushed on, on into the Old City, on to the Temple Mount and on, at last, to the Western ('Wailing') Wall. Although the Six-Day War did not end with the conquest of the Old City, this was its climax. All Jerusalem was liberated and all Israel rejoiced. Soldiers of the IDF on all fronts, weary, wounded and incredulous, would never forget the moment; nor would the hundreds of Israelis who streamed into the Old City, despite the danger, all through the day. The nation had acquired many new heroes, generals and common soldiers, that week, and a host of new legends had come into being. Particular heroes, in addition to the victorious generals, Rabin, Hod, Barlev, Weizman, Gavish, Narkiss and the others, were, above all, the tired paratroopers, the first to break through to Temple Mount, under the command of Brig. Mordechai (Motta) Gur, who reaped the nation's profoundest gratitude.

Around Jerusalem, the battle still swirled and raged, but the Jordanians, despite their often heroic resistance, were finished. By nightfall of 7 June, virtually half of Jordan was lost; Bethlehem and Nablus were taken, Jericho had given in, the Etzion region – scene of the Yishuv's terrible defeat in the War of Independence – was Israel's again. In the face of Israel's advance, deprived of any air cover, suffering thousands of casualties, Hussein's army sued for an end to the fighting. The third day of the war was over. General Rabin summed up the situation: Israel had occupied all of the Sinai Peninsula up to the Suez Canal, had taken Sharm es Sheikh, had captured most of Jordan west of the Jordan River – and had reunited Jerusalem. A total of 441 Arab planes had been destroyed to date – and relative to what had been accomplished, Israel's casualties, though each life lost was bitterly mourned, were 'not great.'

The three divisional commanders of the southern front. *Top to bottom*: General Avraham Yoffe, General Yisrael Tal and General Ariel ('Arik') Sharon

By Thursday, 8 June, Israel's forces were firmly ensconced along the eastern bank of the Suez Canal, all fighting had ended on the central front and only one aggressor nation remained to be subdued, on the third and final front. On Friday, 9 June, the IDF's

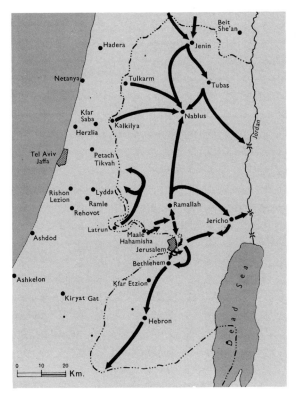
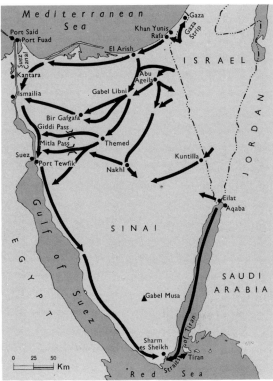

Northern Command, headed by Maj. Gen. David Elazar, readied itself to take on the Syrians, whose artillery had kept up a relentless pounding of the settlements in Galilee for the past two days. The Syrian emplacements were among the most strongly fortified positions in the world, certainly the most formidable ever seen in the Middle East; giant complexes of reinforced concrete, miles of grotesque steel-roofed, bomb-proof bunkers stockpiled with anti-tank guns and artillery; each death-bearing beehive, laced with barbed wire, connected to its neighbour by a deep underground passage. Some of the trenches were eight feet deep and three feet wide and they were seemingly impregnable. But before the emplacements could be demolished, the Syrian Heights had to be scaled; the ascent and the assault lasted for two days and a night. By the morning of 10 June, Gen. Elad Peled's force, the Golani Brigade, the Airforce, the armoured corps and paratroop units had stormed the Syrian positions. The breakthrough was as brutal as it was heroic; engineers in bulldozers struggled up the sheer mine-seeded hills, painfully clearing the way for infantry and tanks, while the Airforce was in constant action. The same ingredients of speed and resolve that had beaten the Egyptians in three days and the Jordanians in two days were now combined to defeat the Syrians.

Israel's campaigns on the central (*left*) and southern fronts

opposite: Victory on the Syrian Heights. Children in the Jewish settlements below now sleep safely above ground – for the first time in 20 years

265

Israel's tanks blast their way
up the blazing Syrian Heights

Damascus sued through the United Nations for a ceasefire; by the time the ceasefire was in force, the IDF was on the slopes of Mount Hermon, the Syrian positions had totally collapsed and the Syrian troops, panic-stricken, were in full flight. The nineteen-year-old threat to the settlements on the plain was ended and the Israel Defence Forces were situated only 25 miles from Damascus.

80 hours of combat   The Six-Day War was over; in reality, it had been won in eighty lightning hours of combat. Israel's armed forces now occupied some 47,000 square miles of enemy territory, an area almost six times greater than Israel itself. The Arab losses were immense – 80 percent of Egypt's military equipment had been destroyed; Nasser himself admitted that 10,000 soldiers and 1,500 officers had been lost, 5,000 more men and 500 officers taken prisoner. Such vast quantities of Soviet-supplied war material were captured that it took months for it to be sorted out. But the Arab states, bruised and humiliated once again, failed to face the consequences of the war; the lesson went unlearned, as it had in 1948 and 1956.

In August, at an Arab summit conference held in Khartoum, the Arab leaders answered Israel's call for peace with three resounding negatives! There would be, they proclaimed, no peace with Israel, no recognition of the Jewish State, no negotiations. Added to this, the terrorist organizations added a fourth statement of their own. Israel must be totally destroyed, even within its pre-1967 boundaries. It seemed the lesson would never be learnt.

266

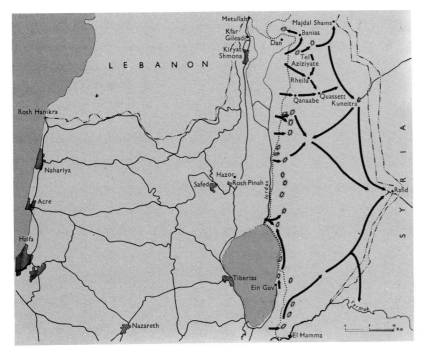

By October 1967, more than 80 percent of Egypt's aircraft, tanks and artillery had already been replaced by the Soviet Union, and Arab terrorists were on the move once again – in Israel itself, on the West Bank, in Gaza and infiltrating, though with small success and at great cost to themselves, from Syria and Lebanon; on the Canal not a day passed without exchanges of fire. But even though the Arabs had drawn no conclusions from the war, Israel had done so; this time, the condition of withdrawal was to be high; it was to be peace. On 12 June, Prime Minister Levi Eshkol gave voice to the nation's determination to hold out until, once and for all, the Arabs came to terms with Israel. The Jewish State, he declared, would never return to the situation that had reigned up to the Six-Day War. 'Alone, we fought for our existence and our security,' he said, 'This land will no longer be a no-man's land, open to sabotage and murder.'

Permanent peace was the issue; peace by treaty, not a series of makeshift truces; peace based on agreed, recognized and secure borders; peace that would give Israel, at last, time and opportunity to develop in tranquillity, to become a beacon in the Middle East, to relinquish the sword so that the ploughshare could be grasped with two hands. The Arabs refused to discuss direct peace talks, the bright immediate post-war vision faded; the IDF remained on its new ceasefire lines, on borders that gave it greater military security than it had ever known, and waited for a permanent set-

The asking price: peace, lasting and real

267

The architect of the victory: Israel's Chief of Staff, Major General Yitshaq Rabin

tlement. And so it awaits today – a citizen's army whose memories of past and crucial concessions are still fresh; an army hoping against hope that the victory of 1967 will somehow bring to an end an ancient futile conflict, an army paradoxically made up of men and women to whom war is anathema. On the 28 June, 1967, General Yitshaq Rabin spoke briefly at a ceremony on Mount Scopus at which he was awarded an honorary doctorate by the Hebrew University of Jerusalem. He accepted it in the name of the thousands of officers and the tens of thousands of men who had fought in the Six-Day War. Speaking on their behalf, he said, '... our soldiers in various branches of the Israel Defence Forces who overcame our enemies everywhere, despite the superior numbers and fortifications – all of them revealed not only coolness and courage in battle but a burning faith in the justice of their cause and sure knowledge that only their personal stand against the greatest of dangers could bring victory to their country and to their families and that if the victory were not achieved, the alternative was annihilation...'

'All this springs from the spirit and leads back to the spirit. Our warriors prevailed not by their weapons but by their sense of mission, by the consciousness of the rightness of their cause, by a deep love for their country and an understanding of the difficult task laid upon them... This army... came from the people and returns to the people – to a people which rises to great heights in times of crisis and prevails over all enemies by virtue of its moral and spiritual strength.'

The sense of mission

None would more deeply have understood the sense of General Rabin's words, more wholeheartedly approved of them, or been more proud of the army he had commanded than its forebears, the small, fabulous band of those who, lacking all alternative, took up arms in Israel's defence. Some belonged to the distant past, to Hashomer and Nili; but others, Legionnaires of World War I and the veterans of the Jewish Brigade of World War II, commanders of the Haganah's nutshell fleet and the volunteers of the Shai, the Palmachniks and soldiers who had fought in the War of Independence and the Sinai Campaign, were among those who heard him speak that day in unified Jerusalem and they knew that he had spoken for all of them.

Glossary

Abaya (A) Long outer garment, usually coloured, worn by many Arabs

Aliyah Literally 'to go up' or ascend: term for immigration to the Land of Israel

Baksheesh (A) A gratuity or bribe

Bar Giora Jewish defence organization established in 1907 named after Simon Bar Giora leader of the Jewish Wars against Rome, 66–70 AD

Bilu–Bilu'im Acronym of the Hebrew 'O House of Jacob, come let us ascend!' Early Zionist pioneering movement founded in Russia in 1882

Bricha Literally 'escape'. The underground railway of Jewish refugees to Palestine

El Fatah (A) Arab terrorist organization established in 1965

Fedayeen (A) Arab terrorist infiltrators

Finjan (A) Arab coffee-pot

Fosh *Plugot Sadeh* – the 'Field Company' units of the Palmach

Gadna Acronym of the Hebrew 'Youth Battalions'. The pre-military cadet corps

Ghafir Supernumary police of the Turkish period and after in Palestine. See also *Notrim*

Ha'apala Term applied to 'illegal' immigration from Europe to Palestine particularly between 1946–1948. Hence *ma'apilim* – 'illegal immigrants

Haganah Literally 'Defence'. The forerunner of the Israel Defence Forces

Hallukah Distribution to the poor of Palestine of funds contributed for their support by the Jews of the Diaspora

'Hatikvah' 'The Hope', the Zionist (later Israeli) national anthem. Composed by Naftali Imber in 1886

Havlagah The policy of self-restraint adopted by much of the Yishuv during the latter part of the British Mandate in Palestine

'Hayedid' 'The Friend', nickname of Captain (later Brigadier) Orde Wingate

'Hazaken' 'The Old Man', nickname for Yitshaq Sadeh, the founder of the Palmach

Him Acronym of the Hebrew 'Home Guard' The militia reserved for defensive duties in the towns and settlements

Hish Acronym of the Hebrew 'Field Army'. The bulk of the Haganah fighting forces

Homa u'Migdal 'Stockade and tower' – Jewish settlements built in 24 hours, and so named after their distinctive features

Irgun Zvai Leumi (*IZL*) The largest of the Jewish underground dissident movements, literally National Military Organization

Khan (A) Arab meeting place; an inn

Kibbutz Jewish collective settlement. Hence *Kibbutznik* – member of a Kibbutz

Kol Israel' 'Voice of Israel' – the Israel Broadcasting Service

Konnenut The state of national preparedness prevailing before a major crisis

Kumsitz Originally from the German – a communal song session round a camp fire at night

Lochamei Herut Israel (*LHI*) An underground dissident organization Literally 'Fighters for the Freedom of Israel', known by the British as the 'Stern Gang'

Ma'apilim See *Ha'apala*

Ma'avak The struggle of the Yishuv against the British

Madfiyah (A) The guest tent of an Arab village

Mifkada Artzit National High Command of the Haganah

Mossad The organization responsible for the Bricha literally 'Institution'

Nili Acronym of the Hebrew 'The Eternal One of Israel will not lie'. Pro-British and anti-Turkish underground intelligence organization in Palestine during World War I

Noddedet 'Mobile Patrols' established by Yitshaq Sadeh

Noter – Notrim The Jewish supernumary police; guards

Oleh – Olim New immigrants

Palmach *Plugot Machatz* – shock companies. The striking arm of the Haganah. Hence *Palmachnik*, member of the Palmach

Palyam The naval units of the Palmach (from the Hebrew *yam* — sea)

Rekhesh The arms and munitions procurement branch of the Haganah

Shai Acronym of the Hebrew 'Information Service'. The underground intelligence network of the Haganah

Ta'asiya Zvai'it. Israel Military Industries, which developed from the home weapons industry

Ugda Self-contained force of approximately brigade strength

Yishuv The Jewish community of Palestine prior to the establishment of the State of Israel

ZAHAL *Zva Haganah Le'Israel*. The Israel Defence Forces

Index